MW01640268

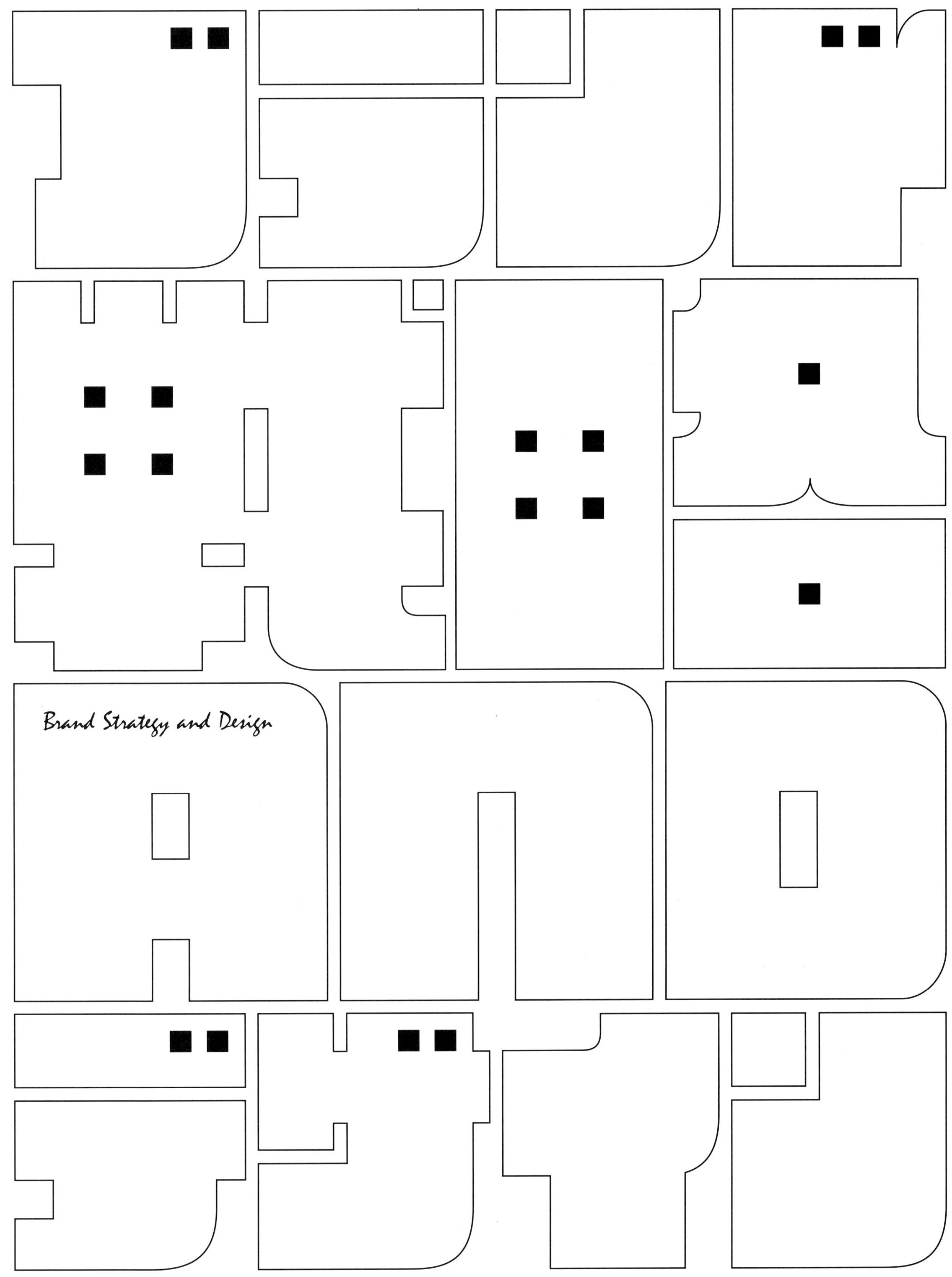
Brand Strategy and Design

Brand Strategy and Design

PIE BOOKS
2-32-4, Minami-Otsuka, Toshima-ku, Tokyo 170-0005 Japan
Tel: +81-3-5395-4811 Fax: +81-3-5395-4812

e-mail:
editor@piebooks.com
sales@piebooks.com
http://www.piebooks.com

ISBN4-89444-295-7 C3070
Printed in Japan

CONTENTS

ブランド戦略におけるデザイナーの役割

永井 X 佐野

（株）HAKUHODO DESIGN　永井一史
1961年東京生まれ。1985年多摩美術大学美術学部デザイン学科卒業後、（株）博報堂入社。2003年5月（株）HAKUHODO DESIGN設立、代表取締役社長に就任。主な受賞に1996年セガ「カモネギ」ポスターにて、1997年産業経済新聞社「白紙広告」の新聞広告にて東京ADC賞受賞、1999年JAGDA新人賞、日経広告賞 グランプリ受賞や朝日広告賞、毎日広告賞、フジ産経広告賞、Clio賞、N.Y Festival、N.Y ADC、ITAACなど受賞多数。ADC会員、JAGDA会員。

（株）HAKUHODO DESIGN　佐野研二郎
1972年東京生まれ。1996年多摩美術大学美術学部グラフィックデザイン科卒業後、（株）博報堂入社。現在、同社と（株）HAKUHODO DESIGNに在籍。主な受賞に2002年日本ラグビーフットボール協会「男」ポスターにてJAGDA新人賞受賞、2003年全日本柔道連盟「WORLD JUDO 2003」ポスター、東京放送「Tブ－S！」ポスターにて東京ADC賞受賞、NY.ADC銀賞・銅賞や東京TDC賞など受賞。

時代とともに変化してきた広告に対する意識

佐野　今日の対談のテーマは「ブランド戦略とデザイン」ということで、まずは自分の今までの仕事を振り返ってみたんです。そうしたら、僕が会社に入ったのは8年ぐらい前なんですけど、その頃に比べると最近は、ブランドの全体というか戦略自体に関わる仕事が多くなっていると改めて思いました。前は「新聞原稿を」とか「ポスターを」とか最初から枠が決められていたんですが、今は「ポスターはやめてパッケージだけにしよう」という風に、こちらからの提案でメディアのチョイスも自由にできるようになってきました。どういうコミュニケーションを重視するのか、幕の内弁当のようにまんべんなく揃えた方向がいいのか、何かに固執する方向がいいのかをアートディレクターが決めるケースが増えてますよね。

永井　そうだね。それはやっぱりデザイナーの意識だけじゃなく、広告に対する世の中の意識が変わってきているからだと思う。これだけ物や情報が氾濫しているなかで、マス4媒体に代表されるような従来のやり方だけでは効かないという認識が送り手にも受け手にも芽生えている気がする。この頃の海外ではメディア・ニュートラルという言い回しがあって、今まではテレビが一番とかメディアのプライオリティーがあったんだけど、それがフラットになってきているという考え方なんだ。確かにコミュニケーションの濃度でいうと今はどれが一番とは言えなくなってきた。

佐野　例えばホンダのモビリオスパイク（本書P132）では、できるだけ商品に近いところでのプロモーションを重視して、店頭で配るフリスビー付きカタログを作りました。ユーザーが実際に手に取れる物の方が、漠然としたポスターよりも効くんじゃないかなと思っているんです。

永井　うん。そういう物の方がよりブランドを伝えられるじゃないかという意識が出てきているよね。これは日本だけじゃなく世界的に言えることだけど、メディアの新しいあり方を模索したり、使い方を評価しようという傾向が生まれている。これからはそういった流れのなかでブランドのコミュニケーション戦略も問われていくんじゃないかな。

店頭で力を発揮するメディアとは何か

佐野　クライアントの意識も変わってきましたよね。例えば飲料だったら、今まではパッケージはクライアントのなかのデザイナーが作って、僕らはその広告を担当するということが多かったんだけど、ここ3年ぐらいはコンセプトやパッケージからデザイナーが担当するというケースがすごく増えてます。ひとりのデザイナーなりアートディレクターが全て一貫してやった方が強いわけで、クリエイターが何人も関わると、それぞれが「オレはこうやりたい！」って変えたくなっちゃうから、コミュニケーションの軸がぶれちゃうんですよね。クライアントもそれを踏まえて発注するようになってきたと思います。

永井　パッケージは象徴的だと思う。従来は商品自体が新しい物であれば、単にそれを伝えるだけで売れるという時代があった。でも今は、同じ物だったらセンスのいい物や、はっきりしている物を選ぶ。受け手の感性も格段に上がっているから、クリエイターが入ることによって、キャンペーンとしての統一性もさることながら、パッケージ自体がひとつの新しい存在感を打ち出せることが重要になっている。コンビニなんてすごいことになってるよね。極端な話、新商品はコンビニの店頭に並べた最初の3日間ぐらいで運命が決まってしまう。広告を打つ前に商品の全ての運命が決まってしまうんですからね。

佐野　そうそう、それぐらいわかりやすくないとダメなんですよね。

永井　だから、店頭では広告よりもパッケージそのものが最大のメディアになっている。世の中の全体的な傾向としても、今までだと付加価値だと言われてきたような部分、中身よりもビジュアルやイメージといった部分が本質的な価値になっているという方向になっていますね。

付加価値の提示がブランド戦略の成否を担う

佐野　付加価値という言葉を聞いて、ふとスターバックスが登場した頃を思い出しました。初めて店に入ったとき、ロゴマークの印象も強かったんですが、店内も茶系で落ち着いた感じになっていて、従来のコーヒーショップとは違うムードが漂っているなと。僕は「これってブランドだなあ」と思ったんですよね。そのうちに、「スターバックスに行くことがカッコいい」ってなったり、「ロゴマーク入りのグッズを持ち歩くのがいい」っていう感じになったじゃないですか。既に景気は下降していたけど、付加価値がしっかり提示できれば、価格が高くても豊かな物、本当にいい物に人は集まるんだなと、すごく興味深かったです。あと、iMacもそうでした。それまではパソコンってみんな同じような感じだったけど、ああやって独自のデザインを打ち出して、コミュニケーションを統一して展開したことによって「買わなきゃ時代に遅れる！」ってなりましたよね。僕はこの2つのブランドがすごくエポック・メーキングだったと思うんです。そして日本でいうと、やっぱりユニクロですかね。

永井　ユニクロは単に商品が安いというだけではなく、その先にきちんとブランドの哲学が感じられたよね。「安かろう悪かろう」には見えない、ユニクロなりの新しい価値観を表現することができたんだと思う。服という物理的な部分だけではなく、それを着ることによってユニクロの哲学や時代の気分を共有できたことが大きい。お客さんは、そういう付加価値にお金を払っているという意味合いが大きいと思うな。

佐野　そうですね。iMacも「これを買ったらきっといろんな事が起こるんだろう」

みたいな予感や期待感がありましたし、商品を買った先にストーリーが見えるところがよかったんだと思います。そういうブランディングって本当に大切だと思いますね。以前に大貫卓也さんがおっしゃっていた言葉に“ブランディングとは企業に色を塗っていくこと”というのがあったんです。青を塗るのか黄色を塗るのか、それができるのはデザイナーだけだから、デザイナーがそういうことを意識すればブランディングはより強いものになるという話で、確かにそうだなーって思うんですよね。永井さんはブランディングってどういうことだと考えていますか？

永井　それは非常に難しい質問だね（笑）。いろいろな表現の仕方があるけれど、ごく一般的に言うならば“受け手の中にある、その企業や商品らしさを強化していくこと”だと思う。企業の提供できるものを明確化して、それを意志をもって伝えていく…　それがどの接点においても感じられることが大切で、そういう姿勢そのものがブランディングだと僕は思うな。

表層的ではないブランディングを目指して

佐野　例えば、リーガル（P042）のケースでいうと？

永井　リーガルは紳士靴のナンバーワン企業なんだけれど、年月とともに、ブランドのイメージがぼけてしまってきた。更に、トラッドがもてはやされた時代はよかったけど、今ではそのスタイルが時代に取り残されてしまっているというイメージもあったんだよね。せっかく、ナンバーワンとしての技術やサービス、システムとか持っているのに、イメージが陳腐化していることが伸び悩んでいる最大の原因だと思ったから、そのイメージを払拭して、ブランドが提供できることやメッセージを明確に伝えることを課題として考えたんだ。最終的に、まっさらな状態にするのではなく、「今の延長上につながるような、リ・ブランディングをしましょう」という提案で落ち着いたんですよ。

佐野　ナンバーワン企業って、普通はどうしても守りに入っちゃうじゃないですか。それなのにリ・ブランディングという冒険ができたというのは、クライアントに決断力があったということなんですか？

永井　クライアント側にイニシアティブをとれる人達がいたというのが大きいね。最初から全員の意志が固まっていたというわけではないんだけれど、プロモーションを進めるうちに結果として商品の売り上げが伸びてきたりして、どんどん社内の人達を巻き込んでいったという感じかな。

佐野　以前はリーガルってトラッドなイメージ以外は見えていなかったけど、今は店頭に行くとロゴがあってシューズボックスがあって、リーガルが何か発言しているというムードが伝わるから、それだけでも気になりますよね。ブランドカラーとしてちょっとくすんだ赤を使っていますけど、あの色を決めるにはどんなこだわりがあったんですか？

永井　もともとリーガルが使っていたのは金赤のような赤だっだんだよね。いい意味でのブランドの資産は継承したいから赤は残そうと思って、渋みを加えた赤に決めたんですよ。

デザインの影響力とそれ故の恐さを感じる時

佐野　色って、ちょっと変えるだけでもすごく印象が変わりますよね。特に飲料なんかだと、色によって味の印象まで変わってしまうし。色のコントロールは重要だし難しいですよね。

永井　そう。だから、さっきの話にもつながるけれど、パッケージというのはすごく大切だよね。パッケージは中身の印象まで恐いぐらいに変えてしまう。デザインの影響力というのは本当に大きい。

佐野　うん、本当に大きい。例えば消費者にパッケージを見せずに飲料を試飲してもらったときと、パッケージを見せて試飲してもらったときだと、結果は全然違いますよね。もう面白いくらいに違う。人気のあるジュースを、パッケージを見せずに主婦層に試飲してもらったときなんか「え〜すごくクスリくさい！　こんなの子供に飲ませられないわ！」なーんて感想が出てくる。でも、普段はそれを子供に飲ませてたりするんですよね（笑）。あと、ビールもそうだった。いくつかのブランドを試飲してもらって一番美味しいのを選んでもらうと、パッケージありだと「やっぱりビールはこれだよね」って自分のひいきなブランドを選ぶんです。で、パッケージなしだと全然違うブランドを選んでる（笑）。

永井　そうそう。パッケージのデザインやブランドイメージの影響力というのは、そういったマーケティング調査でもしっかり結果が出てるよね。

ブランド戦略におけるデザイナーの役割

佐野　結局、ブランディングというのは、世の中の人に目に見える形でブランドを集約して、どんな印象を残すのか、それが重要だと思うんです。そういう部分は今まではコピーライター主導でやってきたんだけれど、デザイナーが主導するとビジュアルですぐに定着できるし、統一感を出せるという強みがありますよね。

永井　クライアント側にブランド･マネージャー的な存在というか、最終的に全てをコントロールができる強力な人がいれば、関わるスタッフが色々いても統一感を出していけると思う。でも、日本ではそういう企業はなかなかないよね。だから、外のクリエイターに任せた方が結果的にうまくいくし、クライアントもそれがわかってきたということだと思う。

佐野　こういうの（本書）を見ると、やっぱり、アートディレクターやデザイナーがマークや広告から全部統括してやっているという最近の傾向がはっきりわかりますよね。

永井　デザイン書というのは、通常はビジュアルだけで、そこに込めた思いだとか企画意図、全体的な戦略までは載っていない場合が多いよね。今回はそういった部分がかなり誌面でさかれていて、ブランドを全体像として理解するのにいい体裁になっていると思いますよ。

佐野　（ページをめくりながら）このマーチ（P126）ってよくできていますよね。顔のマークを見れば車を思い出すし、車を見ればマークを思い出す。ブランドだなーって思います。

永井　そうそう。都内に掲出された大きなバナーとか好きだったな。車のビジュアルはないんだけど、何の広告かすぐわかるしね。

佐野　へ～こんなスクリーンセーバーとかも作っていたんだ！　面白いですね。（更にページをめくりながら）このアイ・スタイラーズ（P174）は白で統一されていて、それが逆に目を引きますね。

“色”が語るブランドの哲学とメッセージ

永井　多種多様な色が氾濫しているなかで引きの美学ということもあるよね。パッケージも含めて広告物というのは、単体で眺めているだけではだめで、実際にそれが使われる環境に置いたときを想定しないといけない。単体で見たときはすごくいいのに、店頭や、その場に置いてみると途端に力を失うということもあるからね。こうやっていろんなブランドを眺めてみると、モチーフも大切だけど、やっぱり色の印象というのは大きいということを実感するね。

佐野　本当に大きいと思います。快活なのか冷静なのか情熱的なのか、そういう言語が色によって表現されていますよね。自分の仕事のなかでも、それが統一感をもってきちんと表現できたときは嬉しいし、商品が売れるという結果に結びついたときは、理解されたという気がして本当に嬉しいですね。そういう実感は、以前のようにポスターだけ新聞広告だけという仕事ではあんまりなかったんです。単体だけの仕事だとどこまで影響力があるのかわからなかった。今はブランド全体に関わるような仕事ができるようになって、ライブ感があって楽しいですね。店頭に行けば自分の作ったパッケージやツールが置いてあって、それを買ったり持って行ったりするお客さんがいる。仕事をしても、その結果が「？」では終わらずに、ダイレクトな反応を感じることができるんですよね。

デザイナーを取り巻く環境は過渡期に入った

永井　もともと田中一光さんなどは、ブランド全体を見据えた考え方でやっていらしたと思うんですけど、広告の分野はどんどん細分化やシステム化が進んでしまって、デザイナーが活躍できる場所が限定されてきてしまったという流れがあるんじゃないかな。でも、ここへきてもう一度ブランドという視点で全部を見直そうという動きが一気に出てきた。僕らのデザイン的なスキルは企業戦略にまで活かすことができるんじゃないかというところまできていると思うな。触れる範囲がどんどん広がってきているというか、デザイナーがダイナミズムをもって仕事ができる環境になってきている。だからこそ、HAKUHODO DESIGNを立ち上げて、佐野君にも加わってもらっているわけだけど。

佐野　ダイナミズムといえば、例えばオゾック（P168）のように建築の分野にまで広告が広がっていますよね。ああいうのを見ると楽しいなって思います。ポスターのようにあっという間に消費されていたものが、しっかりと残っていくんですからね。広告的な感性をもってやれば、建築家だけが関わるものとは違うものができると思うし、他の媒体との統一感も出せる。他にも商品自体を手がけている、メーカー的な役割を果たしているデザイナーもいますしね。そういった例を見ても、デザイナーの役割の幅が広がってきていると実感します。

デザイン領域の拡大が企業の可能性も広げる

永井　やっぱりそれは、コミュニケーションの領域だけをデザイナーが全てディレクションするということだけではないよね。企業がどうなっていけばいいかという大きな意味でのデザインにも関わってくると思う。デザイナーというのはいろいろな要素から取捨選択して、本質的な力を探り出す力をもっている。その能力は企業そのものをどういう方向に導いていくかという戦略を考える場面にも役立つと思うんだ。だから、それぞれの接点へと横展開する水平方向と、戦略性への垂直方向の両方のベクトルに力を発揮できると言ったらいいのかな。僕自身はその両方に興味をもっているし、手がけていきたいと思っている。話は変わるけど、この前、たまたま地方のデザインコンペの審査員をしたんだけど、そこで都会に対しての地方というか、いい意味での地域性を感じたんですよね。作っている人達は「意識していない」と言うんだけど（笑）。でも伝統という言葉に象徴されるような、日本的だったり手作業的だったりするイメージを確かに感じたんだよ。それにすごく刺激を受けた。だから僕もこれからは機会があれば地酒とか、その土地に密着した商品などのデザインもやってみたいな。佐野君はどうですか？

佐野　僕は具体的にこれと言うことはできない漠然とした方向なんですが、やっぱり仕事の幅を広げていきたいと思っています。

永井　今、僕達デザイナーにとってはすごく面白い時代に突入していると思う。世の中も企業も受け手も意識が変化してきているしね。「何かやらなきゃ」という危機感は皆がもっているから、意志と行動力さえあればチャンスのある時代だと思うな。

佐野　そうですよね！　よーし、やる気が出てきたぞ（笑）。

The Role of the Designer in Brand Strategy

NAGAI X SANO

HAKUHODO DESIGN Inc. KAZUFUMI NAGAI

Born in Tokyo, 1961. After graduating from Tama Art University in 1985 with a degree in design, joined Hakuhodo Inc. Founded and became president of HAKUHODO DESIGN Inc. in May, 2003. Major honors include the Tokyo Art Directors Club award in 1996 for the SEGA "Kamonegi" poster and in 1997 for the Sankei Shinbun "White Advertisement" newspaper advertisement series; the Japan Graphic Designers Association's Young Designer Award in 1999; the Nikkei Advertising Award Grand Prix Award; the Asahi Advertising Award; the Mainichi Advertising Award; the Fujisankei Advertising Award; the Clio Award; and awards from the New York Festivals, the New York Art Directors Club, and ITAAC, among several others. Member of the Art Directors Club and the Japan Graphic Designers Association.

HAKUHODO DESIGN Inc. KENJIRO SANO

Born in Tokyo, 1972. After graduating from Tama Art University in 1996 with a degree in graphic design, entered Hakuhodo Inc. Currently works for both Hakuhodo Inc. and HAKUHODO DESIGN Inc. Major awards include the Japan Graphic Designers Association's Young Designer Award for the 2002 Japan Rugby Football Association "Man" poster; awards from the Art Directors Club for the 2003 Japan Judo Federation "World Judo 2003" poster and the Tokyo Broadcasting System "T Boo S" poster; Silver Prize and Bronze Prize from the New York Art Directors Club and the Tokyo Art Directors Club, among others.

Advertising Changing With The Times

S (Sano): Since the theme of today's conversation is "Brand Strategy and Design", I decided to first take a look at my own work to date. I started at this company about eight years ago, and looking back it struck me that comparatively, the amount of work concerned with overall brand strategy has grown dramatically. At first all the work fit into a specific category -- we were asked to produce newspaper advertisements, or posters -- but today companies seem to have more freedom to act on our proposals for other media, like "forget the posters, let's just focus on the packaging". Cases where the art director decides what kind of communication to focus on, whether everything should be made completely uniform, like a boxed lunch, whether to adhere to a specific direction, and so on are increasing.

N (Nagai): Absolutely. I think that's a result not only of a change in designers' mentalities, but also of a change in society's attitude towards advertising. The world is flooded with things and information, and it seems to me that both sender and receiver are beginning to recognize that the old way of doing things, where four media served to represent everything, simply isn't effective anymore. Just as the phrase "media neutral" has become a buzzword outside Japan, the thinking is that whereas what media to use was a big issue before, with television number one and all that, now it's a level playing field. I think that with the sheer density of communication, now no one can say what's number one.

S: For example, in the case of HONDA's MOBILIO Spike (page 132), we placed the greatest emphasis on promotions that occurred near the actual product -- so we handed out catalogs with frisbees attached in the stores. A promotional item the user could actually hold was thought to be more effective than an ambiguous poster.

N: Yes, the perception that that kind of promotion can more effectively communicate brand concepts and message is widening. Not only in Japan but all over the world, a trend is emerging of people evaluating how media is used, searching for the next paradigm. And I think that school of thought will soon turn its attention to brand communication strategy.

Strongest Media in Retail Outlets

S: The client's perceptions have changed as well. In the case of beverages, for instance, it used to be that the client's in-house designer would create the packaging and we would create advertising for it, but lately the number of instances where we're called on to design everything from concept to package is increasing. It's most effective when one designer takes on the role of art director and oversees the consistency of the entire project; when you involve several creative minds, they all start saying, "I want to do it this way!" and the axis of communication begins to slip. I think clients have come to recognize this and are beginning to commission work accordingly.

N: I think the trend in packaging is symbolic of a larger process of change. Up until now if the product itself was "new", you could sell it based on that alone. That era is over. Now, between similar products consumers choose the one with appealing, clearly expressed design. The consumer's sensitivity to design has also markedly increased, and the creative team is depended upon to not only give overall consistency to the campaign but to give a new presence to the packaging itself. Convenience stores have really become incredible places, haven't they. In extreme cases, a product's destiny can be decided within three days of being lined up on convenience store shelves. Even before the advertising hits, the fate of the product is sealed.

S: Yes, yes, if it doesn't communicate intuitively it just doesn't work.

N: So, the package is becoming an even more significant medium than in-store advertising. The trend, even across society as a whole, is for visuals and image to become an even more significant source of what has come to be called "added value" than content.

Brand Strategy Depends on Showing Added Value

S: When I hear the words "added value", I remember the time when Starbucks first came on the scene. The first time I entered a store, of course the logo mark made a strong impression, but I was also struck by the brownish-toned, relaxing interior -- the mood pervading the store that was completely different from the old coffee shops. I thought to myself, "now, THIS is a brand". Soon afterwards, going to Starbucks became the cool thing to do, and people started carrying around Starbucks goods. What I found most interesting about all that was the fact that, even in the midst of an already deteriorating economic climate, good products and services will attract people even at high prices -- if only you can clearly show added value. The iMac was the same way. Before the iMac it seemed like every computer was the same, but they created such an original design, and promoted it with such consistency, that it was almost as if "if you don't buy one you're behind the times". I think these two brands were truly epoch-making. And, in Japan, UNIQLO of course as well.

N: UNIQLO isn't just low-priced goods, consumers really get a sense of the well defined philosophy behind it. UNIQLO has managed to escape the "cheap prices mean cheap goods" mentality by successfully communicating an entirely new value system. Consumers don't just buy the physical clothes, by wearing them they share in a UNIQLO philosophy and era, and that's a huge factor in the brand's success. The implications of the fact that consumers will pay for that sort of added value are huge, I think.

S: That's true. There was a sense of anticipation, or premonition, about the iMac that "if I buy one, interesting things are going to happen", and it helped that consumers were able to visualize good things before buying the product. I think that kind of branding is very important. As Takuya Onuki once said, "Branding is the process of adding color to a business". Whether you add blue or yellow, the only one who can do that is a designer; it's said that if a designer is aware of his or her role the branding becomes that much stronger, and I think that's certainly true. Nagai-san, what do you consider branding to be?

N: That's a very difficult question (laugh). There is a multitude of ways to express it, but generally speaking I think it's "the process of strengthening perception of the business and product in the mind of the consumer". Making clear what a business can offer, and strategically communicating that . . . It's important that the brand can be experienced from any point of contact with a company -- I think that attitude itself is branding.

In Search of Branding beyond the Superficial

S: For example, what about REGAL (page 42)?

N: REGAL is the number one brand of gentleman's shoes, but over time its image had faded. It was an excellent image in an age when traditionalism was applauded, but today that style is also perceived as behind the times. The company's technology, service and systems were unsurpassed, and the obsolescence of its image was the single greatest cause of its business difficulties, so cleaning up its image and clearly communicating the company's message became the issue at hand. In the end, we settled on "rebranding that would remain connected to the current image" rather than trying to start at ground zero.

S: Number one brands usually spend most of their effort trying to protect their position, don't they? So the fact that you were able to go through with a daring rebranding effort means that the company must have strong decision-makers.

N: That the client had people who were able to take initiative was important. I can't say that everyone was behind the effort from the first, but as the promotion continued and sales increased as a result, I felt more and more people within the company came on board.

S: Previously, REGAL was trapped within its traditional image, but now if one goes to the stores, the logo and the shoeboxes and so forth give one a sense that REGAL is making some kind of statement, and that in and of itself grabs attention. You use that slightly subdued red as the brand color --- how did you settle on that color?

N: REGAL had always used a reddish-gold shade of red. We wanted to inherit the valuable brand assets, so we decided to stick with red, finally settling on a slightly subdued shade.

The Power of Design, and the Fear It Inspires

S: A small change in color can really change the effect of a design. Particularly in the beverage sector, color can even change people's perception of taste. Controlling color is important, and very difficult.

N: I agree. So relating to our discussion earlier, the packaging is terribly important. It's almost frightening that the package can even change its contents. The influence of design is truly huge.

S: It certainly is. When you have consumers taste-test a beverage without showing them the package you get completely different results than when you do show them the package. One particular soft drink, if you taste-test it with mothers without showing them the package the general response is, "Ugh, this is really mediciny! I'd never give this to my kids to drink!" But they do give it to their kids to drink! (Laughs) And beer is the same way. If you give consumers various beers and have them choose the best-tasting, if they see the packaging they'll choose their usual beer -- "oh, now this is good beer." And then if you do a taste-test without packaging, they'll choose a completely different brand. (Laughs)

N: Yes, yes. That influence of package design on brand image shows up clearly in marketing surveys as well.

The Role of the Designer in Brand Strategy

S: In the end, when you concentrate a "brand" in a publicly visible package, that is, when you do "branding", I think the impression you leave behind in the mind of the public is most important. That part of the process has generally been left to copywriters, but I think when designers take on that responsibility they can easily establish a message through visuals, even leading to greater overall brand consistency.

N: I think that if there's a brand manager on the client side, someone who has the power to exert final control over all aspects of the project, then even with the inevitably varying suggestions from everyone involved with the project the result will be consistent. However, in most companies in Japan there's no such person. So delegating that to a person outside the company is most effective, and I think that clients have come to realize that as well.

S: Looking at the contents of this book, I think one can clearly see that, as expected, there is a recent trend towards art directors and designers doing everything from logo marks to advertisements.

N: Design books are generally made up only of visuals, and often don't speak to the thought behind them -- the intentions, the overall strategy. Here it is an integral part of the content, and I think it's a good format for understanding overall brand concepts.

S: (turning pages) MARCH (page 126) is really well done, isn't it. Seeing this face-shaped logo mark you remember the car, and if you see the car you remember the logo mark. Now that's a brand, I think.

N: Yes, yes. I really liked the banners and things they had up in the city. There were no pictures of the car, but one immediately understood what they were advertising.

S: Oh? They've even made this screensaver! Now that's interesting. (turning pages again) This I-STYLERS (page 174), done all in white, unexpectedly draws the eye, doesn't it.

What Color Says about Brand Philosophy and Message

N: There's a particular aesthetic to grabbing attention in the midst of a flood of different colors. In advertising, and I include packaging in this as well, if you only focus on the ad it will fail. You have to consider how it would look in the environment in which it will be used. Although on its own it might be superb, it might lose its effect when seen in the store or wherever. Looking at brands in this way, one really senses that while the motif is important, as expected, the impression the color makes is a major factor.

S: Yes, it's very strong. Whether it's playful, calm, passionate -- those sorts of feelings are all expressed by color. In my job, we're happy when we can express emotion clearly and consistently, and when the product sells as a result we're really happy because we feel like we were understood. That feeling we didn't really have when we were making posters and newspaper advertisements like before. Creating a single advertisement, you don't know how much influence your work has. Being able to do jobs that relate to a brand as a whole, it feels like the work lives. You go to a store and the packaging and promotional tools you designed are there, there are customers who bought the products and are carrying them around. Even though it's work, you feel as though there's a direct response -- it doesn't just end in a question mark.

A Transitional Period for Designer's Environments

N: I think that even from the beginning there were designers, such as Ikko Tanaka, who worked with the overall thinking behind the brand in mind, but with the gradual segmentation and systematization of the advertising world, the environments in which designers can work became very limited. But as we reach this point, suddenly there's this movement again towards revisiting everything from the point of view of the "brand". I think we've come to a point where we can make use of our skills as designers even in overall business strategy. The boundaries are widening day by day, and it's becoming an environment where designers can do their jobs with "dynamism". That's why I founded HAKUHODO DESIGN and brought you on board.

S: Speaking of "dynamism", if you look at OZOC (page 168) it seems advertising is even reaching the architectural sector. When I look at something like that I really think it's fun. Like a poster, it's something you consume in an instant yet sticks fast in your mind. If you create it with an advertising sensibility, you can develop something different from what just an architect would do, and make it consistent with other media as well. There are also designers who deal with the product itself, filling a manufacturing role. Seeing examples like that, I feel like the role of the designer is definitely expanding.

Expanding the Role of Design Expands Business Possibilities

N: It's not just that designers are directing communications projects. I think the question of what direction a business should take is also connected to design in a significant way. A designer has the ability to choose between a variety of elements and find the ones that have intrinsic strength. I think that capacity would be of great help in determining the strategic direction of a company. I think one could say that they could exhibit strength in both horizontal and vertical business development. I myself have interest in both areas, and would like to try my hand. To change the subject, I've served as a judge on some regional design competition juries from time to time, and have come away with a good impression of the local flavor of many of these areas, in contrast to the cities. Although it's said the people who create products there "don't even notice". (laughs) But I really felt that "Japanese", "hand-crafted" image symbolized by the word "tradition". It really got to me. So I'd like, if I had the chance, to do some design work for a local sake, or some other product closely tied to its home. What about you, Sano-kun?

S: Though it's too vague an intention to put as concretely as that, I'd certainly like to expand the breadth of my work.

N: I think we've entered a truly interesting era as designers. The sensibilities of the public, of business and of consumers are all changing. Everyone feels like they have to do something, so I think that everyone will find an opportunity as long as they move forward with a sense of mission.

S: Absolutely! I feel like getting to work right now! (Laughs)

クレジットフォーマット
Credit Format

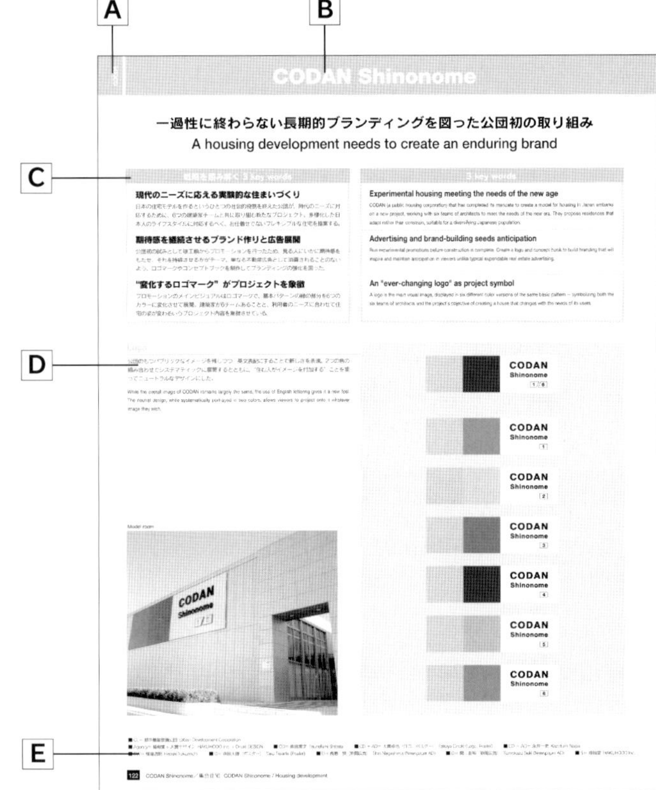

A
カテゴリー
Category

B
ブランド名
Brand name

C
戦略を読み解くキーワード
Key words to understand the strategies

D
ネーミング、ロゴ、キャラクターの紹介
Introduction of name, logo, and character

E

CL：	クライアント	Client
CD：	クリエイティブ・ディレクター	Creative Director
AD：	アート・ディレクター	Art Director
D：	デザイナー	Designer
P：	フォトグラファー	Photographer
I：	イラストレーター	Illustrator
CW：	コピーライター	Copywriter
DF：	制作会社	Design firm
S：	作品提供社	Submittor

・上記以外の製作者呼称は省略せずに掲載しています。
Full name of all others involved in the creation / production of the work.

・媒体名の後ろにつく数字は、クレジット欄の製作者に対するものです。
Numbers following the media name is an explanation for the creators written on credits.

※本書に掲載されている店名、店舗写真、販促ツール、商品などは、すべて2003年4月時点での情報になりますので、ご了承下さい。
All in store-related information, including shop name, photography, promotional items and products are accurate as of April 2003.

※作品提供者の意向によりデータの一部を記載していない場合があります。
Please note that some credit date has been omitted at the request of the submittor.

※各企業名に付随する、"株式会社、(株)"および"有限会社、(有)"は、表記を省略させて頂きました。
The "kabushiki gaisha" (K.K.) and "yugen gaisha" (Ltd.) portions of all Japanese company names have been omitted.

※本書に記載された企業名・商品名は、掲載各社の商標または登録商標です。
The company and product names that appear in this book are published and/or registered trademarks.

COMPANY

Fields フィールズ

業界全体のイメージアップを視野に入れた企業プロモーション

Improving the image of an entire business sector

戦略を読み解く 3 key words

パチンコ・パチスロを国民的娯楽に育てたい

パチンコとパチスロに関わる事業をメインに、様々なエンタテイメント事業を手がける企業。"全ての人に最高の余暇を" を企業理念に掲げ、パチンコとパチスロをより多くの人に愛されるエンタテイメントへ育てることに取り組んでいる。

企業広告を通じて業界全体の活性化を狙う

"The Greatest Leisure For All People" をキャッチコピーに企業広告を展開。自社のブランド力を高めることで、パチンコ・パチスロという娯楽のイメージアップを図る。その一環として、パチンコホールのデザインコンペのプロモーションに力を注ぐ。

人を引きつけ、想像力をかきたてるビジュアル

広告ビジュアルのコンセプトは "パチンコ・パチスロは最高の娯楽だ" と感じてもらうこと。イラストやイメージ写真を効果的に使って見る人の想像力を刺激し、かつ楽しい雰囲気が溢れ出すようなビジュアルを目指している。

3 key words

Making pachinko and slots into popular entertainment

Pachinko and slots are part of the business of bringing people entertainment. Marketing it as "a great way for anyone to pass their free time", work to make pachinko and slots into the entertainment more and more people choose.

Company advertising to enervate the business sector overall

Create advertisements with the catch-copy "The Greatest Leisure for All People". Aim to improve the image of the pachinko/slots entertainment sector as a whole by improving the image of one company. In a coordinated promotion, run a contest to design the interior of a pachinko hall.

Visuals that draw people in and fire their imaginations

Design visuals that tell viewers "pachinko and slots are the best entertainment". Stimulate people's imaginations with the effective use of illustrations and photographs, creating visuals that depict an atmosphere filled with fun.

Naming

エンタテイメントの "フィールド" を広げ、新しい事業を作っていくという企業姿勢を表す社名。

The company name refers to its mission to expand the entertainment "field", and create a new kind of enterprise.

ポスター1 Poster 1

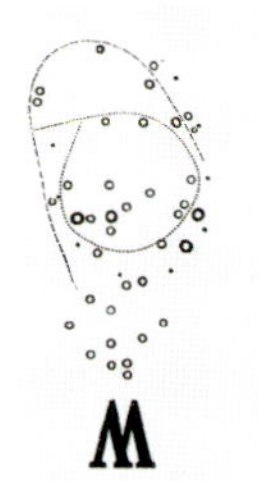

The Greatest Leisure
FOR ALL PeOPLE.
FieLDS
GaMiNg AnD ENTeRtAinmENT

The Greatest Leisure For All People.
Fields
Gaming and Entertainment

ポスター2 Poster 2

The Greatest Leisure For All People.
Fields
Gaming and Entertainment

■ CL= フィールズ Fields Co., Ltd.
■ CD + AD= 青木克憲 Katsunori Aoki　■ AD + D= 関口修男（コンセプトブック） Nobuo Sekiguchi (Concept book)　■ D= 青木克憲（ポスター、コンセプトブック） Katsunori Aoki (Poster, Concept book)
■ D= 高桑佳奈（ポスター） Kana Takakuwa (Poster)　■ D= 寄藤文平（コンセプトブック） Bunpei Yorifuji (Concept book)　■ P= 北島　明（コンセプトブック） Akira Kitajima (Concept book)
■ P= 徳永　彩（コンセプトブック） Aya Tokunaga (Concept book)　■ P= 久家靖秀（会社案内） Yasuhide Kuge (Corporate book)　■ I= 寄藤文平（ポスター3、コンセプトブック、会社案内） Bunpei Yorifuji (Poster 3, Concept book, Corporate book)
■ I= 牧野伊三夫（ポスター2、会社案内） Isao Makino (Poster 2, Corporate book)　■ I= 湯村輝彦（会社案内） Teruhiko Yumura (Corporate book)
■ Art Work= 立花文穂（ポスター1、コンセプトブック、会社案内） Fumio Tachibana (Poster 1, Concept book, Corporate book)　■ Art Work= 福田繁雄（トロフィー） Shigeo Fukuda (Trophy)　■ DF= バタフライ・ストローク butterfly·stroke inc.
■ S= バタフライ・ストローク butterfly·stroke inc.

会社案内 Corporate book

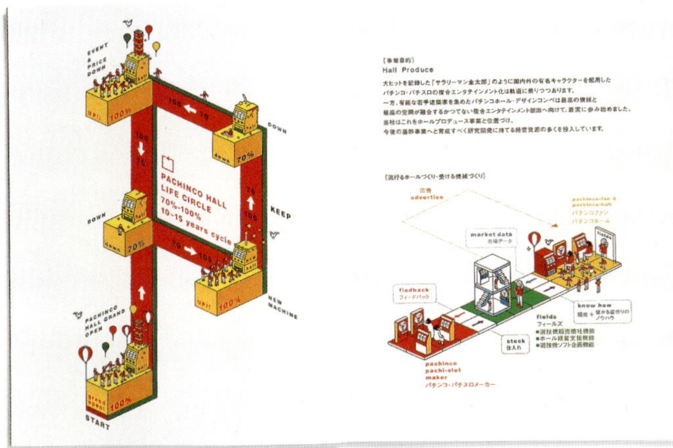

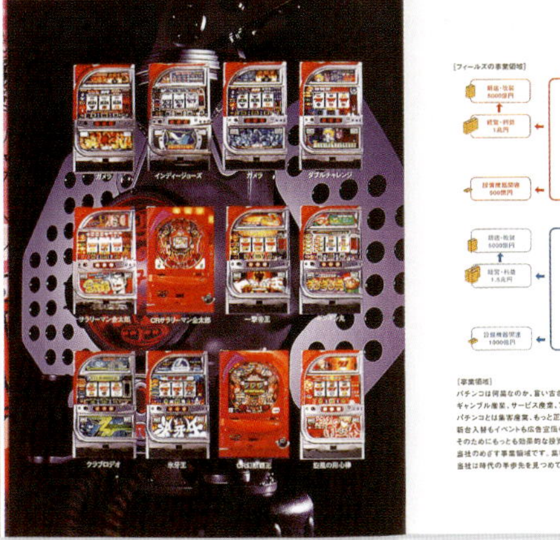

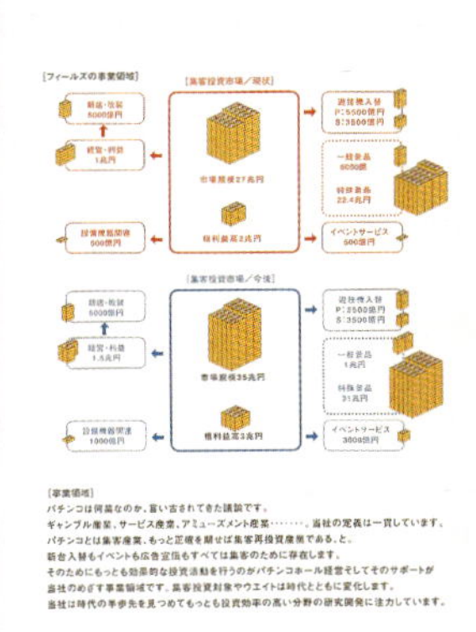

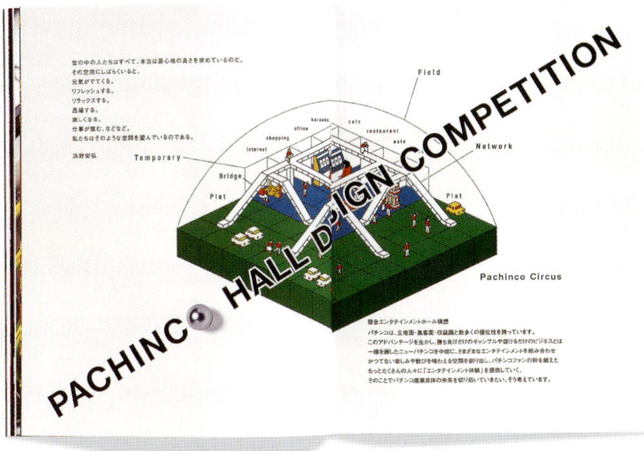

デザインコンペのプロモーションツール

業界としては画期的な、一般公募によるパチンコホール・デザインコンペを実施。プロモーション用にポスターとコンセプトブックを制作した。

Design competition promotional tools

Revolutionary in the industry -- an open competition for the design of a pachinko hall. Promotional poster and concept book produced for the event.

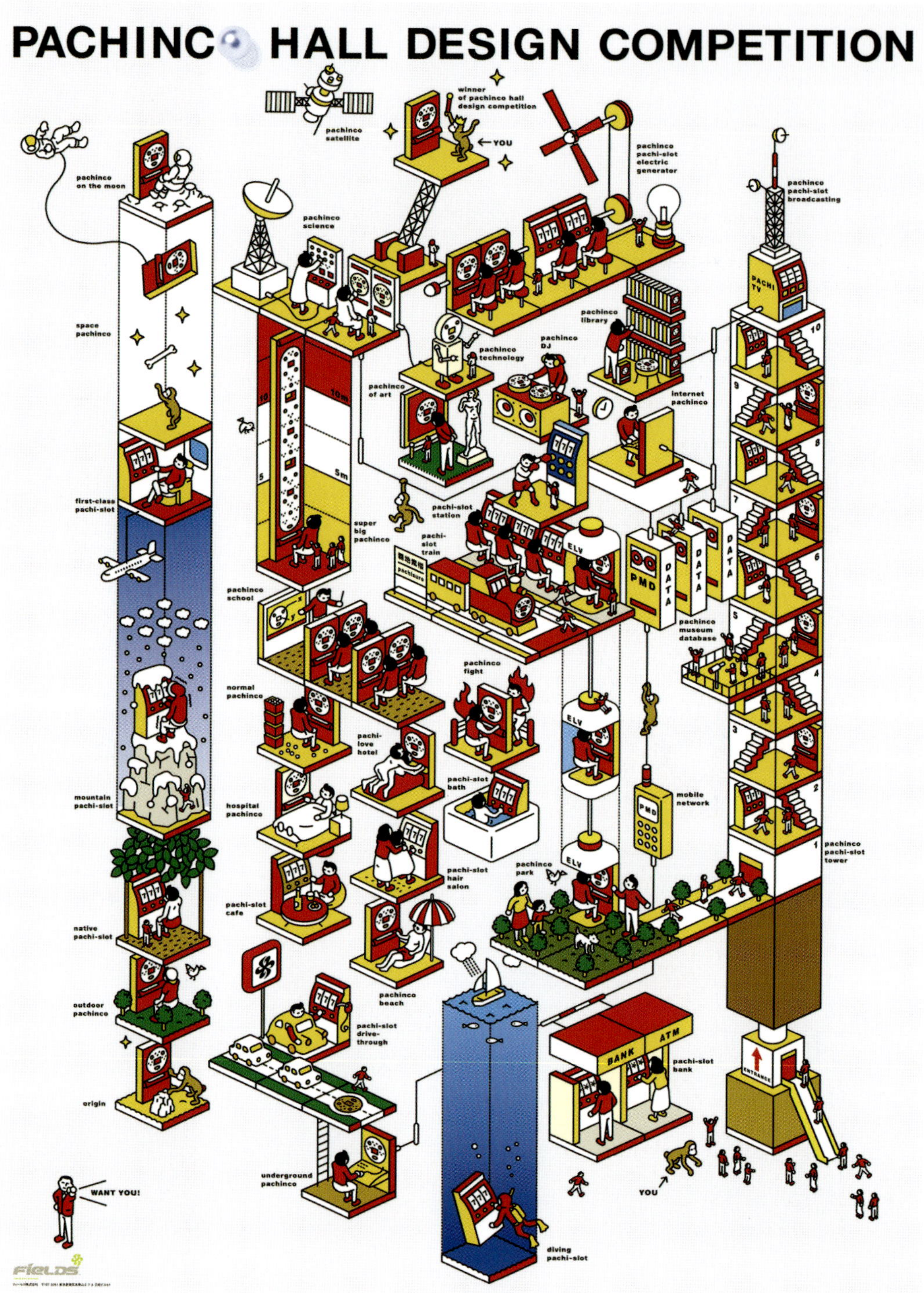

PACHINCO HALL DESIGN COMPETITION

ポスター3 Poster 3

トロフィー

コンペの優勝者に贈ったトロフィー。見る方向によって玉（パチンコを連想させる）や、F（社名の頭文字）に見えるようにデザインした。

Trophy

The trophy awarded the competition winner. Designed to appear like a ball (reminiscent of pachinko) and the letter F (the initial of the company) depending on the viewing angle.

コンセプトブック
コンペの公開審査会場で配布。企業理念を反映したページと、コンペ用ポスターに使われたイラストを使って更にイメージを膨らませたページで構成している。

Concept book
Distributed at the competition judging. A page reflecting the company philosophy and a page that expands the image of the illustration used on the competition poster.

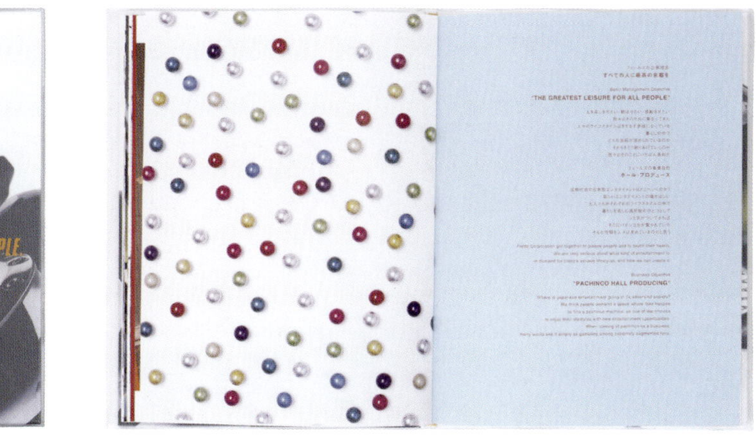

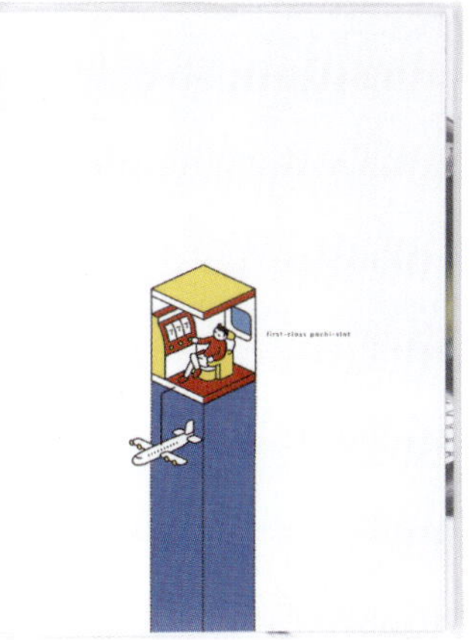

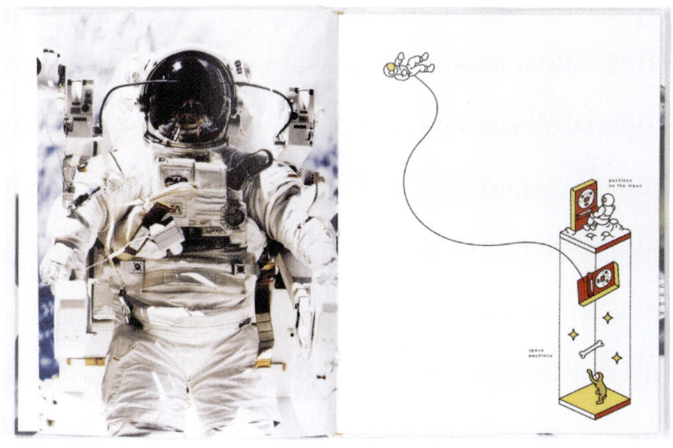

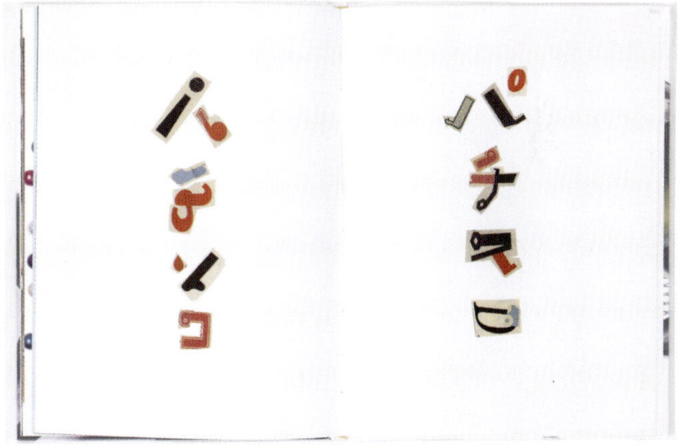

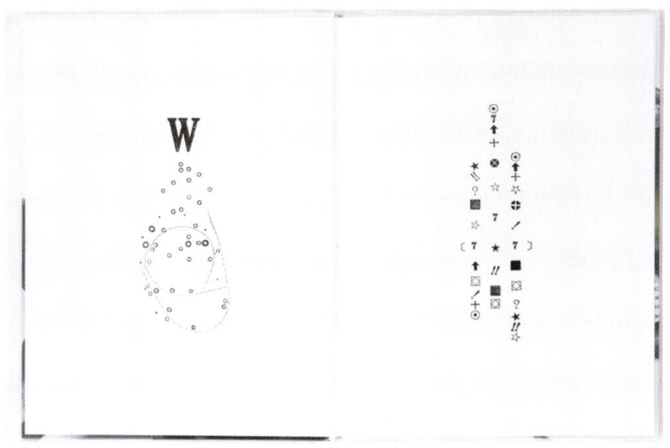

TBS

ウィットに富んだキャラクターがブランドのイメージアップに貢献
Witty characters improve brand visibility

戦略を読み解く 3 key words

堅実さとチャレンジ精神を兼ね備えた企業であること

放送が担うべき責務を着実に果たしながらも、変化を恐れず新たなビジネスチャンスには果敢にチャレンジし続ける企業でありたいと願う。"視聴・聴取者が信頼し、心から楽しめる番組作り"を目標に掲げている。

宣伝マンとして活躍するキャラクターの誕生

単なるアイコンに終わらず、愛称で呼ばれるキャラクター（=企業）としての存在を目指し、Bの文字をキャラクター化して「Tブ－S」と読ませた。その一方で、決して押しつけがましくはない、チャーミングな脇役的キャラクターのイメージも大切にしている。

実用性と遊び心を兼ね備えたツールでイメージアップ

手に取れるツールを魅力的にデザインできれば、マス媒体より高い広告効果が得られると考え、小型ツールの制作を重視。ゴミ袋やトイレットペーパーなど、ウイットに富んだ実用的なツールを制作することで、"知的かつ楽しい"イメージを訴求した。

3 key words

Communicate the trustworthy yet adventuresome spirit of the company

Promotes the company's serious regard for its public responsibility as a broadcaster as well as its desire to continue seizing new business opportunities without fear of change. Defines the mission of the company as "Creating programs that our viewers and listeners can trust, and enjoy wholeheartedly".

Creating effective promotional characters

More than just an icon, we created a character with a friendly image closely tied to the company's by creating "Boo" out of the "B" in TBS and pronouncing the company name as "T 'Boo' S". At the same time, care was given to assuring that the character take on a charming, subordinate role that was in no way obtrusive.

Improve brand image with practical and fun promotional goods

Focus was placed on creating small, useful promotional goods, with the thought that attractively designed, practical goods would have greater effect than advertisements in the mass media. Witty, practical items such as garbage bags and toilet paper were produced, seeking an "intelligent yet fun" image.

Logo

キャラクターの展開のしやすさを図って、ニュートラルなデザインとモノクロのベースカラーを採用した。

With ease of development in mind, the character was designed neutrally, in monochrome.

トイレットペーパー
営業ツールとして利用。ワインバッグに入れることで遊び心を演出した。

Toilet paper
Business tools, carried in a wine bottle bag for a spirited presentation.

■ CL= 東京放送 Tokyo Broadcasting System
■ Agency= 博報堂 HAKUHODO Inc. ■ CD= 山本幸司 Koji Yamamoto ■ AD + I= 佐野研二郎 Kenjiro Sano ■ D= 杉山ユキ Yuki Sugiyama ■ CW= 中村恭子 Kyoko Nakamura ■ S= 博報堂 HAKUHODO Inc.

Tシャツ T-shirt

ゴミ袋＆番組表

ゴミ袋は、番組観覧者へのプレゼントや、社内やロケ現場での掃除に使用。東京都の認可も取得済み。

Dust bag & Program list

A giveaway for program audiences, used for cleaning within the company and on location as well. Approved by the government of Tokyo.

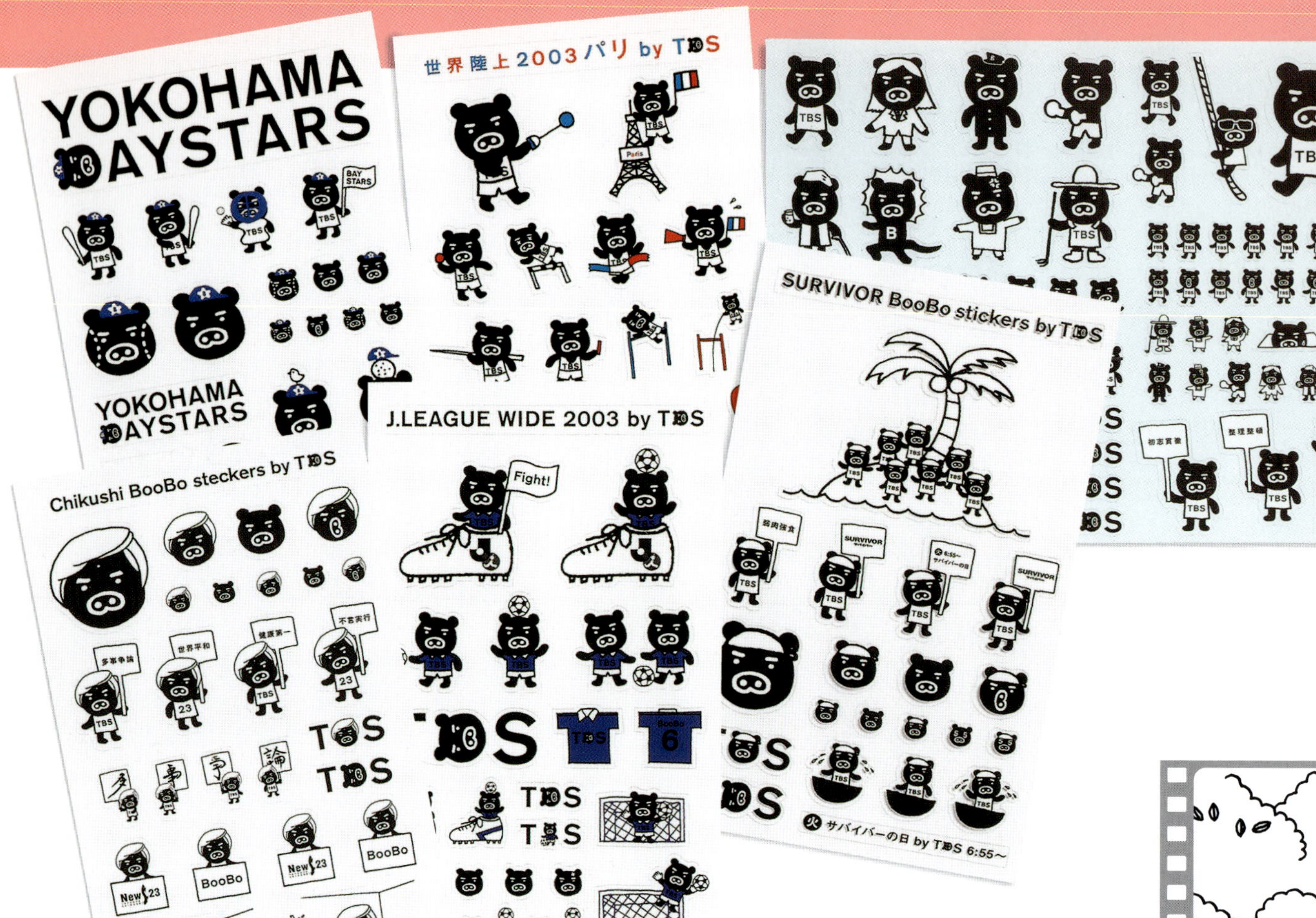

シール Sticker

TVCM

TBS

月 水戸黄門の日

木 ここがヘンだよ日本人の日
TBS

TBS
日 ウルルン滞在記の日
TBS

TBS
土 USo!? ジャパンの日
TBS

月 月曜ミステリーの日

TBS
たかし元気でやりおる？
日 からくりTVの日
TBS

Virgin Atlantic Airways ヴァージン アトランティック航空

空の旅をさらに楽しく快適に。デザインとユーモアで個性をアピール
Strong Style and humour promotes more enjoyable and exciting air travel

戦略を読み解く 3 key words

ブランドバリューは革新性。独自のスタイルを追求

英国に拠点を置く航空会社。「革新性」をブランドバリューのひとつに掲げ、スタイル性やセンスの高さを意識し、追求している。搭乗客に機内で快適に過ごしてもらうことはもちろんだが、ユーモアを交えながら楽しい、個性的な旅を提案している。

デザイン性の高さが語る「信頼」と「安心」

デザイン性の高さは、航空会社としての信頼性や安全性の高さを反映するものと考え、ツール制作に力を入れている。また、楽しい旅を願い、ユーモアも欠かさない。これらの背景には会長のサー・リチャード・ブランソンの考え方が強く影響している。

日本独自のツールでヴァージンらしさを表現

機内で使用するツールは世界共通、その他のノベルティやリーフレットは日本独自に制作。日本の文化や感性を踏まえ、「ヴァージンらしさ」をより効果的に伝えることを目指す。自由で洗練され、かつユーモアに富んだツールで企業の個性を表現している。

3 key words

Style Objective: Individuality builds brand value

This UK based airline, strives to maintain it's innovativeness as a form of brand value in a conscious quest for a superior and individual sense of style. In-flight comfort is provided with a mixture of humour resulting in a unique way of travel.

High-sense design conveys "reliance" and "security"

Every attention to details is made when it comes to producing high quality promotional material, resulting in the feeling of reliability, consistency and safety. In addition, an injection of humour adds to the feel good factor of travel - the foundation of which is strongly upheld and encouraged by Chairman Richard Branson.

Japan-specific tools express Virgin's uniqueness

In-flight tools are consistent worldwide; other promotional material is designed to be Japan-specific, drawing on Japanese culture to effectively convey Virgin's unique character. Promotional tools that are complimentary, good quality and full of humour express the company's individuality.

Logo

「レッド」「パープル」「ホワイト」がブランドカラー。「Cool、Trend、Design」といった要素を含んでいる。

Brand colors are red, purple and white. Cool and trendy design elements are incorporated.

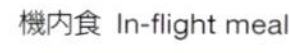

手提げ袋 Paper bag

機内食 In-flight meal

■CL= ヴァージン アトランティック航空 Virgin Atlantic Airways
<In-flight meal, Paper bag> ■Project production= ヴァージン アトランティック航空 Virgin Atlantic Airways ■S= ヴァージン アトランティック航空 Virgin Atlantic Airways

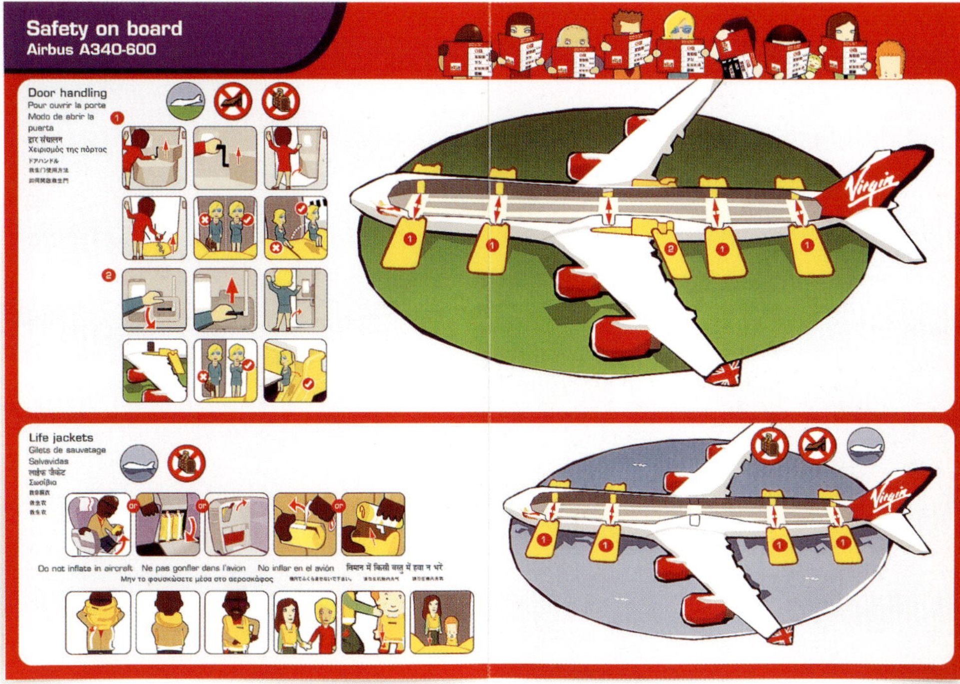

機内セーフティ・カード
離陸前に上映する「セーフティービデオ」に登場するキャラクターを連動。

Safety card
Relates to the characters appearing in the safety video shown before take-off.

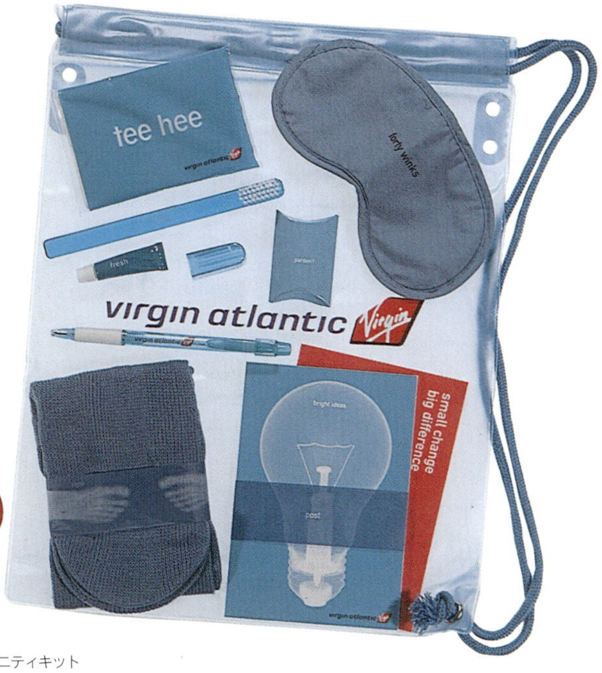

アメニティキット
エコノミークラスで提供している歯ブラシやアイマスクなどのグッズが入ったキット。
スケルトンカラーで全5色をそろえている。

Amenity kit
Economy class kit containing toothbrush, eye mask and other personal products comes in five colors, randomly placed in the seat pockets.

<Safety card> ■ I= ヴィークル Vehicle ■ Project production= ヴァージン アトランティック航空 Virgin Atlantic Airways <Amenity kit> ■ Project production= ヴァージン アトランティック航空 Virgin Atlantic Airways

2001年春
新アッパークラス（ビジネスクラス）導入時のプロモーション。

Spring 2001
Promotion for the launch of Virgin's new upper class (business class).

ノベルティ（アイマスク） Novelty (Eye mask)

ノベルティ（メモキューブ）
Novelty (Memo cube)

駅貼りポスター Poster

<Spring 2001 Novelty> ■CD + AD= 鵜野沢佳祐 Keisuke Unosawa ■DF= ウノサワデザイン Unosawa Design
<Spring 2001 Poster> ■CD= 金森周一 Shuichi Kanamori ■AD= 水谷孝次 Koji Mizutani ■I= Paul Davis ■DF= 水谷事務所 Mizutani Studio

2003年初夏

ショーファーカー無料送迎サービスの日本導入記念「No Problimo」プロモーション。

Early summer 2003

"No Problimo" promotion celebrating the launch of Virgin's complimentary limo service to and from the airport in Japan.

ノベルティ（ペンホルダー）
Novelty (Pen holder)

雑誌広告 Magazine AD

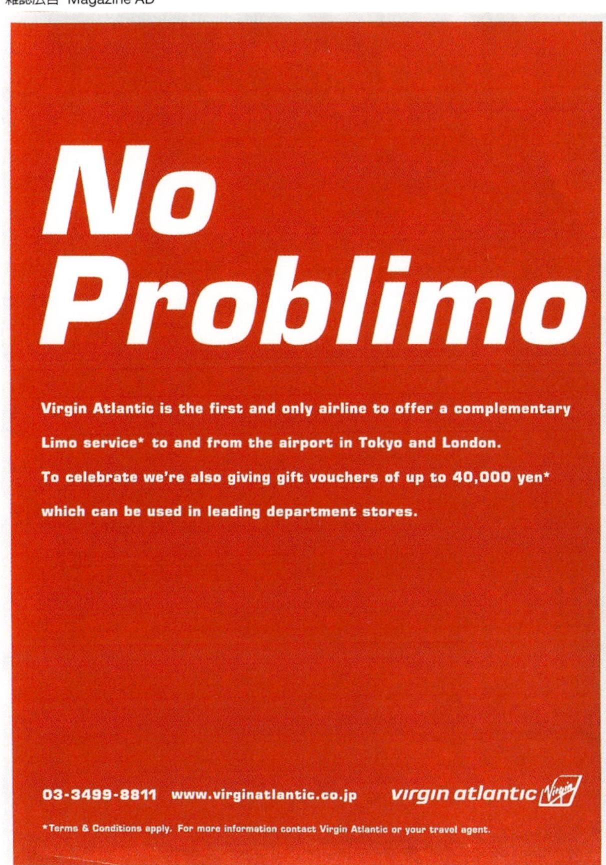

リーフレット Leaflet

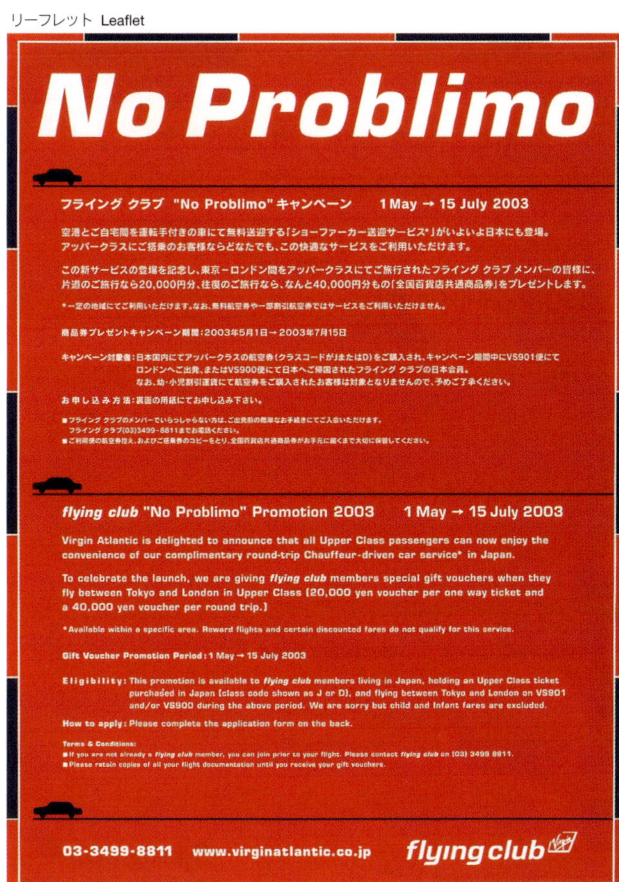

<Early summer 2003 Magazine AD, Leaflet, Novelty> ■ CD + AD + D= 鵜野沢佳祐 Keisuke Unosawa ■ DF = ウノサワデザイン Unosawa Design

2002年秋
エアバス最新鋭機A340-600型が日本路線に導入されたことを記念するプロモーション

Autumn 2002
Promotion celebrating the introduction of the new Airbus A340-600 jets on Japan flights.

雑誌広告 Magazine AD

ノベルティ（フライトソックス） Novelty (Flight socks)

リーフレット Leaflet

<Autumn 2002 Leaflet, Magazine AD, Novelty> ■CD + AD + D= 鵜野沢佳祐 Keisuke Unosawa ■DF= ウノサワデザイン Unosawa Design

フライングクラブ

マイレージプログラム「フライングクラブ」会員向に発送されるツール。

Flying Club

Materials sent to "Flying Club" mileage programme members.

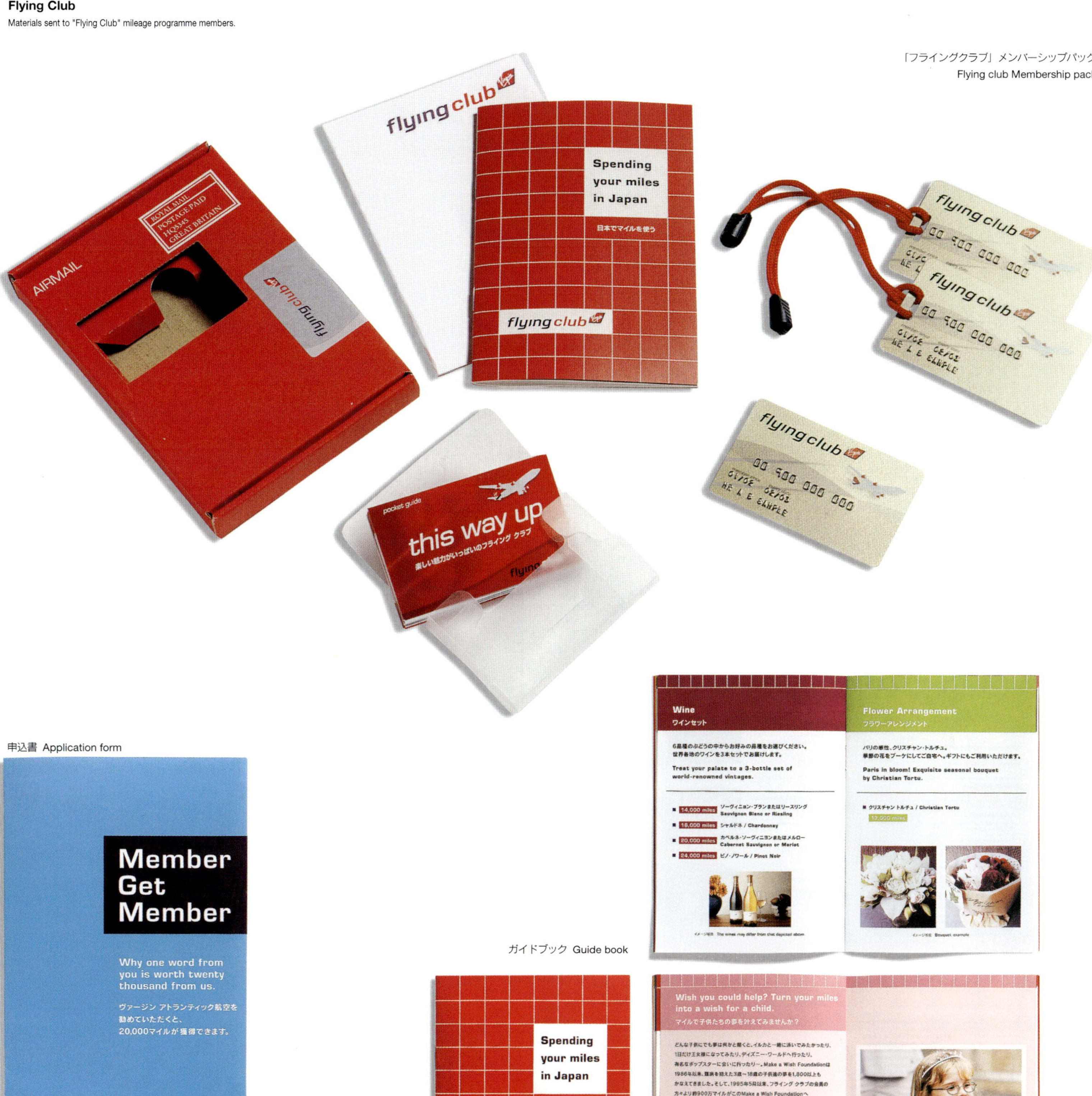

「フライングクラブ」メンバーシップパック
Flying club Membership pack

申込書 Application form

ガイドブック Guide book

<Flying Club Guide book> ■CD + AD + D= 鵜野沢佳祐 Keisuke Unosawa ■DF= ウノサワデザイン Unosawa Design <Flying Club Application form> ■AD + D= 鵜野沢佳祐 Keisuke Unosawa ■DF= ウノサワデザイン Unosawa Design
<Flying Club Membership pack> ■Project production= ヴァージン アトランティック航空 Virgin Atlantic Airways

社内報 In house newsletter

サービスガイド Service guides

会社案内 Company profile

社内報 In house newsletter

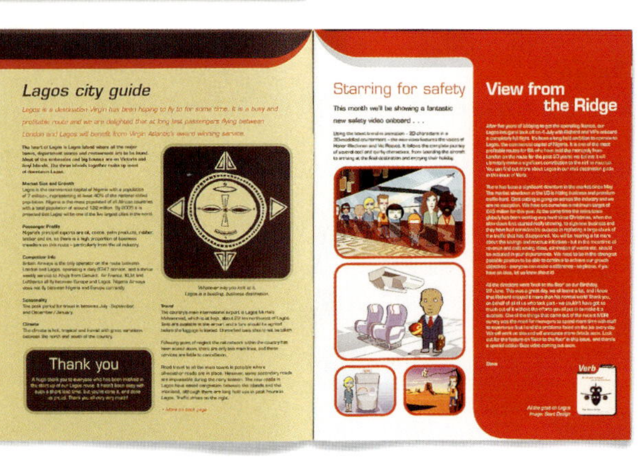

<Service guides> ■CD + AD + D= 鵜野沢佳祐 Keisuke Unosawa ■DF= ウノサワデザイン Unosawa Design <Company profile> ■CD= 川崎 誠 Makoto Kawasaki ■AD + D= 稲生聡宏 Akihiro Inou ■CW= 武田 透 Toru Takeda ■CW= 新藤明彦 Akihiko Shindo ■CW= 風穴 団 Dan Kazaana ■CW= 金子真樹 Masaki Kaneko ■D= 和田玲児 Reiji Wada ■DF= ジオグラフィックス GEO Graphics
<In house newsletter> ■Project production= ヴァージン アトランティック航空 Virgin Atlantic Airways

広告 Advertisement

まるで夢を見ているような心地よさ。

飛行機の中でマッサージが受けられる、世界でたった1つの航空会社「ヴァージン アトランティック航空」。
ビューティ・セラピストによるマッサージやネイルケアで、ロンドンまでの快適フライトをお約束します。
ご予約やサービスに関するお問い合わせ：03-3499-8811 www.virginatlantic.co.jp

upper class　virgin atlantic Virgin

「チェックインの長い列から抜け出したい・・・」と思ったことありませんか？

ヴァージン アトランティック航空は東京-ロンドン間を毎日運航。アッパークラスにご搭乗のお客様なら、
運転手付きの車がホテルまでお迎えにあがり、車の中でスムーズなチェックイン手続きをお済ませいただけます。
ご予約やサービスに関するお問い合わせ：03-3499-8811 www.virginatlantic.co.jp

upper class　virgin atlantic Virgin

ヴァージン アトランティック航空が「プレミアムエコノミー」を導入してから、今年で10周年を迎えます。業界の中で、つねに革新的なサービスをお届けし続けているヴァージン。
専用キャビンと、広々としたシートをご用意した「プレミアムエコノミー」が、スタイリッシュでゆったりとした空の旅をお約束します。
ご予約やサービスに関するお問い合わせ：03-3499-8811 www.virginatlantic.co.jp

premium economy　virgin atlantic Virgin

<Advertisement>　■ Project production= ヴァージン アトランティック航空 Virgin Atlantic Airways

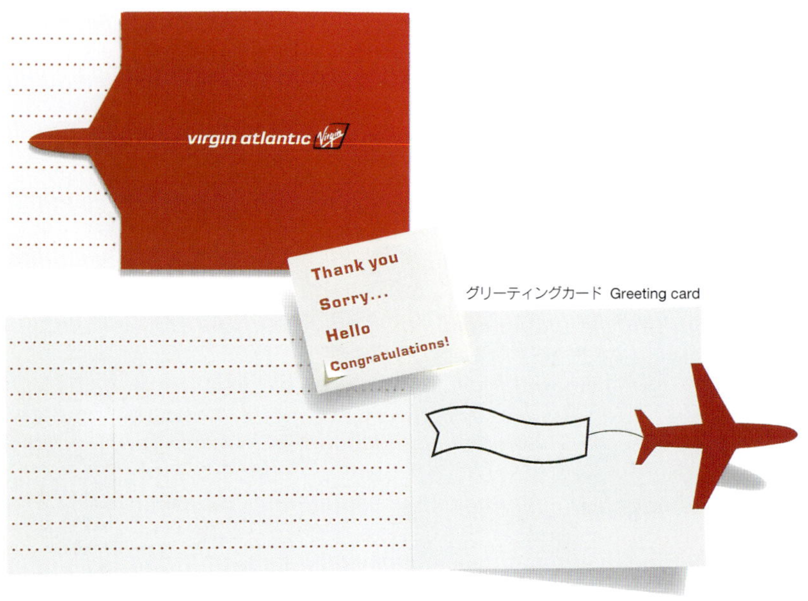

グリーティングカード Greeting card

2003年 カレンダー Calendar 2003

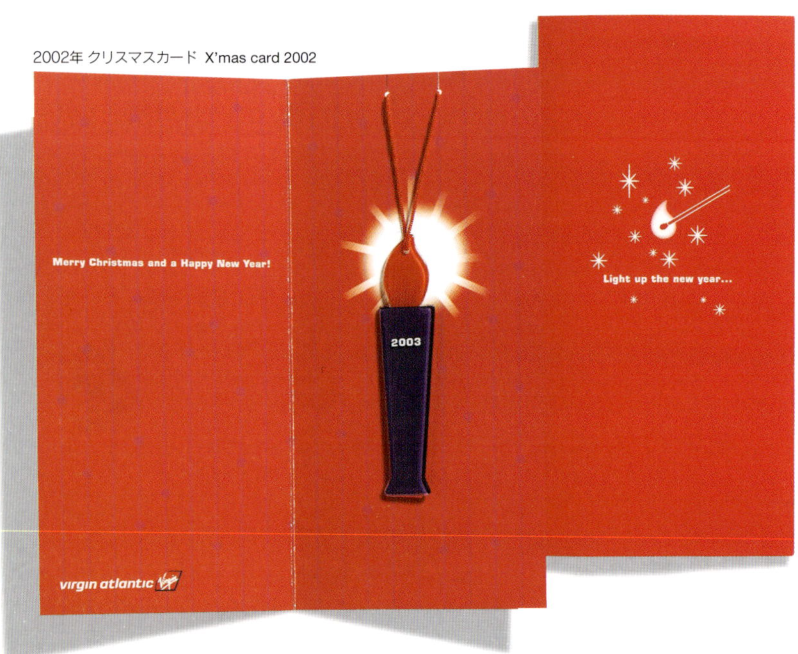

2002年 クリスマスカード X'mas card 2002

2001年 クリスマスカード X'mas card 2001

2001年 年賀状 New years card 2001

2003年 年賀状 New years card 2003

<Greeting card> ■CD + AD + D= 鵜野沢佳祐 Keisuke Unosawa <Calendar 2003> ■AD= Martin Muir ■I= Anthony Williams ■CW= Derek Waddy ■CW= Glen Law ■D= James Sterling ■DF= Start Design
<X'mas card 2001, 2002> ■CD + AD + D= 鵜野沢佳祐 Keisuke Unosawa ■DF= ウノサワデザイン Unosawa Design <New years card 2001> ■AD + D= 高田正治 Masaharu Takata ■DF=タカタデザイン Takata Design
<New years card 2003> ■CD + AD + D= 鵜野沢佳祐 Keisuke Unosawa ■DF= ウノサワデザイン Unosawa Design

2002年春

ホームページリニューアル時に展開した、新ウエブアドレスの認知度を高めるプロモーション。

Spring 2002

Promotion to increase recognition of Virgin's newly renovated website address.

ノベルティ（ポストイット&クリアファイル）
Novelty (Post it & Document holder)

雑誌広告 Magazine AD

ポストカード Post-card

ホームページ HP

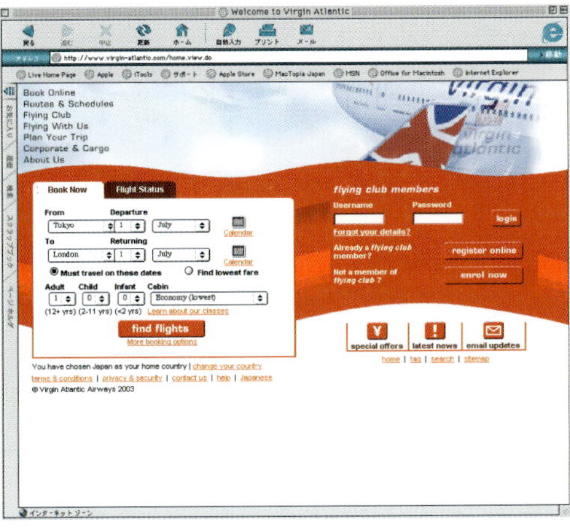

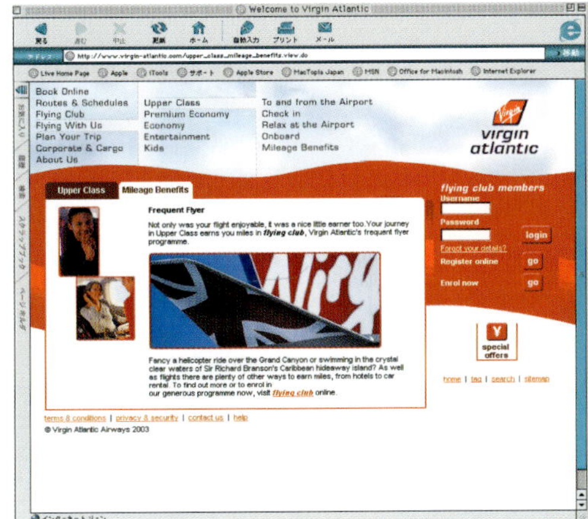

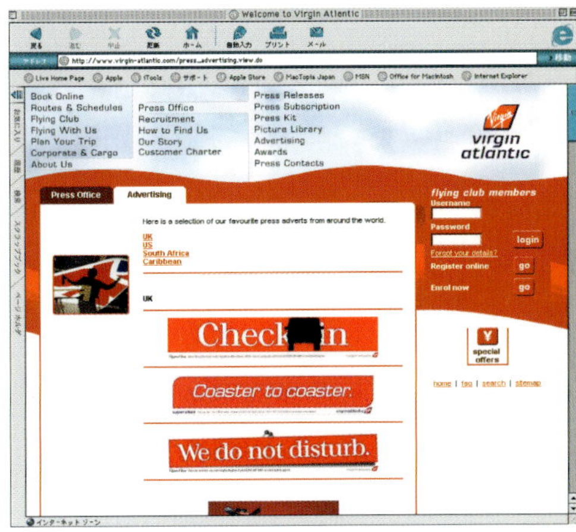

<Spring 2002 Novelty, Post-card> ■CD + AD= 鵜野沢佳祐 Keisuke Unosawa ■DF= ウノサワデザイン Unosawa Design
<Spring 2002 Magazine AD> ■CD= 川崎 誠 Makoto Kawasaki ■AD + D= 稲生聡宏 Akihiro Inou ■DF= ジオグラフィックス GEO Graphics
<HP> ■Project production= ヴァージン アトランティック航空 Virgin Atlantic Airways

FULLCAST フルキャスト

"短期バイト"を連想させるユニークな広告で知名度向上に成功

Increasing brand awareness through a unique ad campaign

戦略を読み解く 3 key words

登録制アルバイトを通して"若者を応援する"

18〜25歳の男女がメインスタッフとなりアルバイトの短期業務を請負う。スタッフ登録の希望者はウェブサイト「tankibaito.com」を経て登録し、希望のアルバイトを探すというシステム。業務を通じて"若者を応援する"企業でありたいと願う。

登録スタッフとクライアントの双方に発信

社名とウェブサイトの知名度を上げ、登録スタッフを増やすことを目的にプロモーションを展開。マス媒体での露出がメインだが、手に取ってもらえるSPツールにも注力。また、仕事を発注するクライアントに向けたブランディングも視野に入れる。

若さ溢れるビジュアルと、アイデアが光る広告手段

短期バイトを連想させるダンボールやタオルを使用したり、等身大の若者をモデルに起用したりと、"若さ、情熱、勢い"といったイメージを全面に打ち出す。特にダンボールを使ったポスターは発想のユニークさで注目を集め、スタッフの登録増に成功した。

3 key words

"Supporting young people" with a part-time employment site

The website contracts part-time jobs for 18-25 year olds. Job seekers register at the website "www.tankibaito.com" and search for the job they want. The company hopes to "support young people" through its work.

Targeting job seekers and employers alike

Develop a promotion to increase awareness of the company and its website, and increase the number of registered job seekers. Focus mainly on mass media, but also produce flyers and other promotional tools. Design each advertisement to effectively brand the website among employers as well.

Youthful visuals and bright ideas for delivering them

Use towels and cardboard -- things young people associate with part-time jobs -- to create life-size models that communicate a "young, hungry, strong" image. The cardboard poster attracts particular attention due to its unique concept, and compels many young people to register on the website.

Naming

"若さをフルにキャスト"するという企業コンセプトをストレートに表したネーミング。

The company name is derived from its mission -- "casting young people in fulfilling roles".

2001 - 2002年

ダンボールポスターをひとつのタレントと見立て、本物のタレントと共に"キャスティング"したり、単独で海岸や街に登場させたりした。

2001 - 2002

A cardboard poster of a TV personality is "cast" with other popular young TV personalities, and makes appearances alone on the beach and around town.

雑誌広告 Magazine AD

ポスター Poster

■CL= フルキャスト FULLCAST CO., LTD.
■CD + CW= 初海 淳 Jun Hatsuumi ■AD= 原 耕一 Koichi Hara ■D= 渡邊隆雄 Takao Watanabe ■P= 三浦憲治 Kenji Miura ■P= 円山正史 Masashi Maruyama ■Producer= 小泉 学 Manabu Koizumi
■SP Planner= 砂田チエ Chie Sunada ■Planner= 西 和彦 Kazuhiko Nishi ■Planner= 岡 雅敏 Masatoshi Oka ■Planner= 寺嶋秀則 Hidenori Terashima ■Agency= ジェイ・アイ・シー JIC Corp. ■DF= トラウト TROUT INC.
■S= ジェイ・アイ・シー JIC Corp.

2001年キャンペーン

フルキャストが運営するウェブサイト「tankibaito.com」へのアクセス誘導を目的に展開した。

2001 Campaign

Developed as an access guide to the website "tankibaito.com" operated by FULLCAST.

その日にもらえる
tankibaito.com

ポスター
折り畳んだ状態のダンボールをそのまま駅貼りポスターとして使用。1週間後、組み立てたダンボールを撮影したポスターを同じ場所に掲出した。

Poster
A flattened cardboard carton used as is as an in-station billboard poster. A poster featuring a photograph of the assembled carton was hung in the same location one week later.

ノベルティ
ポスターの掲出期間に合わせ、駅周辺で配布した圧縮タオル。表面を銀紙で包み、サイトのロゴを型押しした。

Novelty
A compressed towel, handed out around the station timed with the appearance of the poster, foiled wrapped and embossed with the website logo.

ポスター Poster

雑誌広告 Magazine AD

2003年キャンペーン

フルキャストの企業広告を展開。“若者を応援する” という企業スタンスを強く印象付けることが狙い。

2003 Campaign

FULLCAST's corporate advertising. Aims to convey the company's commitment to "supporting young people" and make a strong impression.

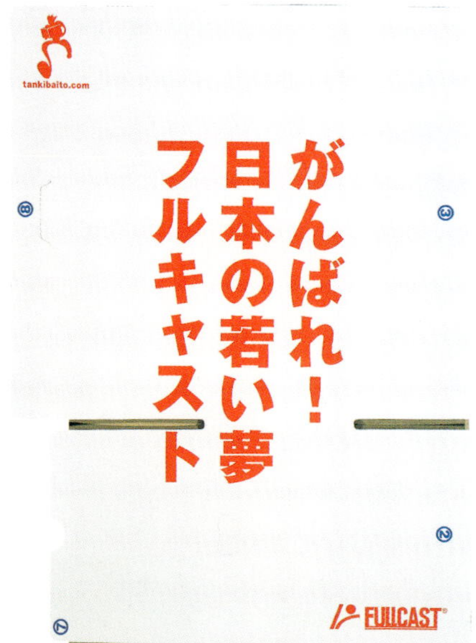

ポスター

2001年キャンペーンと同様のダンボールポスター。ターゲット層と同世代のサッカー選手やタレントをモデルに起用し、それぞれの夢を語ってもらうという作り。

Poster

The same cardboard poster as used in the 2001 campaign. Soccer players and TV personalities in the same age group as the target user each describe their dreams.

ポスター Poster

アドカード AD card

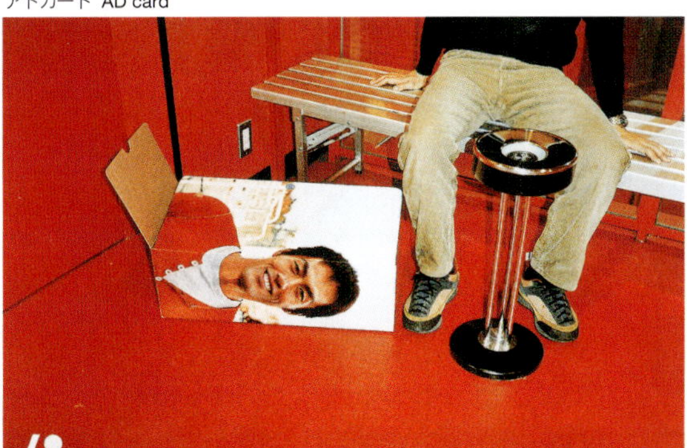

フリーペーパー Free paper

DENTSU 電通

100色の名刺で社員の個性・能力の多様性を表現

Business cards in 100 colors express staff diversity

戦略を読み解く 3 key words

世界で認知される企業を目指し、VI導入

創立100周年、株式上場、新社屋への移転を契機に、2002年12月1日、パブリックカンパニーとして、世界中だれでも社名を認知できる新たなブランド・ロゴを中心にした、VIを導入。ロゴのデザインでは、等身大で世界と対話する企業イメージを表現した。

3本柱のカラー・システムを構築

サイン、社章など社の統一性を示すアイテムには白・黒・グレーのベースカラーを使用。名刺は社員の個性、能力の多様性を示す100色のサブカラーを展開。コーポレートカラーはデンツウ・エクセレント・ブルーおよびデンツウ・エクセレント・レッドの2色。

高い視認性を追求したブランド・ロゴ

21世紀のプロフェッショナルなコミュニケーション企業としての電通および電通グループのイメージをブランド・ロゴで表現。印刷物から電子メディアまで、視認性の高いデザインを目指した。シンプルな書体を使いながら、そこに変化をつけて独自性を出した。

3 key words

A visual identity builds worldwide recognition

Established 100 years ago, the company went public and moved to its new headquarters on December 1, 2002. Introduce a new visual identity, centered around a new brand logo, that will make the public company's name recognizable around the world. The logo design expresses a corporate image that dialogues with the world on a human scale.

Building a color system around three base colors

Signage, badges, and other corporate applications indicating corporate consistency use three base colors: white, black and gray. Business cards, which express the diverse staff personalities and abilities are available in 100 sub-colors. The corporate colors are Dentsu excellent blue and Dentsu excellent red.

A brand logo striving for high visual recognition

Express the image of Dentsu and the Dentsu group as a 21st century professional communications company through the brand logo. Strive for design with high visual recognition across all applications from print to electronic media. Use a simple typeface transformed to give the logo originality.

Logo

ベーシックなVerdanaという書体を使い、そこに手を加えてデザインした。小文字にしたことで、ソフトでカジュアルなイメージが高まった。

Design using a basic typo called Verdana. By using the typo of small letters, a soft and casual image has grown.

名刺
名刺の色は、サブ・カラーの100色のなかから自由に選ぶことができる。

Business Card
Staff can choose from 100 sub-colors for business card colors.

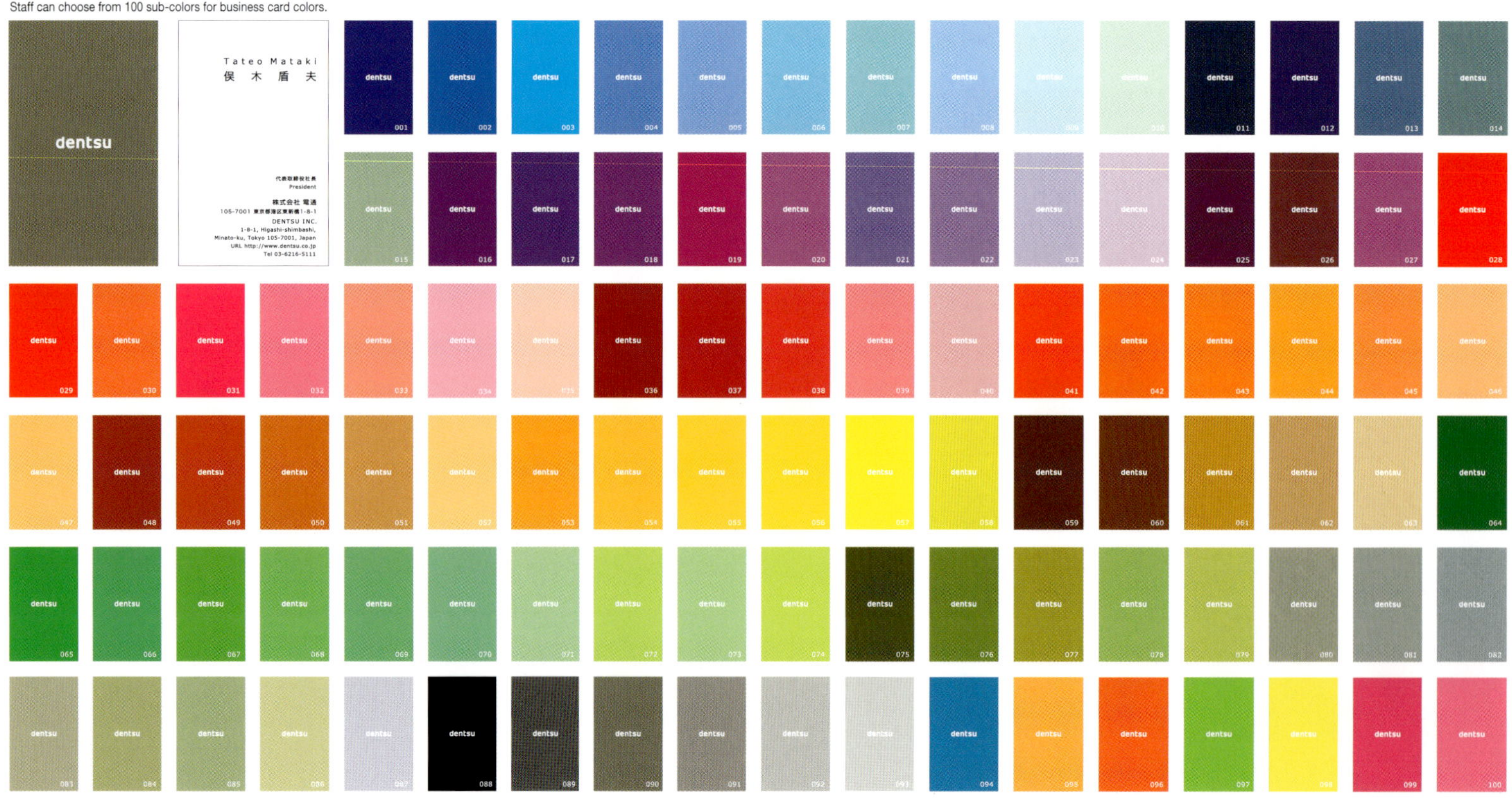

■CL= 電通 DENTSU INC.
■CD + AD + D= 河合雄流 Takeru Kawai ■D= 金井理明 Tadaaki Kanai ■Producer & ECD= 油谷勝海 Katsumi Yutani ■Producer= 中澤真純 Masumi Nakazawa ■Application producer= 古川彰俊 Akitoshi Furukawa
■Project production= 電通 DENTSU INC. ■S= 電通 DENTSU INC.

デザイン・マニュアル Design system manual

一般封筒
地にベースカラー、ワンポイントにサブカラーを使用。

General envelope
Envelope: base color for the stock, with a sub-color as an accent.

クラフト封筒 Manila envelope

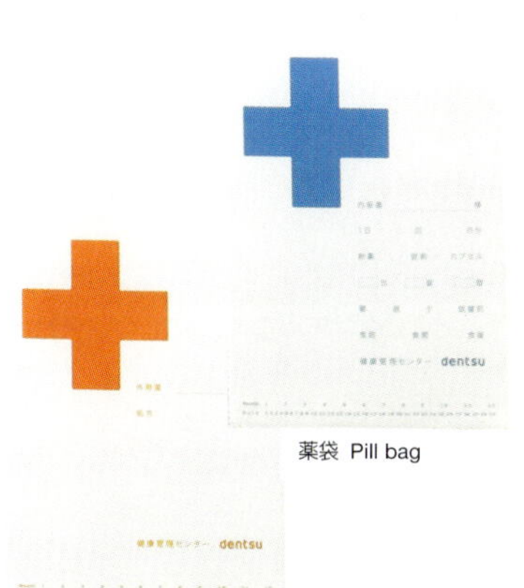

薬袋 Pill bag

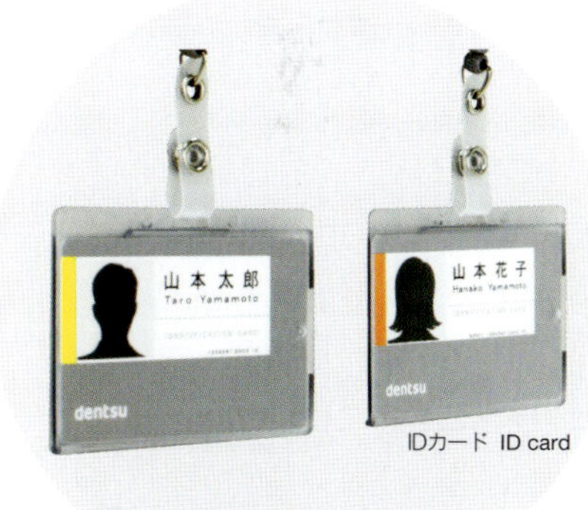

IDカード ID card

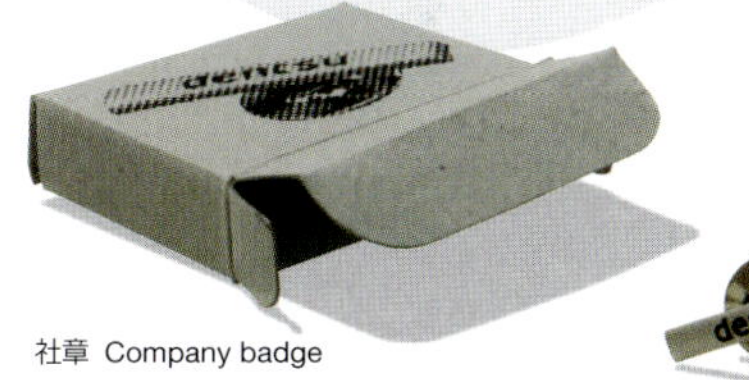

社章 Company badge

レターセット Letter set

紙袋 Paper bag

はっぴ Happi coat

Cyber Agent サイバーエージェント

常に変化するアメーバ＝常に成長・進化する企業

Like an amoeba, business that grows and changes

戦略を読み解く 3 key words

進化するインターネット専門の広告代理店

1998年に設立されたインターネット専門の広告代理店。新たなインターネットメディアの開発、運営、コンテンツ制作など事業の幅が広がっているのに伴い、2002年、新たな企業広告を制作した。若々しいエネルギーで常に新しい挑戦を続けている。

成長し続けるアメーバをイメージにCI展開

サイバーエージェントが持つ、常に成長・進化を続けるイメージを、いろいろなものを吸収して成長するアメーバととらえ、CIのデザインに据えた。そして、この新たなCIをスピーディに浸透させるため、広告からグッズまで幅広く取り入れている。

オリジナルフォントはあえて読みにくく

サイバーエージェント独特のフォント「アメーバボールド」を開発。あえて解読するのが難しい形にし、読み解きたいという欲求を導き出すことを狙った。遊び心のある、時代の流れを読んだ解読型コミュニケーションを展開している。

3 key words

Specialists in the evolving world of Internet advertising

Established in 1998 as an Internet advertising agency. As the business of developing, managing and producing content for the Internet becomes ever greater, the company decided to create a new advertising campaign. Continues to take on new challenges with fresh energy.

CI imaged after an ever-growing amoeba

The corporate identity likens the company's image of constant growth and change to that of an amoeba, assimilating everything in its path as it grows. In order to speed penetration, the CI incorporates a wide variety of goods and advertising.

Obscure lettering grabs the eye

Develop an original Cyber Agent font, "Amoeba Bold", which is daringly obscure and difficult to read -- catching the viewers' eyes as they struggle to make out what it says. Continually developing playful, contemporary forms of written communication.

Naming

インターネット専門の広告代理店という新たな企業の形をストレートに社名に据えた。

A simple, direct name that clearly expresses the company's role as an Internet advertising agency.

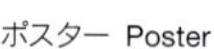

ポスター Poster

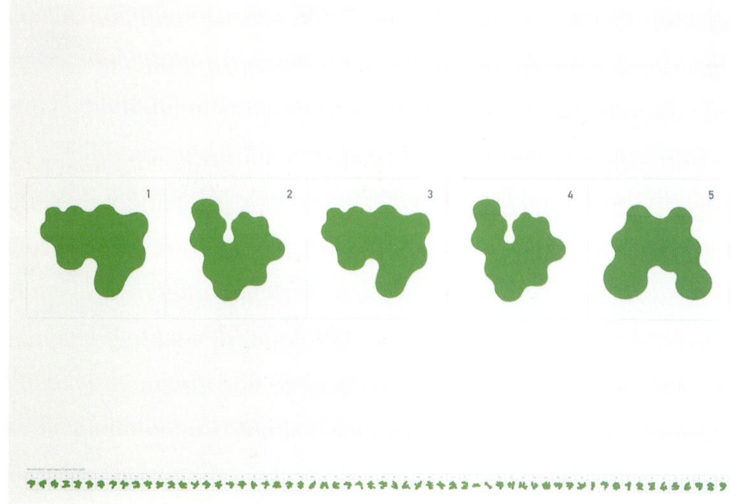

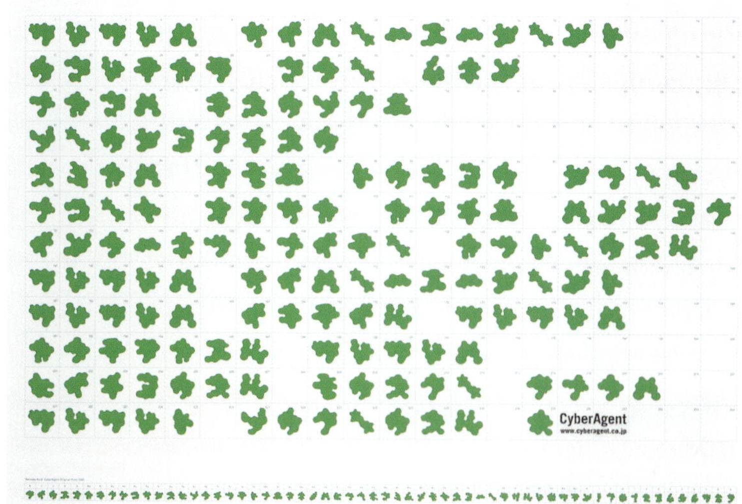

■CL= サイバーエージェント Cyber Agent
■CD= 須田 伸 Shin Suda ■CD＋AD= 金子 敦 Atsushi Kaneko ■AD＋D= 金子泰子 Yasuko Kaneko ■CW= 小西利行 Toshiyuki Konishi ■Advertising agent= 博報堂イン・プロブレス hakuhodo in progress
■DF= ブラッド・チューブ・グループ Blood Tube Group ■S= 博報堂イン・プロブレス hakuhodo in progress

ステーショナリー Stationery

名刺 Business card

紙袋 Paper bag

ぬいぐるみ Stuffed animal

Tシャツ T-shirt

雑誌広告 Magazine AD

DIC COLOR & DESIGN ディックカラー&デザイン

「色」の可能性を追求して新ツールを開発、情報発信

New promotional tools explore the possibilities of color

戦略を読み解く 3 key words

デジタル時代に対応したカラーツールを開発・提供

デジタル・DTP時代に対応した、カラーリング環境を提供。「色で生きるデザイン」「デザインで生きる色」を念頭に、DICカラーガイドのデータソースを基盤とした新カラーツールを開発している。

メンバーズクラブやギャラリーで色の多様性を発信

DICカラーガイドシリーズより1580色をベースに搭載した「カラートレイン」の制作など新規商品の開発に力を入れつつ、さらに、色に関する情報を伝える「DIC カラークラブ」やギャラリー「DIC COLOR SQUARE」の運営に力を入れている。

「色」を重要視した媒体を作成

すべての媒体において、「色」が重要な要素。デザインの細かなところまで、色彩を意識したつくりになっている。企画展『色の旅』のパンフレットやグッズも企画意図に基づき、色をテーマにした仕上がりで統一を図った。

3 key words

Color promotional tools for the digital age

The company offers coloring environments created for the age of digital and desktop publishing. Keeping the twin concepts of "design brought to life with color" and "color brought to life through design" in mind, we create new, colorful promotional tools using the DIC Color Guide as our palette.

Convey the multiplicity of color via a members' club and gallery

While concentrating on developing new products, such as the "Color Train", the 1,580 colors from the DIC Color Guide Series ready for use with computer design programs, manage the "DIC COLOR CLUB", a discussion forum about color, and the "DIC COLOR SQUARE" gallery.

Stressing color in every medium

The creative process focuses on color down to the smallest elements of design, using color as an essential element in every medium. Everything hews to a consistent color theme, down to the promotional pamphlet and goods for the planned exhibition "A Voyage of Color (Iro no tabi)".

Logo

CIカラーはフランスの伝統色「ルージュ・アルダン」。生き生きとして輝き、強烈に燃える炎の色のように、インパクトや勢いに富み、先進性を保ち続ける企業姿勢、「カラー&デザイン」への情熱を表現している。

The color used in the corporate identity is "Rouge Ardennes" from the DIC Traditional French Colors series. Bright and vivid, like a raging fire, it is a strong, impactful color that represents the company's business attitude of constant advancement and fervor for "color and design".

会員誌 Bulletin journal

メンバーズカード Membership card

DIC カラークラブ

カラーに関するさまざまな情報を伝える会員制のクラブ。メンバーには年4回、会員誌が届けられる。

DIC COLOR CLUB

A members club conveying a wide range of information on the subject of color.

会社案内 Company guidance

■CL= ディックカラー&デザイン DIC COLOR & DESIGN
<Company guidance> ■D= 町田英保 Hideyasu Machida ■CW= 田畑宏恵／スタッフコミュニケイション Hiroe Tabata / STAFF COMMUNICATIONS <Logo> ■D= 中村俊樹 Toshiki Nakamura
<DIC COLOR CLUB> ■AD + D= 相田貴子 Takako Aida ■S= ディックカラー&デザイン DIC COLOR & DESIGN

Gallery

ディック カラー スクエア

ギャラリー。企画展「色の旅3000年」は自社で企画・運営した展覧会。オリジナルツールも制作している。

DIC COLOR SQUARE

The gallery. "The History of Color in 3000 Years", an exhibition planned and operated by DIC for which original promotional tools were produced.

RGBスケールキット RGB scale kit

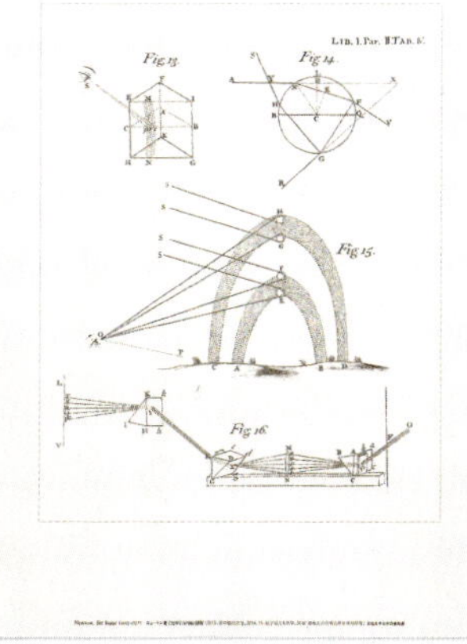

パンフレット

「色の旅展」は連続する企画展。毎回、新たにパンフレットとスタンプを作成する。来場者がスタンプを押し、旅のイメージを膨らませる。

Pamphlet

"The History of Color" is staged in series of exhibitions. A new pamphlet and stamp is produced for each, stamped on visitors' passes to project the image of travel.

企画展カタログ Plan exhibition catalog

雑誌広告 Magazine AD

デジタルカラーガイド「カラートレイン」
Digital color guide「Color Train」

<DIC COLOR SQUARE> ■AD + D= 相田貴子 Takako Aida ■AD= 永原康史／永原康史事務所 Yasuhito Nagahara / The Nagahara Office
<Color Train, Magazine AD> ■D= 町田英保 Hideyasu Machida ■D= 別府さやか／永原康史事務所 Sayaka Beppu / The Nagahara Office
<RGB scale kit> ■CD= 山口正幸 Masayuki Yamaguchi ■D= 井口仁長／永原康史事務所 Jincho Iguchi / The Nagahara Office

REGAL リーガル

時代に合わせて存在感をアピールする、老舗ブランドのイメージ戦略
Creating a modern presence -- brand image strategy for an old label

戦略を読み解く 3 key words

課題は従来のブランドイメージからの脱却

トラッドシューズの代名詞的存在として広く認知されてきたが、多様化するファッションの流れに伴い、今一度ブランドとしての存在感をアピールすることが課題となっていた。そこで従来のトラッドイメージから脱却するべく、VIの再構築を行った。

残すべきところは残しながら新たなVIをデザイン

VIの再構築にあたり、ロゴデザインは従来のローマン系をゴシック系に変えてモダンさを強調。ブランドカラーは金赤に近かった従来のカラーを“今”にアジャストさせたいと考え、シアンを入れて落ち着いたイメージを打ち出した。

商品見直しとの相乗効果でイメージ戦略に成功

ショールームや店頭も含めた全ての媒体において、VIを前面に出した統一感のあるビジュアルで新たなイメージの浸透を図った。更にプロモーションに合わせて商品ラインの見直しも行い、結果として売り上げ及び展示会での受注は前年比140%を達成した。

3 key words

Escaping from a long-established brand image

While widely recognized as synonymous with traditional shoes, the Regal label needs to reestablish its presence as a modern brand in order to succeed in a fragmenting fashion market. Redesign the visual identity in order to escape from the confines of the previous brand image.

Redesigning visual identity with an eye for what should be saved

Redesigning the visual identity involves changing the serif logo to a san serif face, emphasizing a modern sensibility. The reddish-gold brand color is adjusted to the "now" by adding a touch of cyan, projecting a cooler image.

Successfully combining product redesign with image strategy

Use the visual identity consistently and prominently across all media, including in showrooms and retail outlets, to increase penetration of the new brand image. Simultaneously, introduced new-look products in conjunction with promotions, leading to an increase in retail sales and industry orders of 40%.

Naming

ブランド名は英語で「王者らしい、堂々とした」という意味で、モノ作りに対するブランドの誇りが込められている。ロゴに添えた“The pride to share.”というコピーは“ブランドの誇りを履く人と分かち合いたい”というポリシーを表すもの。

The "kingly, stately" connotations of the Regal brand name imply the company's pride in craftsmanship. The copy used in the logo, "The pride to share.", reflects the company's policy of "wanting to share our pride with our customers".

Shop

Showroom

■CL= リーガルコーポレーション REGAL CORPORATION
■Agency= 博報堂 HAKUHODO Inc. ■CD + AD= 永井一史 Kazufumi Nagai ■D= 関 友和 Tomokazu Seki ■D= 中島 清 Kiyoshi Nakajima ■CW= 加藤麻司 Asaji Kato ■P= 数井啓介 Keisuke Kazui
■S= 博報堂 HAKUHODO Inc.

靴箱 Shoe box

Showroom

プレート&台 Plate & Stand

靴まわりアイテム Shoe tool

ポスター Poster

コンセプトブック Concept book

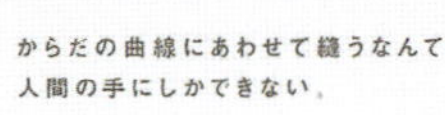

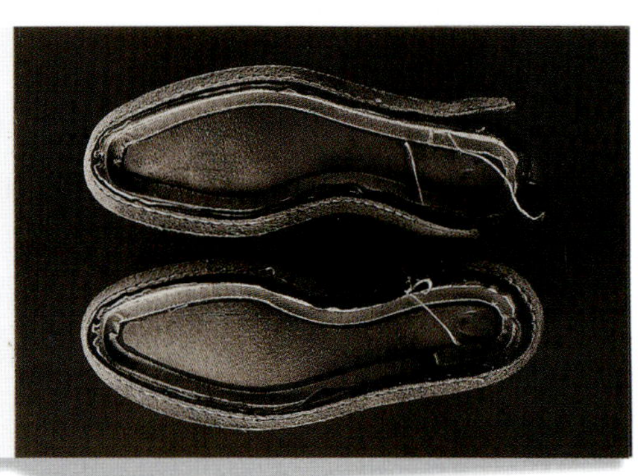

木型
靴の木型は、その靴を履く国で作るべきです。
骨格がまったくちがう、自分では履くことができない人に
履きやすさを追求することは不可能でしょう。
リーガルは、足の長さ、幅、指の付け根の位置、親指から
小指にかけてのカーブなど日本人の足を知り尽くしています。

素材
強さ、しなやかさ、光沢。靴に使用する革は、
他の革製品に比べてはるかに高い品質が要求されます。
当然のことながら、上質な革の生産量は少なく、
リーガルでは、ヨーロッパ、アメリカ、日本など
世界の革市場に出かけ、自らの基準に合う革を仕入れています。

グッドイヤーウェルト製法
リーガルがこだわり続ける靴の製法のひとつ。
他の製法より縫う工程が多く、時間も手間もかかりますが、
そのぶん丈夫で型くずれしない靴を作る
ことができます。グッドイヤーウェルト製法による
靴の生産量はリーガルが世界No1です。

縫って、縫って、また縫って。

靴は思想である。

靴を履くことは、道を歩くことだ。
社会のなかを進むことだ。
美しい靴であるまえに、
正しい靴でありたいとリーガルは思う。
世界のどこの場所でも胸をはって歩ける
品質とデザインを約束する靴であること。
正統のなかにも、自分らしさを表現する楽しさを
教えてくれる靴であること。
この哲学を、いつの時代にも通用する
普遍的な価値とするために、
リーガルは、新しいスタイルと機能性を
伝統のなかに注ぎ込みつづけていく。
リーガルを履くこと、それは誇りを分ちあうこと。

The pride to share.
REGAL

カード Card

新聞広告 Newspaper AD

minä perhonen ミナ・ペルホネン

ブランドコンセプト、商品、ショップ、顧客を有機的に結ぶ取り組み
Organically linking brand concept, products, shops and customers

戦略を読み解く 3 key words

長期的ビジョンで"モノ作りの方法論"をデザイン

レディースのファッションブランド。10年、100年先を見据えたモノ作りにこだわり、表面的な新しさを追わず、ワンシーズンで消費されないモノ作りを追求。既成概念にとらわれず、常にモノ作りの方法論そのものからデザインするスタンスを貫く。

人と人でつなぐ"手渡しのプロモーション"を重視

ブランドの認知には、"本当に情報を必要としている人に向けた、確実な情報とサービスを提供すること"、つまり来店者を満足させることが最も効果的だと考える。マス媒体は使わずに、手に取ったユーザーが"嬉しい"と感じるツール作りに努めている。

ブランドの姿勢と特長をグラフィックを使って表現

グラフィックでのブランディングで大切なのは"商品の質感や、使われている技術を表現すること"。ブランドの特長である、イマジネーション豊かなオリジナル・テキスタイルを視覚化することをベースに、常に実験的なデザイン手法に取り組んでいる。

3 key words

Designing a "craftsmanship methodology" along a long-term vision

A ladies' fashion brand. Focusing on craftsmanship that will last ten, one hundred years, the company ignores the superficially new to create products that will last beyond the current season. Unconfined by pre-existing concepts, the starting point for its product design is a "methodology of craftsmanship".

"Hand-to-hand promotion" links people

The most effective brand recognition comes from "providing trustworthy information and service to customers who need information" -- that is, satisfying each customer who visits the store completely. Eschewing mass media, put efforts into creating promotional tools that embody the "happiness" of each customer that holds it.

Expressing brand attitude and characteristics through graphics

The most important contribution the graphics make to the brand is "describing the quality of the product, materials and craftsmanship". Graphics are developed through experimentation based on a visualization of the imaginative, original textiles that are the hallmark of the brand.

Naming

minäはフィンランド語で"自分"という意味で、不揃いの小さな点の集合は"いろいろな自分"を表す。当初はこのminäがブランド名だったが、ブランドが次なるステージに入ったところでperhonen（同じくフィンランド語で"蝶々"の意味）という名称をプラス。"蝶々の羽の柄"のように、更にたくさんのテキスタイルを創っていきたいという思いを込めた。

"minä" means "oneself" in Finnish, and the aggregation of various slightly different versions of the word expresses the multitude of "selves" that exist. "minä" was originally the brand name, but when the brand hit its next stage of development, "perhonen" (meaning "butterfly" in Finnish) was added. Like the "pattern on the wings of a butterfly", the company will create even more beautiful varieties of textiles.

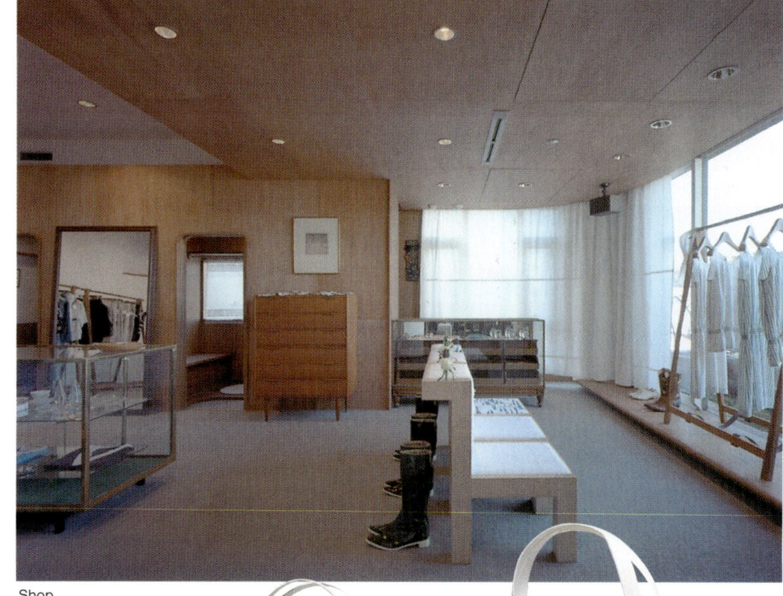

Shop

ショップカード Shop card

タグ Tag

ラッピング Wrapping

ショップバッグ Shop bag

■CL= ミナ MINA Co., Ltd.
■CD + Textile Design= 皆川明 Akira Minagawa　■AD + D= 菊地敦己 Atsuki Kikuchi　■S= ブルーマーク Bluemark Inc.

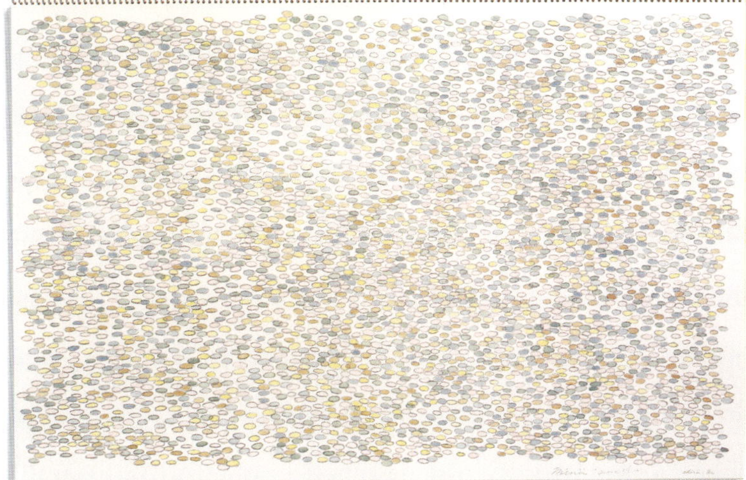

ノベルティ
商品のテキスタイルパターンを全ページにプリントした大型スケッチブックで、顧客には1枚ずつプレゼント。ポスターや包装紙など、様々な使い方をしてもらいたいと制作した。

Novelty
The pages of a large scale sketchbook printed with product textile patterns are torn off and given to customers one each. Produced with the hope that customers will use them as posters, wrapping paper, and in many other ways.

ポスター Poster

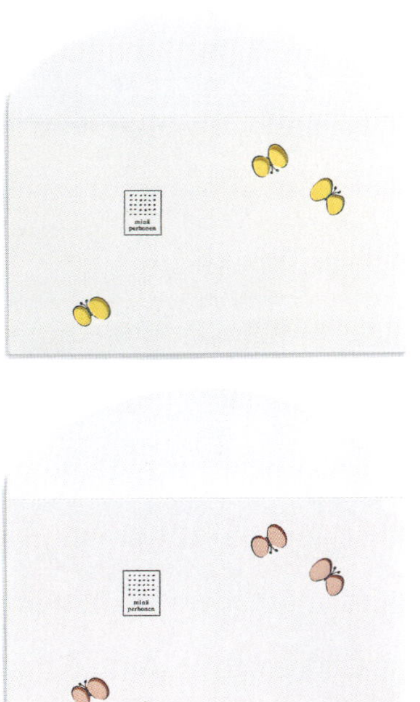

招待状 Invitation

招待状 Invitation

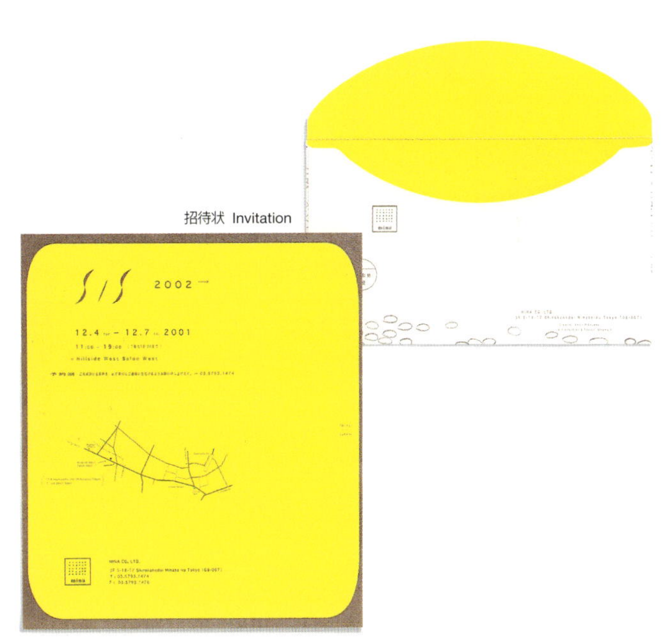

2002年に行った「粒子」展

洋服だけではなく、洋服を作るまでのプロセスや、モノを作るとはどういうことかを見せるための展覧会。ADは、プロデュースから会場構成、付随するツールまで全てを手がけた。

Exhibition of minä's works "Ryushi" in 2002

An exhibition that shows not only clothes, but the process of making them and what making things in general entails. The art director was involved in every aspect of production, from the design of the exhibition space to all peripheral materials.

カタログ Catalog

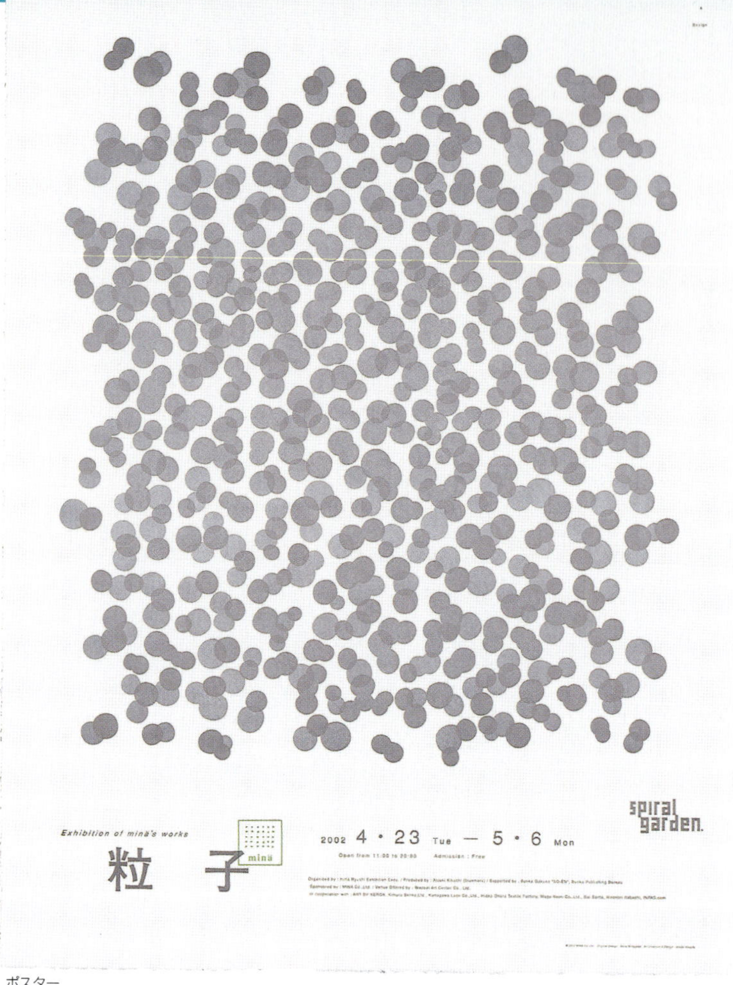

ポスター

デジタルで制作したデザインを、活版印刷でフランス製の版画用紙にプリントするという手法をとった。均一ではない仕上がりも織り込み済みで、独特の風合いを出すことに成功。

Poster

Digitally produced design letterpress-printed on French woodblock print paper. Factoring in an uneven finish rendered an unique texture.

フライヤー Flyer

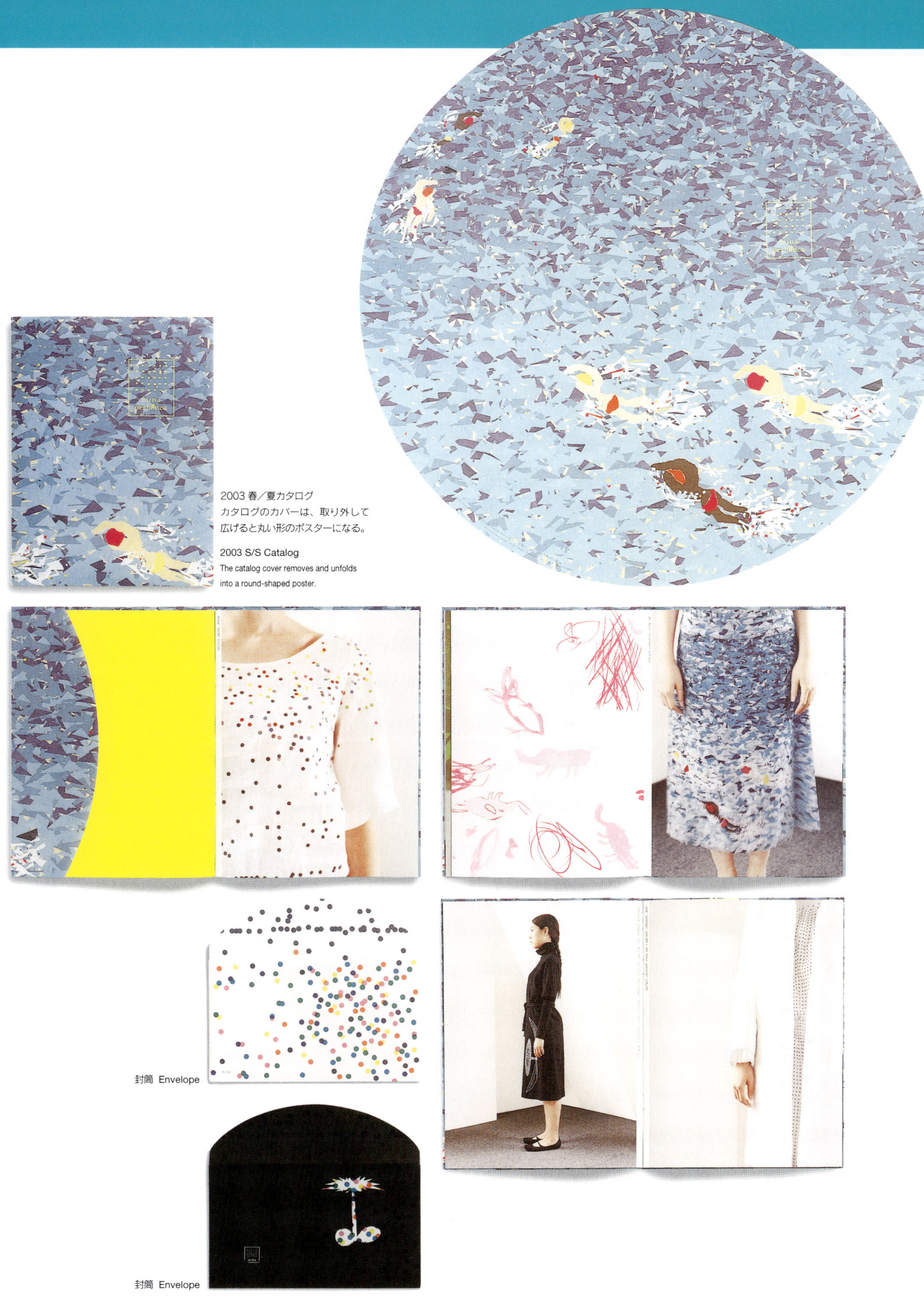

2003 春／夏カタログ
カタログのカバーは、取り外して広げると丸い形のポスターになる。

2003 S/S Catalog
The catalog cover removes and unfolds into a round-shaped poster.

封筒 Envelope

封筒 Envelope

ノベルティ（コースター）と商品（ミニバッグ）

定番アイテムのミニバッグは、様々なテキスタイルを使って制作。そのデザインに合わせたコースターは顧客にプレゼントする他、セット販売も行った。

Novelty (coaster) & Product (mini bag)

The mini-bag, a regular item, is produced using various textiles. Matching coasters were presented to visitors, and sold as sets.

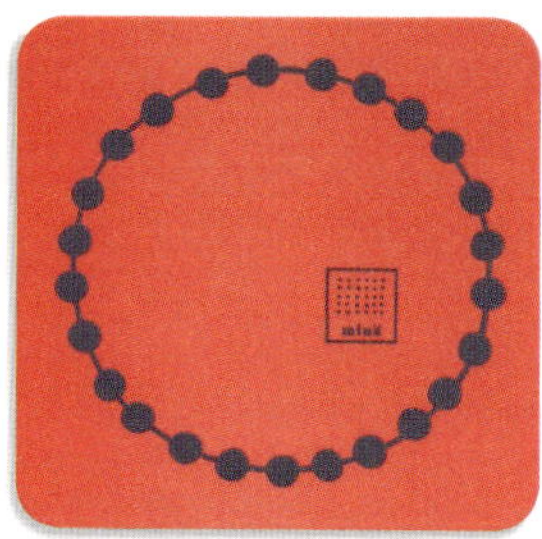

■ Textile Design= 皆川　明　Akira Minagawa

Camper カンペール

すべての媒体を通してカンペールのフィロソフィーを発信
Promoting the Camper philosophy through every medium

戦略を読み解く 3 key words

毎日履けるカジュアルで機能的な靴を製造

1877年から時を経て、スペイン最古の靴会社へと成長。毎日履けて、カジュアルで、機能的なコンフォートシューズをつくり続けている。地中海の歴史、文化、景色から受けるインスピレーションを大切にしたフェミニン〜ユニセックスまで幅広い商品がそろう。

自然がいっぱいの田舎の世界と都会との掛け橋に

地中海の豊かな自然を都会で暮らしている人たちにも感じてもらいたいと、地中海の自然をモチーフにした商品を採用。さらに、ポスターやカタログ、ショップにも地中海の要素を取り入れ、自然とのふれあい、環境を尊重することの大切さを伝えている。

各媒体を連動させ、企業の理念をかたちに

ポスター、ショート・フィルム、ショップ、カタログ、ホームページなど各媒体を連動させ、靴づくりにとどまらず、人生の哲学や考え方まで含めた企業理念を幅広く発信している。

3 key words

Functional shoes for casual, everyday wear

Spain's oldest shoemaking company, founded in 1877, the company makes a line of casual style, functional shoes comfortable enough to wear every day. Drawing on the history and culture of the Mediterranean region for inspiration, the line comprises a wide range of shoes including both feminine and unisex styles.

Bringing the city to the countryside

Introduce products with motifs of Mediterranean nature, so that even city-dwelling customers will feel as though they're in the lush Mediterranean countryside. Use the Mediterranean element in posters, catalogs and in stores, communicating the company's connection to nature and high regard for the environment.

Coordinate efforts in every media to embed brand concept

Coordinate posters, short films, shops, catalogs, websites -- in short, a lockstep movement to widely and consistently promote a brand concept that includes not only shoes, but also the company's humanistic philosophy and way of thinking.

Naming

マヨルカの言葉で「農夫」を意味する。

The brand name is a Mayorcan word for "farmer".

マガログ（カタログ）
Magalog

■CL= カンペール Camper
■CD= Shubhanker Ray ■AD= Pablo Martin ■P= Stefan Ruiz ■I= Marti Guixe ■Project production= カンペール クリエイティブ チーム Camper Creative Team ■S= カンペール Camper

¿PROBLEMA DE GASES?

El trabajo que realiza el aire comprimido es bien conocido. Basta con recordar los martillos neumáticos que perforan las calles de la ciudad. Hoy el aire comprimido acciona el motor de un coche. Ésta es la contribución a la familia humana del ingeniero francés Guy Nègre, cuyo sueño está a punto de realizarse a través de la empresa MDI que él mismo creó. Tras superar todo tipo de trabas administrativas, el primer coche homologado con motor de aire se anuncia para principios del 2003. Este vehículo se fabricará en factorías de tamaño humano con unos cien obreros y una producción anual de entre dos mil y cuatro mil unidades.

El motor de aire no sólo no contamina el aire, sino que lo purifica. Ronronea como una cafetera y por el tubo de escape escupe aire fresco y limpio. De momento la historia y la situación administrativa del motor de aire parecen una broma. Seguro que las energías renovables nos depararán nuevas sorpresas para la necesaria autonomía energética.

Rompe todos los esquemas de los automóviles actuales. Su carrocería es de fibra de vidrio para reducir al máximo el peso y se ensambla como se hace con los aviones. Su estructura es tubular para que, siendo liviana, otorgue máxima protección al conductor como sucede con los bólidos. Todo el circuito eléctrico, que en los coches tradicionales llega a pesar hasta 20 kg, se reduce a un solo cable gobernado por un pequeño emisor de radio que a su vez hace de antirrobo. El sistema de información del panel del conductor es una pequeña pantalla de ordenador. Con una bombona de aire comprimido de 300 litros puede recorrer más de 200 km arrastrando unos 500 kg con un coste de 0,75 euros por 100 km. Este vehículo puede cargarse en nuestra casa en unas tres o cuatro horas con electricidad convencional de 30 amperios o bien en unos tres minutos cuando existan compresores de carga en las gasolineras. Se estima un precio base de unos 9.500 euros.

GAS PROBLEMS?

The role of compressed air is well known. One only has to think of pneumatic drills hammering away at city streets. Now compressed air can activate a car's motor. This contribution to the humanity is that of Frenchman Guy Negre whose dream is soon to be realised thanks to MDI, a company he founded. At the beginning of next year, 2003 and after overcoming all sorts of administrative traps the first officially recognised air motor car will be announced. This vehicle will be built in human sized factories employing around a hundred workers and producing annually between 2000 and 4000 units.

The air motor not only does not contaminate but also purifies. It purrs like a coffee maker and from its exhaust belches clean fresh air. For now the history and the administrative situation of the air motor read like a joke. To be sure renewable energies will provide new surprises so that a necessary energetic self-sufficiency can occur.

It breaks with all the present definitions of a car. Its frame is of fibreglass to reduce maximum weight and it is assembled in the same way that aeroplanes are. Its structure is tubular so that although it is light it can provide maximum protection for the driver much as a racing car does. The electrics of traditional cars can weigh up to 20kg but in this one is reduced to one cable controlled by a small radio transmitter which at the same time works as a car alarm. The driver's dashboard is a small computer screen. With one 300 litre compressed air cylinder one can cover more than 200km carrying 500kg for around 0,75 Euros every 100km. This vehicle can be charged in our homes in 3 to 4 hours with conventional 30 amp electricity or in three minutes when one can charge up at gas stations. Estimated basic price is 9.500 Euros.

TOTALLY MAD TOTALLY NORMAL

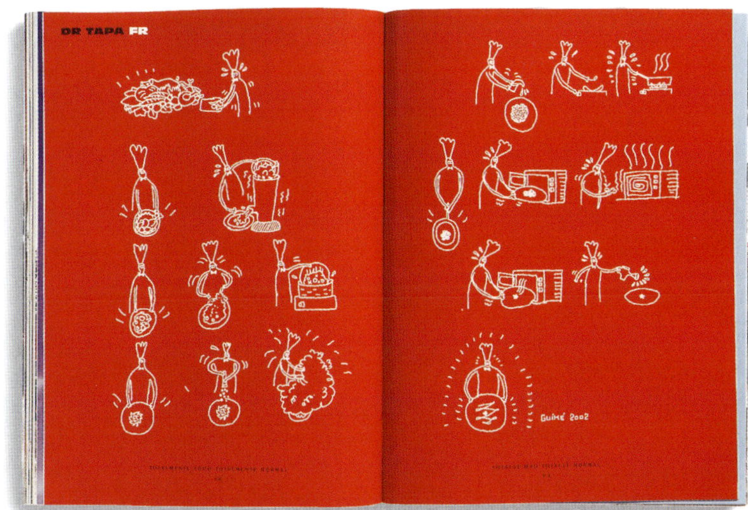

P.O.P.

P.O.P.

ノベルティ（軽石） Novelty (Pumice)

P.O.P.

ショップバッグ Shop bag

ミニカタログ Mini catalog

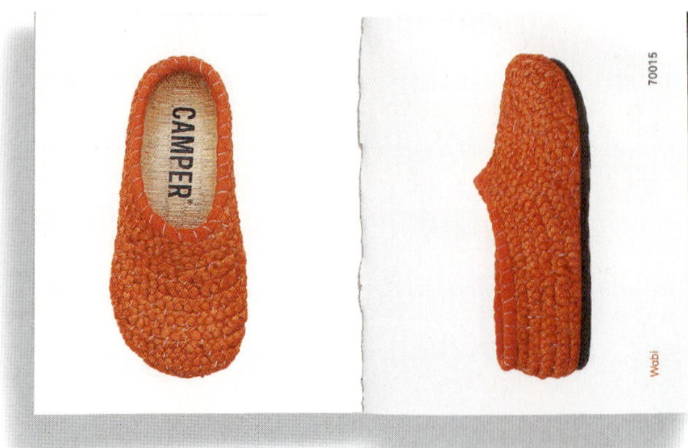

Shop

ポスター Poster

Nisshin Petfood 日清ペットフード

ペットを飼うって楽しい！ 幸せ！ を感じるキャンペーンを展開

Campaigning on the fun and happiness of caring for your pet

戦略を読み解く 3 key words

高品質、安全、おいしいペットフードを提供

大切な家族の一員であるペットが、健康で長生きできるよう、高品質なペットフードの研究開発、製造、販売を行っている。製品は食品衛生法にも配慮し、確かな安全性を保持。さらに、ペットが喜んで食べるおいしさ・味も追求している。

ペットが登場する遊び心いっぱいのカレンダー制作

キャンペーンやプレゼント企画などペットライフをより楽しくするプロモーションを展開。2002年に実施した「第1回ココロの叫び大賞」では、ユニークなコメントを添えたペット写真を募集。特賞および入賞ペット写真をカレンダーに掲載し、プレゼントした。

絵本にペーパークラフト。仕掛けが詰まったセット

2003年版カレンダーはペットをモチーフにデザインしたピンクと白のバインダーにセット。365匹の愛犬・愛猫の写真入りカレンダーのほかに、ペットを描いたミニ絵本、組み立てて遊べる家型のペーパークラフトをつけた。

3 key words

Offering safe, delicious, high-quality pet food

The company researches, develops and sells high-quality pet food designed to help that most important member of your family live a long and healthy life. The company also scrupulously follows the food safety regulations to ensure the safety of its products. Furthermore, they work to develop pet food with the taste pets enjoy.

Creating a pet calendar with a playful attitude

The promotion is designed to make living with your pet even more fun with special campaigns and giveaways. In 2002, call for entries of pet photos with unique comments for the "First Annual Cries of the Heart Prize". Use the prize-winning photographs to create a calendar for giveaways.

Picture book, paper crafts -- a calendar set filled with fun

The 2003 pet calendar is distributed in a set with a pink-and-white binder. In addition to the 365 pictures of pet dogs and cats, it contains a mini picture book illustrating pets, and paper cutouts that assemble into house for play.

Naming

「ペットの元気と長生きのために」というテーマを掲げ、犬、猫をはじめ鑑賞魚、小動物、小鳥用などのアイテムがそろう日清製粉グループの会社。

The company is part of the Nisshin Flour Milling group of companies, which provide items for a variety of pets, including dogs and cats but also fish, rodents and birds, under the banner "For Healthy and Long-Living Pets".

日清製粉グループ

カレンダー(2002年版)
2001年に実施したキャンペーン「ホットエピソード2001」の入賞ペットをモチーフにした2002年版カレンダー。多数ある犬・猫カレンダーと差別化するため紙芝居型にした。

Calendar (2002)
2002 calendar featuring award winning pets from the "Hot Episode 2001" campaign. Produced in the form of a picture-story show to distinguish it from the many dog and cat calendars on the market.

■ CL= 日清ペットフード Nisshin Petfood
■ CD= 狩野光一 Koichi Kanou ■ AD= 田中 元 Gen Tanaka ■ CW= 赤石正人 Masato Akaishi ■ CW= 細川美和子 Miwako Hosokawa ■ D= 保坂丈二 Joji Hosaka ■ D= 折田笑子 Emiko Orita ■ P= 進藤祐光 Yukou Shindo
■ I= ワタナベケンイチ Kenichi Watanabe ■ Creative producer= 柏崎成幸 Shigeyuki Kashiwazaki ■ Coordinator= ライブアネックス Live Anex ■ Advertising agent + Project production= 電通 DENTSU INC.
■ Project production= 電通テック DENTSU TEC ■ Project production= アドブレーン ADBRAIN ■ S= 電通 DENTSU INC.

カレンダー(2003年版)
2002年に実施したキャンペーン「第1回ココロの叫び大賞」の入賞ペットをモチーフにした2003年版カレンダー、ミニ絵本、ペーパークラフトのセット。

Calendar (2003)
2003 calendar, mini picture book and papercraft set featuring award winning pets from the "First Annual Cries of the Heart Prize" campaign.

新聞広告 Newspaper AD

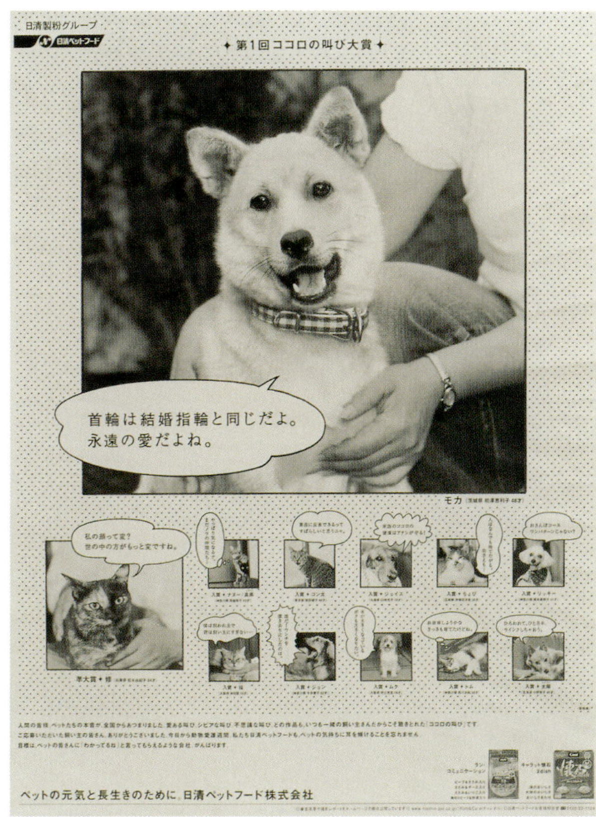

AIWA アイワ

“ペット感覚で愛されるブランド”のイメージを動物のアイコンで表現
An animal icon makes a brand as lovable as a pet

戦略を読み解く 3 key words

ユーザーの“コンパニオン”としてアプローチ

ソニーに吸収合併された同ブランドが、新たなイメージを打ち出すために行ったキャンペーン。ユーザーの生態系（住環境）になじむ仲間（家電）であることの訴求を戦略の柱とし、“コンパニオン・エレクトロニクス”をキーワードに据えた。

メインビジュアルは動物のキャラクター

“生態系になじむ仲間”を象徴する存在として、動物のキャラクターをアイコンに起用。豊富なバリエーションと柔軟な汎用性をもたせたデザインによって、グローバルやユニバーサルといったブランド方針を反映しやすくした。

プロモーション展開はユーザーの“生態系”で

メインターゲットである若者の“生態系”でのアプローチを重視し、原宿や渋谷を中心にプロモーションを展開。原宿駅でポスタージャックをしたり、日本初登場のベロタクシーを広告媒体として活用するなど、ブランドイメージの普及に努めた。

3 key words

Casting the product as "companion"

A campaign to reestablish the brand with a new image after the company's merger with Sony. The strategy's main thrust is to establish the company's products as trusted acquaintances (home appliances) within the customer's ecosystem (living environment). "Companion electronics" is the keyword.

Animal characters star in ad visuals

Use animal characters to symbolize the existence of the company's products as "trusted living companions". Make the brand campaign easy to implement universally with richly variable and adaptable design.

Bring the promotion to the user's ecosystem

Run promotions in Harajuku and Shibuya, the "ecosystem" of the young people who are the targets of the ads. Promote brand image through a variety of initiatives, including exclusive campaigns occupying all available poster space in the Harajuku station and advertisements on the velotaxis just being introduced to Japan.

Naming

“使い手も作り手も楽しめるブランド”という意味を込めたキャッチフレーズ。AV家電のイメージとキャラクターの角張ったイメージに合わせ、デジタルな書体で表現した。

The company name implies "a brand users and creators alike can enjoy". The brand name is written in a digital font that matches the image of home electronics and the angular form of the promotional characters.

Enjoy 100%,
AIWA

紙袋 Paper bag

キャラクターキット Character kit

■ CL= ソニー・マーケティング Sony Marketing Inc.
■ CD= 大島征夫 Masao Ooshima ■ CD + AD + D= 青木克憲 Katsunori Aoki ■ I= 久保誠二郎 Seijiro Kubo ■ CW= 芳谷兼昌 Kensyo Yoshitani ■ Agency & Production= フロンテッジ FRONTAGE INC.
■ DF= バタフライ・ストローク butterfly·stroke inc. ■ S= バタフライ・ストローク butterfly·stroke inc.

連旗 Flag

ティッシュ Tissue paper

段ボール Corrugated cardboard

マット Mat

ベロタクシー
ドイツで生まれた3輪の自転車タクシーで、日本国内での運用は
アイワが初めて。東京・青山付近を走らせて注目を集めた。

Velotaxi
AIWA is first to operate the three-wheeled peditaxi invented in Germany promotionally in Japan. The vehicles drew much attention running around the Tokyo Aoyama area.

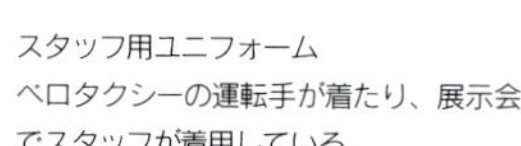

スタッフ用ユニフォーム
ベロタクシーの運転手が着たり、展示会
でスタッフが着用している。

Staff uniform
Uniform worn by Velotaxi drivers and exhibition staff.

ポスター Poster

ポスター Poster

Enjoy 100%, AIWA
We only have now.
So now is the time to play, laugh, enjoy.
Give it 100%.

Enjoy 100%, AIWA
We only have now.
So now is the time to play, laugh, enjoy.
Give it 100%.

Enjoy 100%, AIWA
We only have now.
So now is the time to play, laugh, enjoy.
Give it 100%.

Enjoy 100%, AIWA
We only have now.
So now is the time to play, laugh, enjoy.
Give it 100%.

Enjoy 100%,
AIWA
We only have now.
So now is the time to play, laugh, enjoy.
Give it 100%.

Enjoy 100%, AIWA

Enjoy 100%, AIWA

Enjoy 100%,
AIWA
We only have now.
So now is the time to play,
laugh, enjoy.
Give it 100%.

Enjoy 100%,
AIWA
We only have now.
So now is the time to play, laugh, enjoy.
Give it 100%.

PINO ピノ

ブランドの新たな顔と、モノづくりにかける変わらぬ情熱を訴求
Promote the new face of the brand and its enduring zeal for craftsmanship

戦略を読み解く 3 key words

日本国内の職人と手を組んだ妥協無きモノづくり

規格商品やフルオーダーだけでなく、小さなニーズにも対応できるセミオーダー・システムを採り入れ、"使いやすい道具であると同時に、創造的な生活を演出するモノ"を提供。単なるビジネスに留まらず、家具を中心とした人の輪を育てたいと考える。

ブランドの世界観を伝える営業ツール

創立10周年を機にCIを一新し、従来の大口顧客に加え、新たに個人客も視野に入れたプロモーションを展開。営業ツール=顧客とのコミュニケーション・ツールとして捉え、CI及びブランドコンセプトの訴求に力を注いだ。

目指すはユーザーの想像力と創造力の牽引

新しくなったCIを前面に出すとともに "見る人に楽しい驚きを与え、想像力や創造力をかきたてる" ビジュアルを目指す。多用される丸い形には、"ピノという会社を双眼鏡で覗くような気持ちで見て欲しい" という気持ちが込められている。

3 key words

Allied with Japanese artisans in uncompromising craftsmanship

Offers "easy-to-use goods that promote the creative lifestyle" with a semi-custom production system that responds to even small customer needs better than standardized or made-to-order systems. The company's goal is to be a link between people, centered around home furnishings -- not just a business.

Management tools communicate the brand's worldview

Taking the company's tenth anniversary as an opportunity to retool its corporate image, develop a promotion intended to appeal to individual consumers in addition to the company's previous market of bulk purchasers. As a tool for management and communication with the consumer, efforts are concentrated in the areas of corporate image and brand concept.

Promoting creativity and imagination in the user

Promote the new corporate image with visuals that "pleasantly surprise the viewer and arouse their imagination and creativity". Circles are used abundantly, implicitly communicating that "we want the viewer to look at PINO the company through binoculars (i.e., in a new way)".

Naming

PINOはイタリア語で「松」の意味。コーポレートカラーの深緑は、豊かに育つ森をイメージしている。

PINO is Italian for "pine tree". The corporate color is dark green, recalling the image of a lush forest.

商品
創立10周年を記念して制作したソファ。使う人によって様々に表情を変え、生活を創造的に楽しくするという特性は、ブランドコンセプトを象徴している。

Product
Sofa produced to commemorate the company's tenth anniversary. Changes in expression according to its users making living more creative and fun, thus symbolizing the brand concept.

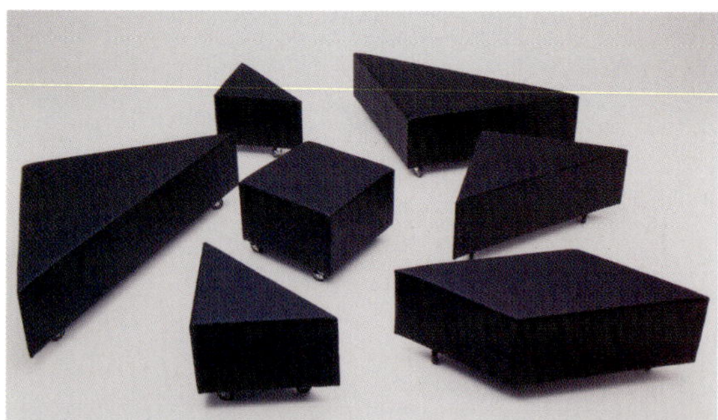

Showroom

■CL= ピノ・コーポレーション PINO CORPORATION
■D= 髙橋正実 Masami Takahashi ■P= 藤井 真 Makoto Fujii ■DF= MASAMI DESIGN ■S= MASAMI DESIGN

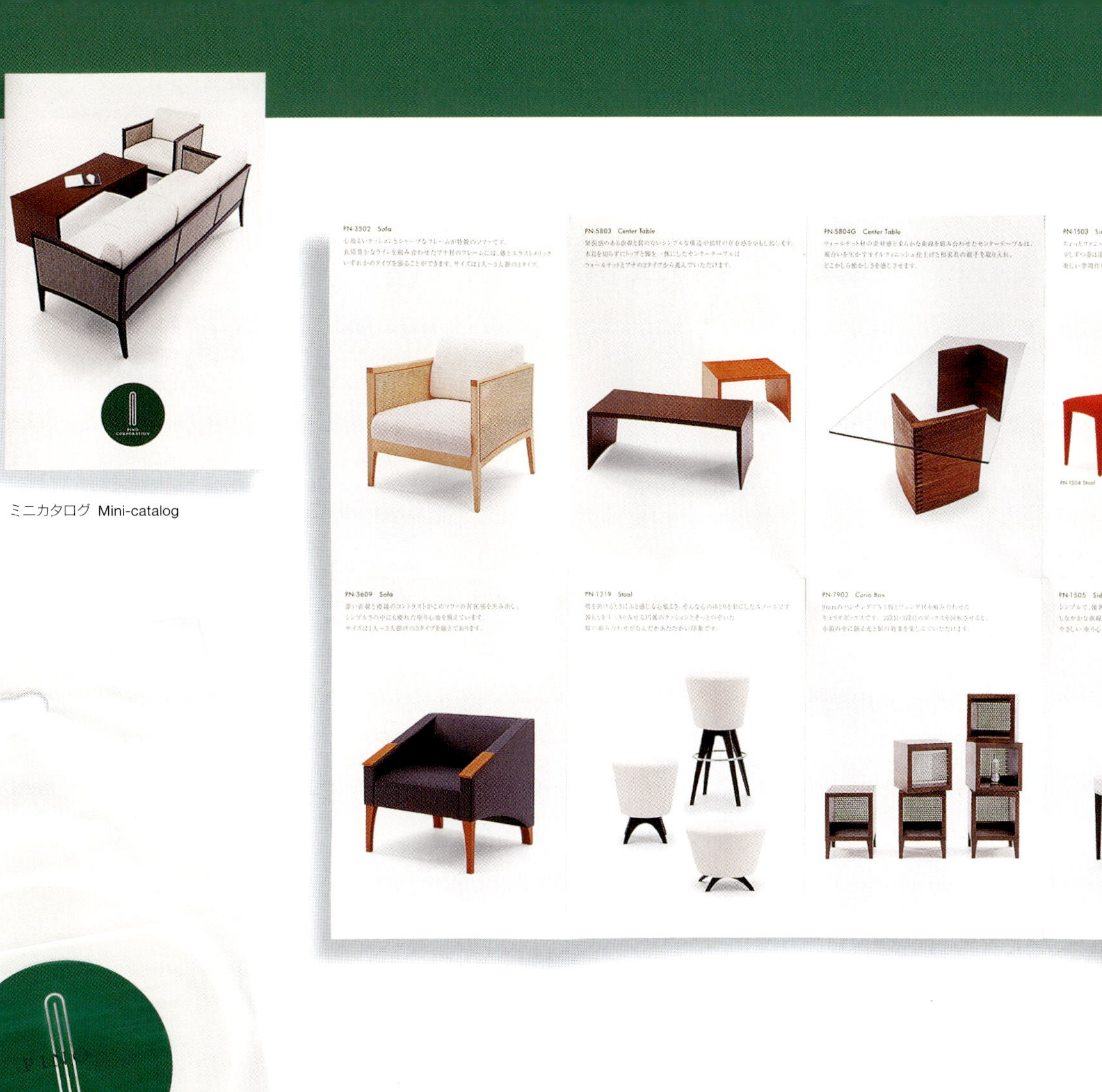

ミニカタログ Mini-catalog

カタログ＆プライスリスト Catalog & Price list

GlaxoSmithKline グラクソ・スミスクライン

アレルギー性鼻炎の治療をガイドする、子供向けのキャラクター

Child-oriented characters teach how to treat allergies

戦略を読み解く 3 key words

厳しい規制のなかでこそ生まれたアイデア

医師を顧客とする医薬品メーカーとして病院に配布するツールの制作を重視しているが、規制が厳しいためにストレートな広告表現はできない。そこで、企業の姿勢をキャラクターに語らせるというアイデアを採用。

子供にとって意味のあるキャラクターを設定

今回のツールは、小児のアレルギー性鼻炎の治療を行う病院で使用してもらうためのもの。そのためキャラクターには単なるアイコン的な意味ではなく、子供にとって"一緒に鼻炎を治す友達"という存在意義をもたせ、絵本風の小冊子でコンセプトを明確に表した。

ポジティブで可愛らしいビジュアルを追求

ツールのベースとなる色にはカラフルなオレンジを選び、ポジティブなイメージを付加した。病院内でP.O.P.のように使ってもらうことで子供たちに「カワイイ！」と感じてもらい、ブランド力を高めることにつながるビジュアルを目指している。

3 key words

Tight restrictions actually inspire ideas

With serious restrictions on the promotional tools pharmaceutical makers can use to advertise to doctors, their customer base, in hospitals, standard advertising is not an option. This gave rise to the idea that the company's position could be expressed through educational characters.

Defining characters that have meaning for children

In this case, we created materials to be used in facilities that treat children with allergies. The concept was realized with characters in illustrated pamphlets that, rather than just being icons, exist to "help you (children) get better together".

Seeking, positive, appealing visuals

Orange was selected as the base color for the promotional materials, adding a positive image. The goal was visuals that children would think were cute and friendly when used like P.O.P. materials in the context of a hospital, and at the same time would strengthen the brand of the company.

Character

キャラクター名の「ハナッペ」は、"鼻たれ"を可愛らしくアレンジしたもの。子供が親しみを感じるキャラクターとして、クマをモチーフにした。

The character's name, Hanappe, is a playful rearrangement of hanatare (runny nose). He was designed on a bear motif so children would sense they could have fun with him.

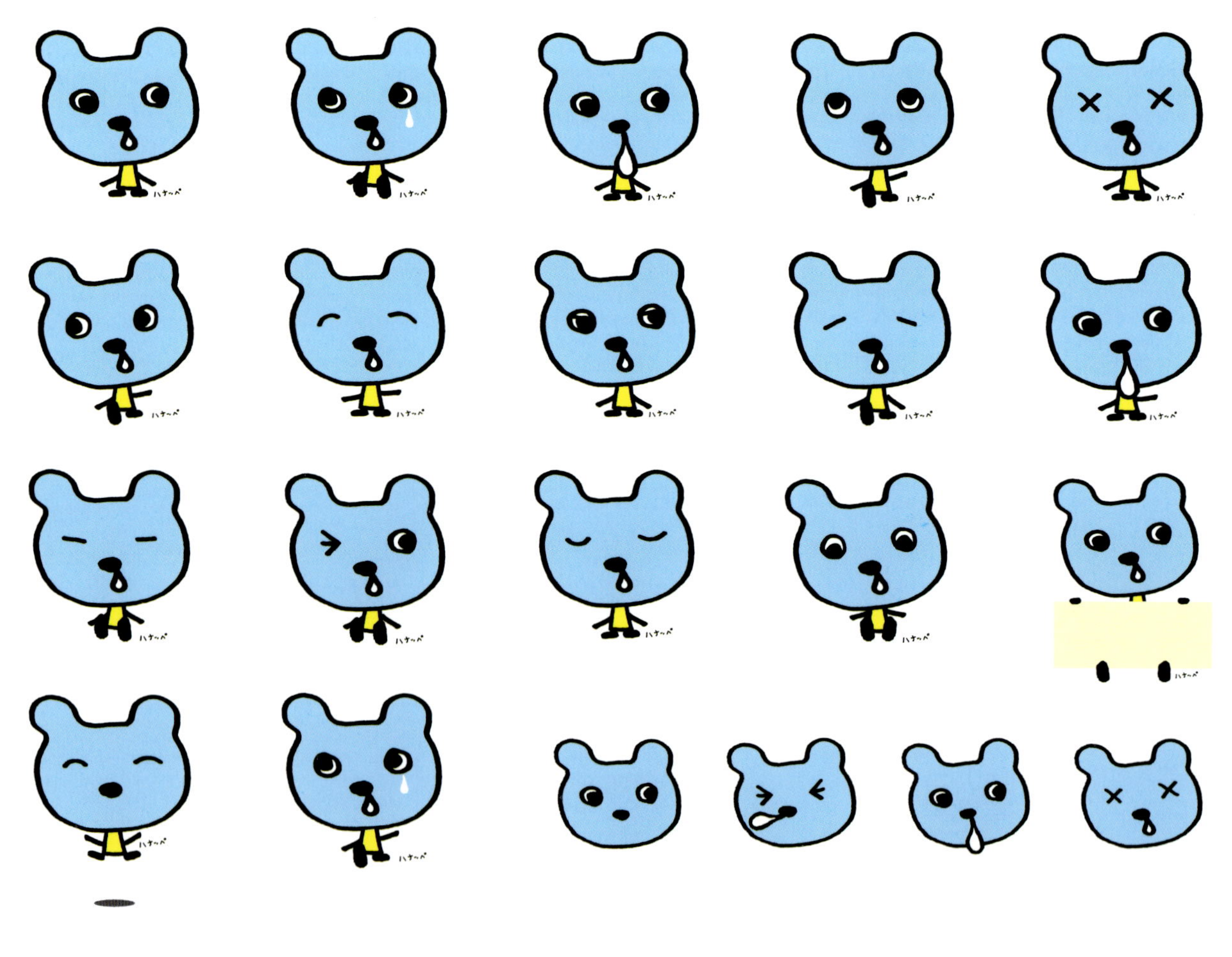

■CL=グラクソ・スミスクライン GlaxoSmithKline
■Agency= 博報堂+スパイス HAKUHODO Inc. + SPICE INC. ■CD= 澤田浩二 Koji Sawada ■AD + I= 佐野研二郎 Kenjiro Sano ■D= 遠藤祐子 Yuko Endo ■D= 戸塚亮子 Ryoko Totsuka ■S= 博報堂 HAKUHODO Inc.

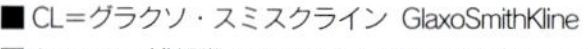

ティッシュボックス
Tissue box

シール Sticker

ポスター Poster

ボールペン Ball pen

メモ帳 Memo pad

小冊子 Pamphlet

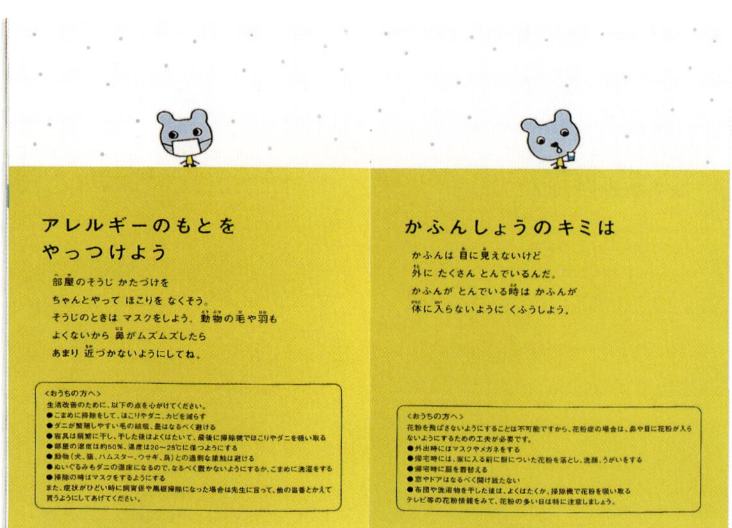

GOODS

HOPE MENTHOL ホープ メンソール

商品を覆う＝隠すという逆説的発想で“購入する楽しみ”を創出

Wrapping = hiding -- a paradoxical idea leads to "fun you can buy"

戦略を読み解く 3 key words

新たな購買層の獲得を目指して発売した新商品

HOPEの愛煙家は30～40代が中心で若者は比較的少なかったため、20代を中心とする若年層にターゲットを絞ったメンソールを新発売。“若者に人気”のメンソールをブランドの一角に加えることで、HOPEブランド全体のイメージの若返りも狙う。

店頭で力を発揮するプロモーションを重視

キャンペーンの主軸に着脱式のシガレットケース（デザインスリーブ）を据え、そのビジュアルを使ったライターや化粧箱なども制作。このようなノベルティグッズを重視した展開で“購入する楽しさ”を演出し、“最終的に店頭で勝ち残る”ことを目標にした。

コレクション欲をくすぐるビジュアルと仕掛け

デザインスリーブには“センスの良さや遊び心”を感じさせるビジュアルを採用。全25種とバリエーションをもたせベンダー（自動販売機）からはどれが出てくるか分からない。そんな“次は何が出るんだろう”という期待感の演出が好調な売れ行きに結び付いた。

3 key words

A new product to capture a new consumer group

With a core customer base mainly consisting of habitual smokers in their thirties and forties, HOPE develops a new menthol cigarette to appeal to younger smokers in their twenties. The objective is to use the popularity of menthol with young people to inject some youth into the HOPE brand as a whole.

Focusing on strong in-store promotion

The visuals on the easy-open-and-close cigarette case (design sleeve), the centerpiece of the campaign, are used on matching lighters and makeup containers. The novelty-goods centered display promotes "fun you can buy", with the intention of winning the battle at the point of sale.

Visuals that tickle "collector's desire"

Visuals that convey "good taste and a fun-loving spirit" are used on the "design sleeve". With 25 variations in all, the consumer never knows which will emerge from the vending machine. This creates anticipation in the purchaser that one they do not yet have will come out, and is linked with positive sales results.

HOPE
MENTHOL
FILTER CIGARETTES

Logo

商品パッケージはデザイン、ロゴともにHOPEを踏襲し、カラーのみメンソールを連想させる緑に変更。広告ビジュアルでは本来のロゴを覆う感覚、いわばデザインスリーブ的発想で全く別のゴシック系ロゴを使用し、モダンさを印象付けた。

The product packaging design and logo stays true to HOPE's image, but the color is changed to a menthol-inspiring green. The advertisement visuals overlay the original logo, i.e. the design sleeve approach allows for the use of a completely different san-serif style logo that gives a "modern" impression.

ティーザーポスター
デザインスリーブのビジュアル要素だけで構成したポスターで、発売前に「何の広告？」と疑問を抱かせるのが狙い。そのタネ明かしとして、発売時にはアドスリーブと商品を並べたポスターを掲出した。

Teaser poster
A poster composed entirely of "design sleeves" aims to make viewers wonder what is being advertised. The secret is revealed when sales open in poster showing art sleeve and product side by side.

■CL= 日本たばこ産業 JT
■CD= 太田恵美 Megumi Ohta ■CD + AD= 沢田耕一 Koichi Sawada ■D= 河合雄流 Takeru Kawai ■D= 根岸明寛 Akinori Negishi ■D= 岩田敏昭 Toshiaki Iwata ■D= 上松智樹 Tomoki Uematsu
■P= 白鳥真太郎 Shintaro Shiratori ■P= 瀬尾 隆 Takashi Seo ■I= VASARELY ■I= 宇和島太郎 Taro Uwajima ■CW= 辻野 裕 Yutaka Tsujino ■Agency= 電通 DENTSU INC. ■S= 電通 DENTSU INC.

P.O.P.

ベンダー用の化粧箱 Cigarette case for vendor

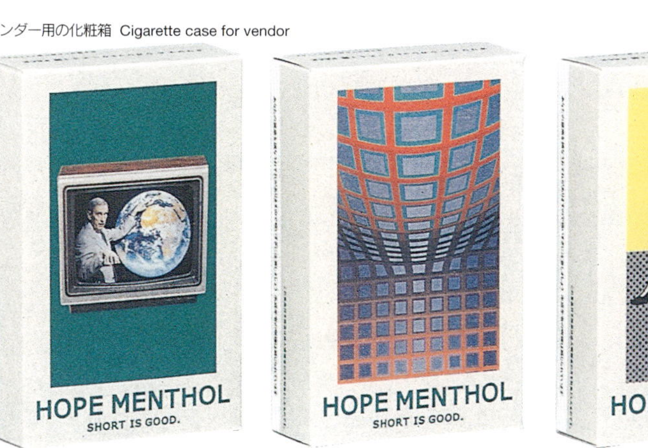

デザインスリーブ
上段から海外のTVプログラム編、タイポグラフィ編、モダンアートの巨匠バサルリーの作品編、プロレス技編の4シリーズを制作した。

Design sleeve
Produced in four series: Foreign TV program edition, typography edition, master modern artist Vasarely edition, and pro-wrestling techniques edition.

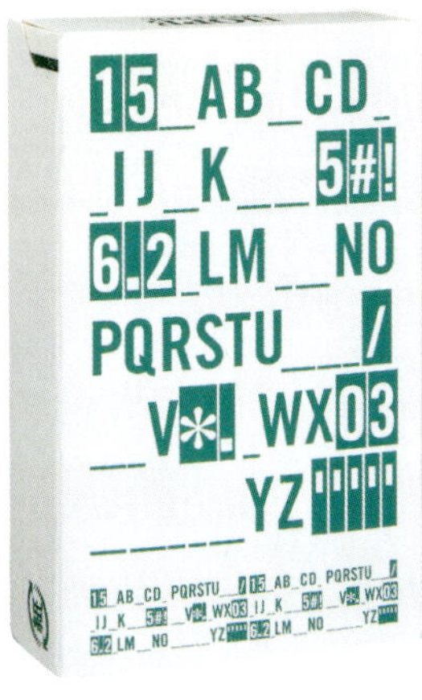

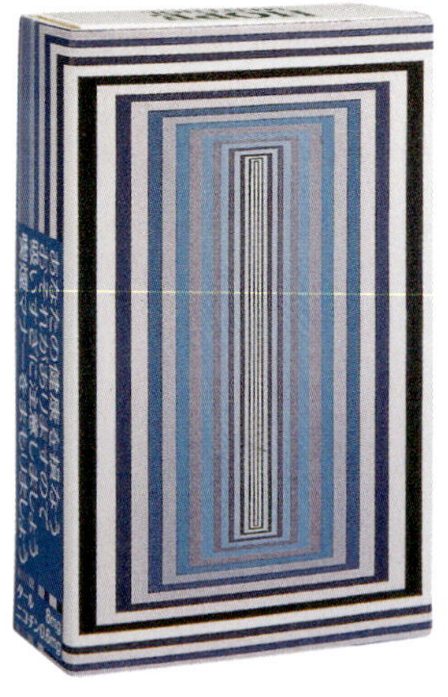

ノベルティ Novelty

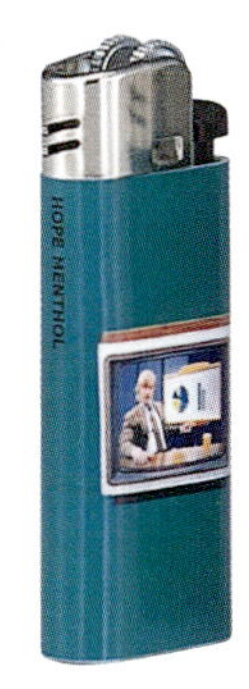

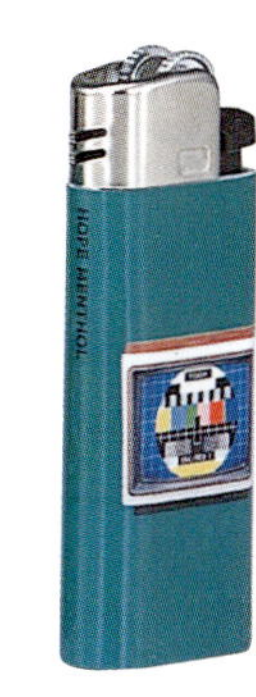
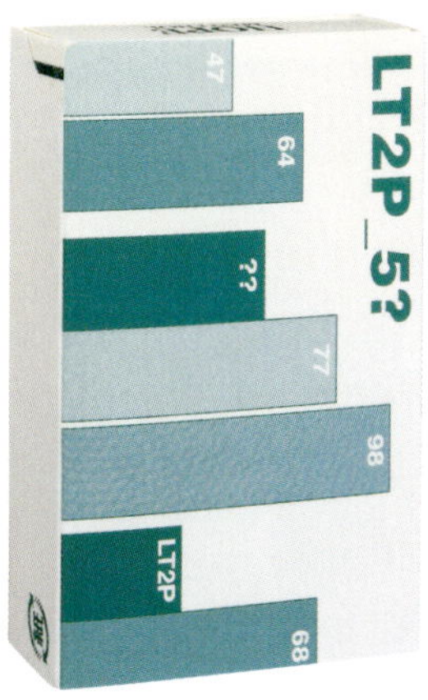

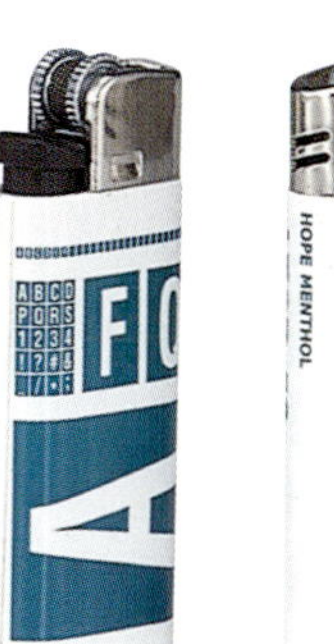

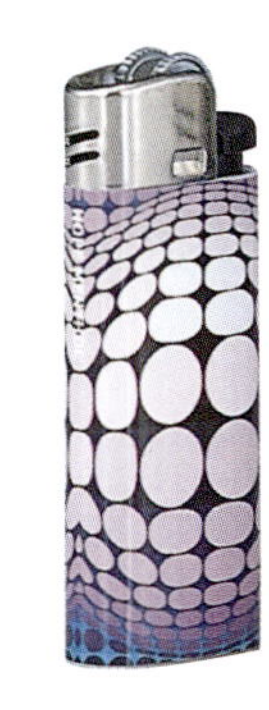

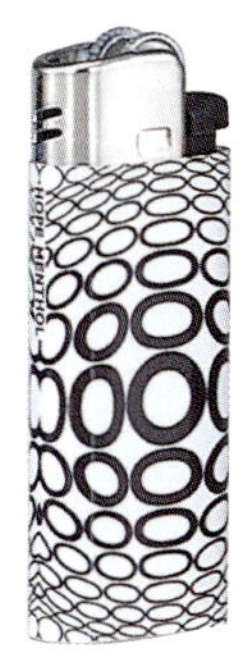

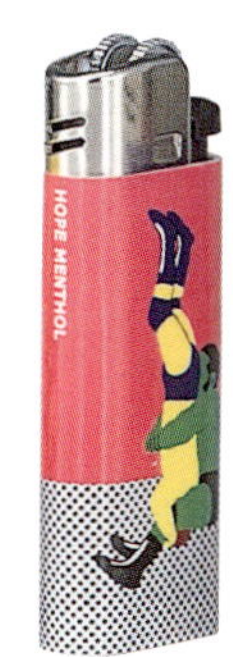
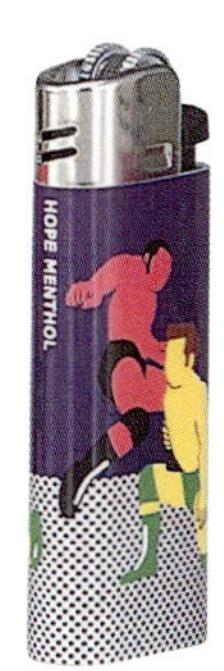

55 HOPPY 55 ホッピー

「温故創新」伝統を大切にしながらも新しく、クリエイティブに

Valuing tradition while pursuing the creative and new

戦略を読み解く 3 key words

目指すはノンアルコールビール市場のオンリーワン

ホッピー発売55周年を記念し、開発した新製品。麦芽100%、従来の2倍の時間をかけて醸造・熟成。コクがありながらも後味すっきりのノンアルコールホップ飲料。10年ぶりの定番新製品としてノンアルコールビール市場のオンリーワンを目指す。

健康志向派・女性に向けてヘルシーをアピール

「ホッピーの3ハッピー」と銘打って、1.プリン体ゼロ、2.低カロリー、3.低糖質を積極的にアピール。さらに海洋深層水使用というヘルシーさを前面に押し出すことで、健康志向派、女性、アンチビール派をもターゲットにしている。

「ホッピー=赤ちょうちん」からのイメージ革新

2002年より始まった、「ホッピー=赤ちょうちん」にとらわれないイメージ革新。商品には開拓者精神の伝統・品格を含ませながらも、スタイリッシュで今を感じさせる、新たなホッピー像を追求。懐かしくて新しい21世紀のホッピーを表現した。

3 key words

Pursuing dominance of the non-alcoholic market

Hoppy Beverage releases a new product as it celebrates its fifty-fifth anniversary. 100% malt, brewed and matured for twice as long as previous beverages, the non-alcoholic beer is has a full, rich body and a refreshing taste. The company hopes to achieve dominance in the non-alcoholic beer market with this, its first new product in ten years.

A healthy alternative for women and the health-oriented

Play up the appeal of the "Three Happinesses of HOPPY": its no purine content, its low calorie content and its low sugar content. Combine this with an emphasis on the healthiness of the water, drawn from the depths of the ocean, used to brew the beer, and target the health-oriented, female and anti-beer market segments.

Escaping from the "HOPPY = Akachochin" image

The campaign to revolutionize the HOPPY image away from "HOPPY = Akachochin" begins in 2002. The target is a stylish, new image for the product that retains its refinement and pioneer-spirit. The result is a sweetly nostalgic, 21st century HOPPY.

Naming

「ホッピー（HOPPY）」とは、原材料に本物のホップを使った麦芽飲料であることに由来する。そのホッピー発売55周年を記念し、"ゴーゴー（go go）"の意味合いも含め、「55ホッピー（55HOPPY）」が誕生した。

The product name derives from the genuine hops used in making the malt beverage. As the company reached its fifty-fifth anniversary, "Go! Go! HOPPY!" was coined as a play on the Japanese for fifty five (gogo) for its newest product.

チラシ Flyer

■CL= ホッピービバレッジ HOPPY BEVERAGE
■AD= 臼田香太 Kota Usuda ■D= 植草麻奈美 Manami Uekusa ■DF= アトリエタイク. atelierTAIK. ■S= アトリエタイク. atelierTAIK.

ホッピー専用ジョッキ＆グラスセット
中に飲み方の説明付き。

HOPPY special mug & glass set
Instructions on how to drink enclosed.

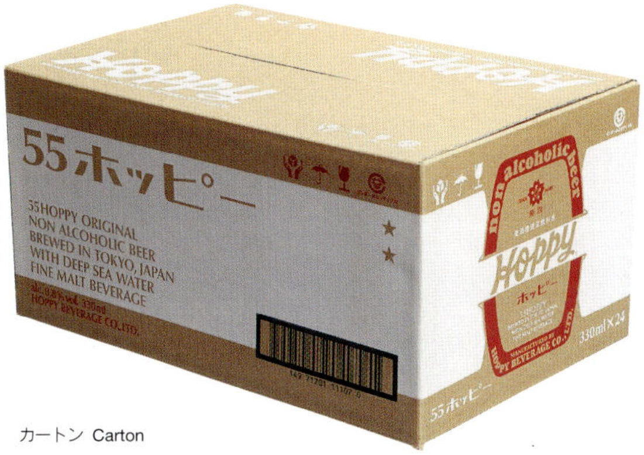

カートン Carton

2003年年賀状 2003 New Year's card

カートン Carton

商品
Goods

チラシ Flyer

55復刻版HOPPY

ホッピー発売55周年を記念し、発売当初使われていたラベルを復刻した。

Fifty-fifth reprinted edition HOPPY

In celebration of the fifty-fifth anniversary of Hoppy's release, the original label was reproduced.

P.O.P.

P.O.P.

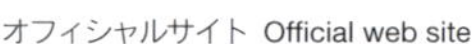
オフィシャルサイト Official web site

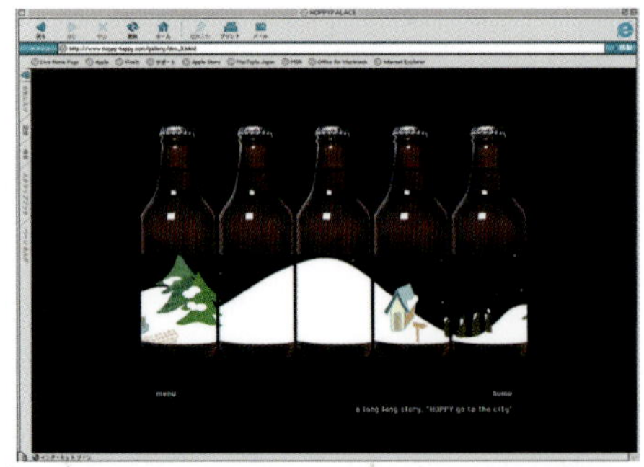

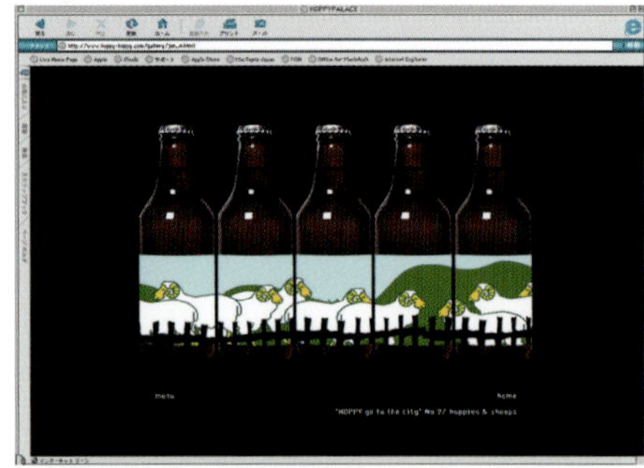

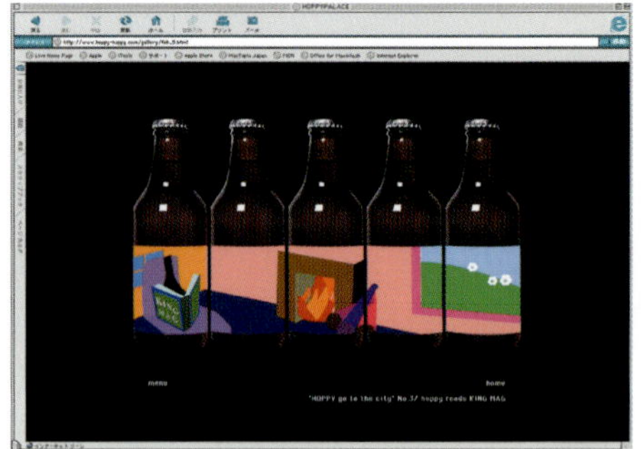

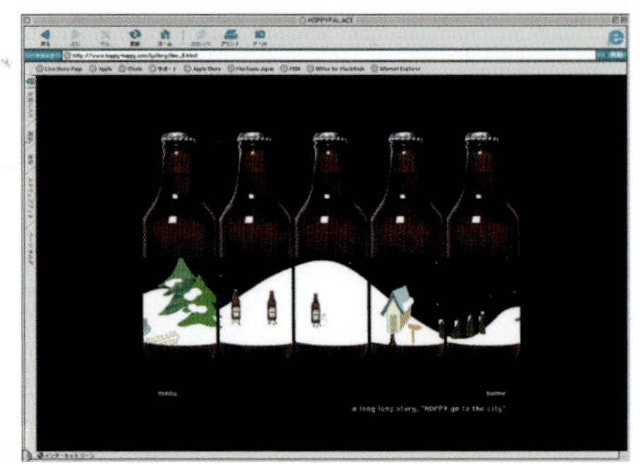

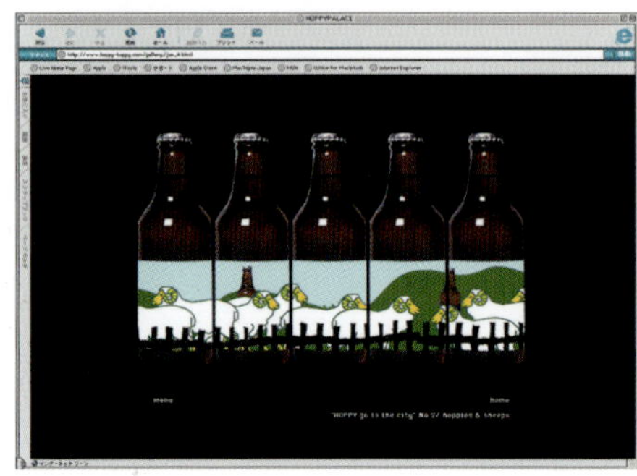

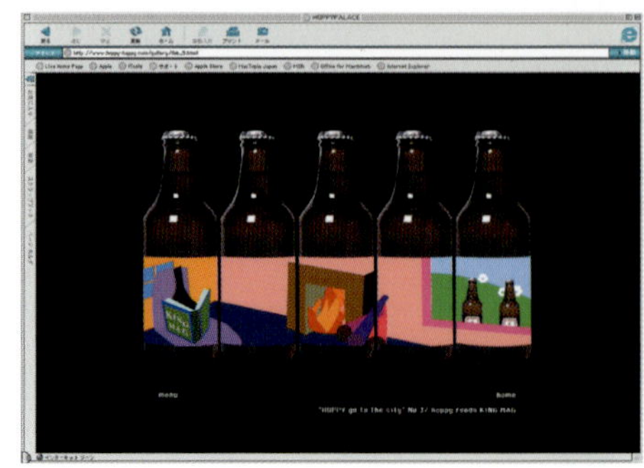

miz no eau 水の王

すっきりとした飲み口をボトルに写りこんだ風景で表現

Clear, refreshing taste represented by a landscape

戦略を読み解く 3 key words

「大吟醸ライト」水のような飲み口の良さを実現

「水の如し」は、古来、日本酒の本質的価値である一方、低アルコール・低甘味志向のニアウォーター世代にも受け入れられると考えた。日本酒的王道に最新の技術を合わせることで、普遍的かつ斬新なプロダクトを目指した。「カフェで飲める日本酒」がコンセプト。

女性誌への広告出稿でターゲットの女性にアピール

20代〜30代の女性がイメージターゲットであるため、読者層が重なる雑誌を中心に広告を出稿。新聞広告はお中元・お歳暮のギフト特集の号に出稿するなど、狙いを定めたプロモーションを行っている。

ボトルに写った風景をそのままに生かして

水のように透明で天然なイメージを表現するため、ボトルに写り込んだ風景をそのままに生かした撮影をし、すべての媒体に展開した。また、店頭用のリーフレットは、手に取りやすく、持ち帰りやすいよう、カード型を採用。

3 key words

Expressing the clear, refreshing taste of Daiginjou Light

Traditionally a prized quality in Japanese sake, being "like water" has recently become associated with the low-alcohol, low-sweetness "near-water" of recent years. By adding modern production methods to the traditional way of sake, the company created a product that was both novel and universal. The concept is "sake you can drink in a cafe".

Reaching women by advertising where they read

Target the desired market segment, women in their twenties and thirties, by placing advertisements in women's magazines with broad reader bases. Also make use of targeted promotions, such as advertisements in special newspaper supplements focused on mid-year and end-of-year gift ideas.

Bringing the landscape on the bottle to life

In order to emphasize the image of clear, natural water, use photographs based on the landscape imprinted on the bottle throughout advertisements in all media. Also employ card-style in-store promotional leaflets that are tempting to pick up and easy to take home.

Naming

酒の味を大きく左右する水。その「水」の良さをストレートに表現した。

The name of the company, Mizu no Eau (literally meaning King of the Water) is a direct reference to the fact that the water used in the production process is perhaps the greatest factor in the taste of a sake.

雑誌広告 Magazine AD

リーフレット Leaflet

■ CL= あさ開 ASABIRAKI Inc.
■ CD= 植村潤吉 Junkichi Uemura ■ CD= 三宅達也 Tatsuya Miyake ■ AD= 遠藤礼奈 Reina Endo ■ P= 辻 佐織 Saori Tsuji ■ Calligrapher= 富永泰弘 Yasuhiro Tominaga ■ CW= 高橋 真 Makoto Takahashi
■ D= 上島健二 Kenji Joshima ■ Producer= 須藤尚子 Hisako Sudo ■ Producer= 佐藤純一郎 Junichiro Sato ■ Media AE= 浦上海平 Kaihei Uragami ■ Advertising agent= 盛岡博報堂／博報堂 MORIOKA HAKUHODO Inc. / HAKUHODO Inc.
■ S= 盛岡博報堂／博報堂 MORIOKA HAKUHODO Inc. / HAKUHODO Inc.

MALT'S モルツ

シンボリックな顔のマークとカラーだけで“商品の全てを語る”
Symbol mark and color "tell it all"

戦略を読み解く 3 key words

“自然の恵み”をとことん生かした生ビール

1986年の発売以来のヒット商品で、素材には麦芽100%、天然水100%を使用。麦のコクとうまみを一層ひきたてることにこだわって、地下深くから汲み上げた良質の天然水を使う。キャッチコピーは“天然水の生ビール。生が自慢のモルツです”。

“旨い生ビールはモルツ”とアナウンスするマーク

既に成熟したブランドであるため、“新鮮さ”を打ち出そうと広告ビジュアルを一新。まずは、数ある生ビールのなかでも“旨い生ビールといえばモルツだ”と主張する記号を作りたいと考え、キャラクター的意味合いも兼ねた顔のマークをデザインした。

品質保証印＋キーカラーで“旨い生ビール”を表現

マス媒体だけでなく、ノベルティなどユーザーの手に届くツールも含めたキャンペーンを実施。“品質保証の印”を押していく感覚で、“顔のマーク”を全てのツールに使用した。キーカラーの黄色は、ビールから連想する色を素直に表したもの。

3 key words

Draft beer that exploits "nature's bounty"

A hit product since its debut in 1986, brewed from 100% barley malt and natural water. Use high quality deep spring water to bring out the body and rich flavor inherent to barley. The copy line, "The spring water draft beer. The MALT'S we take pride in, draft".

A mark that announces: "Good tasting draft beer: MALT'S"

Imbue the already mature brand with "freshness" by using all-new advertising visuals. Begin by creating a mark that among the many draft beers advocates: "talk about good-tasting draft beer -- MALT'S"; make it a face to also give it a cartoon character-like quality.

Quality assurance seal + color express "good tasting draft beer"

Effect a campaign that includes not only mass media, promotional tools that consumers take in hand such as novelties. Use the "face mark" on all product-related tools in the way a "quality assurance seal" would be stamped on a product. The key color yellow forms a direct association to color of beer.

Naming

商品名は、“麦芽（Malt）100%の生ビール”という商品特徴をストレートに表現したもの。

The product name is a direct expression of the product's distinguishing feature -- a "100% barley malt based draft beer".

ポスター Poster

■CL= サントリー SUNTORY LIMITED
■CD= 高上 晋 Shin Takaue ■CD= 佐々木 宏 Hiroshi Sasaki ■AD＋I= 沢田耕一 Koichi Sawada ■D= 沢田 真 Makoto Sawada ■P= 白鳥真太郎 Shintaro Shiratori ■CW= 谷山雅計 Masakazu Taniyama
■S= 電通 DENTSU INC.

紙コップ Paper tumbler

ノベルティ Novelty

輸送用ケース Cardboard containers

SKIP スキップ

おいしい、たのしい、あんしん、なっとく

Taste, fun, safety, satisfaction

戦略を読み解く 3 key words

安心して食べられる食品を食卓へ

ユニクロが2002年秋から行っている食品事業。永田農法で栽培された野菜を中心に、卵、米、牛乳、ジュースなどの商品を扱っている。安全性はもちろん、おいしくて買いやすい、そして楽しいを目指す。現在、通信販売と常設店舗での販売を行なっている。

マス広告は控え、クチコミを重視

「おいしさ」を表現するために、有名シェフや消費者の意見を積極的に収集。本当にいい商品をいい伝え方で提供すれば、ブランドの信頼感も自然に確立されると考え、マス広告よりも「クチコミュニケーション」を重視している。

ポップなデザイン・イラストで親しみやすさを表現

パッケージに描かれているキャラクターは、ストレートに商品情報を伝えるアイコン。ポップなデザイン、イラストを使い、親しみやすいブランドを訴求した。さらに、各媒体・ツールでは素材の良さを素直に表現している。

3 key words

Bringing safe and delicious food to your table

A new line of food products launched by Uniqlo in fall 2002. Centered around vegetables grown using the Nagata method, it also includes eggs, uncooked rice, milk, juice and other products. Safety, taste, convenience and fun are the selling points of the new brand. At present, the products are sold on the Internet and in brick-and-mortar establishments.

Word-of-mouth, not mass communication

Gather comments from famous chefs and gourmands talking about the high quality of the brand. Focus on "oral communication" rather than "mass communication" -- transmit these positive comments to consumers in a positive way and trust in the brand will build naturally.

Expressing approachability through pop illustrations and design

Illustrated characters on the packaging provide clear information about the product. Use pop design and illustrations to create a friendly brand image. Clearly express the high quality of the products in every promotional tool in every media.

Naming

おいしものを食べると、ウキウキしてスキップしたくなる楽しさを「SKIP」で表現。生産から販売まで一貫して自社でコントロールするという理念から、スキップして途中段階をとばす、の意味も持つ。

The brand name expresses the light, happy feeling one gets from eating healthy, delicious food. It also refers to the company's control over the product from production to sales, skipping the middleman.

商品 Goods

■ CL= エフアール・フーズ FR FOODS
■ CD + CW= 糸井重里 Shigesato Itoi ■ AD= 秋山具義 Gugi Akiyama ■ P= 阿部伸治 Shinji Abe ■ P= 蒲生弘政 Hiromasa Gamo ■ I= 天明幸子 Sachiko Tenmyo ■ D= 一見貴重 Takashige Kazumi
■ Project production= 東京糸井重里事務所 TOKYO ITOI SHIGESATO OFFICE ■ DF + Project production= デイリー・フレッシュ Dairy Fresh ■ S= デイリー・フレッシュ Dairy Fresh

トレーナー
Trainer

キャップ Cap

エプロン Apron

レジ袋 Cash register bag

カートン Carton

トラックストア
以前はトラックによる移動販売も行なっていた。

Truck store
Mobile sales were originally conducted out of a truck.

このちらしをご覧のみなさまへ

無料お試しキャンペーン!!
(2月28日まで)

「話題のおいしい野菜」は、もうお試しいただけましたか?

まだのかたは、入会金と初回代金が無料になる今がチャンス!

ユニクロからうまれた野菜とくだもののブランド

SKIP

0120-084-831

チラシ Flyer

CD

ショップバッグ Shop bag

Shop

初店舗オープン

2003年5月、松屋銀座に初の店舗がオープンした。

First retail store opens

First retail store opens at Matsuya Ginza in May 2003.

カタログ Catalog

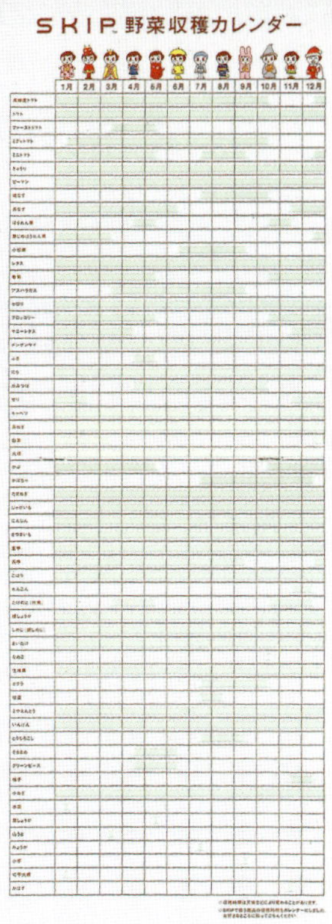

ホームページ HP

会報誌 Bulletin journal

CONTAC コンタック

製品を擬人化したユニークなキャラクターが"自分自身を宣伝"

Cartoon character personifies the product and promotes itself

戦略を読み解く 3 key words

キャッチコピーは"1日2回で長く効く"

鼻やのどの諸症状を持続的に改善し、"1日2回服用するだけで、昼はアクティブに過ごせ、夜はぐっすり眠れる"市販薬。くしゃみと鼻水をとめる「CONTAC 600SR」と、咳や痰をとめる「CONTAC せき止めSR」の2種類がある。

製品が"自分をセールス"して他社と一線を画す

風邪薬のCMではタレントを起用するのが一般的。CONTACでは他社製品との差別化を図って、タレントの代わりになるような存在感をもつキャラクターを考案。カプセル型という製品の形状をそのまま活かした、ユニークなキャラクター「Mr.CONTAC」を創出した。

店頭でのプロモーションを強化して増収に成功

プロモーションでは、まずテレビCMへの露出でキャラクターの浸透に成功。その後は、キャラクター人形を店頭に設置したり、携帯ストラップをおまけとして製品にベタづけしたりと、店頭でのコミュニケーションを展開して売り上げ増に結び付けた。

3 key words

Catch copy: "Twice a day for continuous action"

An over-the-counter medicine that delivers long-lasting relief from nose and throat symptoms, "one capsule two times a day, in the morning to stay active, at night to rest comfortably". There are two formulas: Contac 600SR for relief of sneezing and runny nose, and Contac Cough Control SR for coughing and phlegm.

Self-promoting to distinguish it from its competitors

Cold remedies typically use TV personalities for their commercials. Create a cartoon character with strong presence to use in lieu of a TV personality to distinguish Contac from competitive products. Thus the creation of the unique character, Mr. Contac.

Strengthening in store promotion increases sales

Promotion calls initially for TV commercial exposure to achieve penetration of the new character, followed by the development of on-going communications at the point of sale, including character figure store displays and giveaways such as cell-phone straps attached to product packages -- direct links to increased sales.

Naming

商品特性を反映した名前にしたいと考え、長く効く＝Continuous Actionを縮めてCONTACとした。

The name is an acronym from the distinctive feature of the product -- Continuous Action.

店頭用の人形
キャラクターは製品に合わせて2種類。左の「600SR」は陽気で明るい大阪人、右の「せき止めSR」はクールで知的な東京人という性格づけもした。ファンの間ではそれぞれ「大阪くん」「東京くん」と、通称で呼ばれるほどの人気キャラクターに成長。

Window-AD doll
The two characters developed for the two products. At left, for 600SR, a bright, cheerful Osakan; at right, for Cough Represent SR, a cool, intelligent Tokyoite. They have subsequently become so popular that among fans they go by the names Osaka-kun and Tokyo-kun respectively.

中吊りポスター Traffic AD

■CL= グラクソ・スミスクライン GlaxoSmithKline
■CD + AD= 沢田耕一 Koichi Sawada ■D= 河合雄流 Takeru Kawai ■P= 白鳥真太郎 Shintaro Shiratori ■CW= 磯島拓矢 Takuya Isojima ■Agency= 電通 DENTSU INC. ■S= 電通 DENTSU INC.

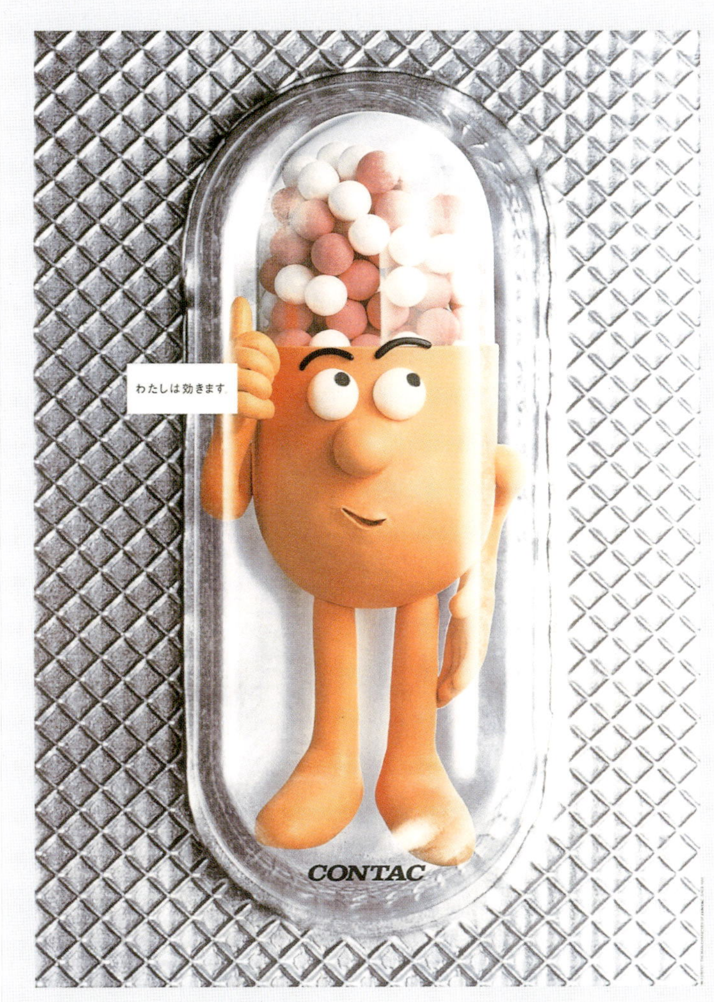

ポスター Poster

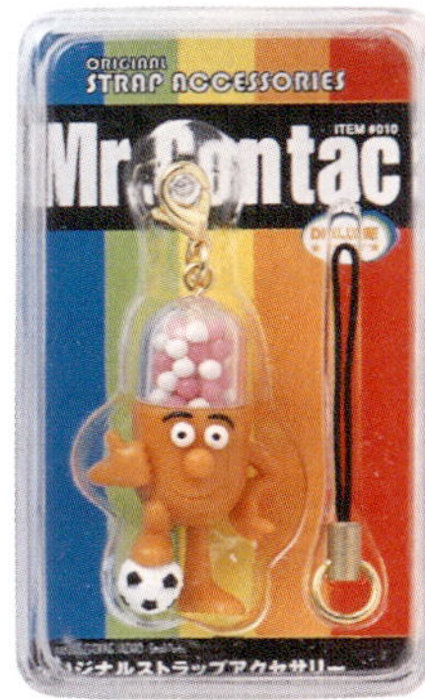

ノベルティ（携帯ストラップ） Novelty (Handyphone strap)

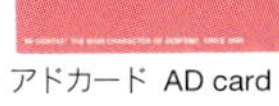

アドカード AD card

INOUI ID インウイ アイディー

商品の色は隠して、見る側の想像力を引き出すビジュアルを展開

Visuals hide product color, inspiring viewers' imagination

戦略を読み解く 3 key words

メーキャップは素顔よりも自分らしさを表現する

ブランドコンセプトは「ILLUSION(イリュージョン)」。メーキャップには各人の感性や考え方がこめられるものであり、その人らしさを伝える自由で多様な表現手段である。こうしたメーキャップの創造的な可能性に目を向け、その楽しさを伝えていく。

資生堂から独立した単独コーナーを展開

従来の資生堂コーナーから独立した単独コーナーを展開。専属スタッフが、その人らしい美しさを表現するメーキャップのテクニックや色使い、顔だけでなく髪型が与える印象をも含めた「パーソナルスタイリング提案」を実践している。

商品の色を隠して想像力を刺激

ブランド立ち上げ時に制作したビジュアルは、見る人の想像力でプロダクツのカラーバリエーションをイメージしてもらえるよう、あえて色をみせずブランドカラーである赤を前面に展開。モデル写真はモノクロにした。さらに、そのイメージを店頭にも連動させた。

3 key words

Makeup expresses personality better than the naked face

The brand concept is "Illusion". Makeup reflects the wearer's sensitivity and way of thinking, offering the wearer many ways to express herself. Communicate the fun inherent in the creative possibilities of makeup.

Establishing independent sales corners

Develop dedicated department store sales corners for the brand, independent of Shiseido's. Specialized staff offer "personal styling suggestions", including tips on makeup technique, color and even hair styling that will express each person's individual beauty.

Coyly hiding product color inspires consumer imagination

Visual imagery created for brand launch emphasizes the brand color, red, while hiding the colors of the products themselves -- inspiring consumers' imaginations. Photographs of models are monochrome. The use of the imagery extends even to the inside of stores.

Naming

フランス語で「たぐいまれな」という意味の「INOUI」と、独自性という意味のアイデンティティーの「ID」を組み合わせた。ブランドカラーは赤。

"Inoui", French for "rare", is combined with the connotations of individuality attached to "ID" to make up the brand name. The brand color is red.

INOUI ID

雑誌広告 Magazine AD

■CL= 資生堂 SHISEIDO
■CD + AD= 澁谷克彦 Katsuhiko Shibuya　■P= 清水行雄（商品） Yukio Shimizu (Goods)　■P= イネス＆ヴィヌー（人物） Inez & Vinoodh (Person)　■CW= 吉田聖子 Shoko Yoshida　■D= 新村則人 Norito Shinmura
■S= 資生堂 SHISEIDO

Shop

商品 Goods

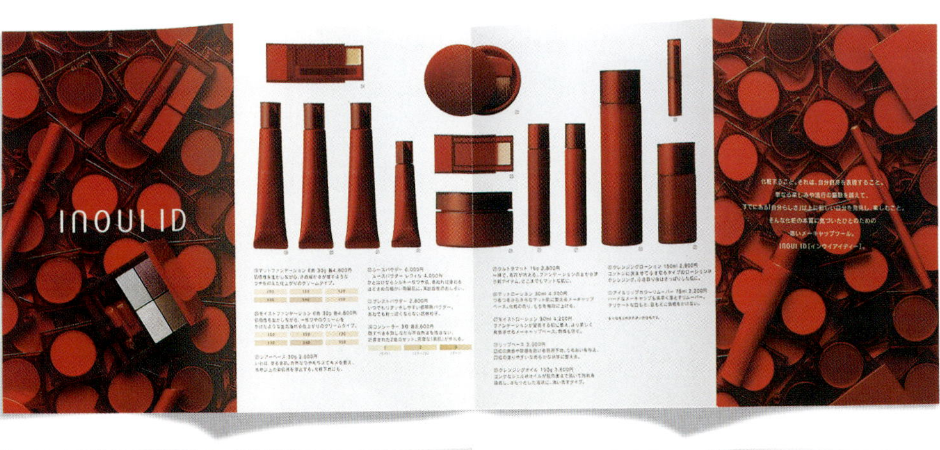

パンフレット Pamphlet

パンフレット Pamphlet

コンセプトブック
そこに写った人がカバーガールになるという意味をこめて、表紙は鏡。

Concept book
Mirror-coated cover makes whoever is reflected a cover girl.

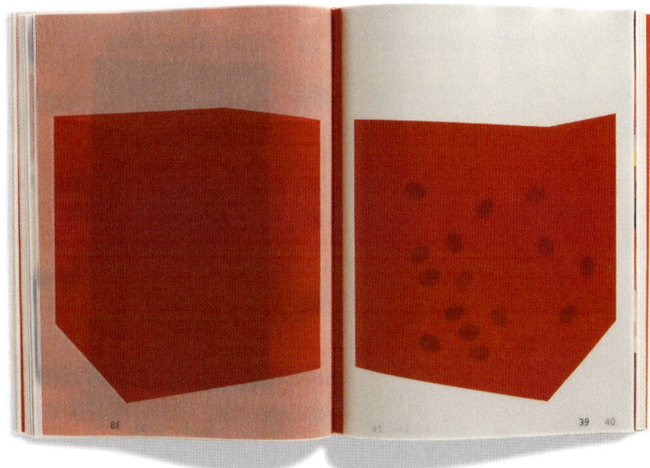

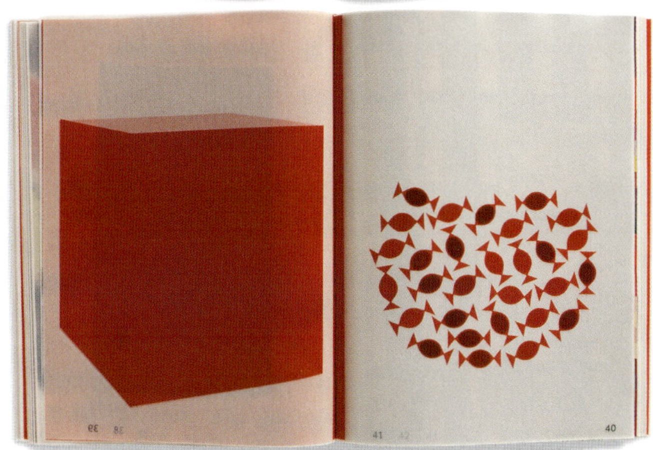

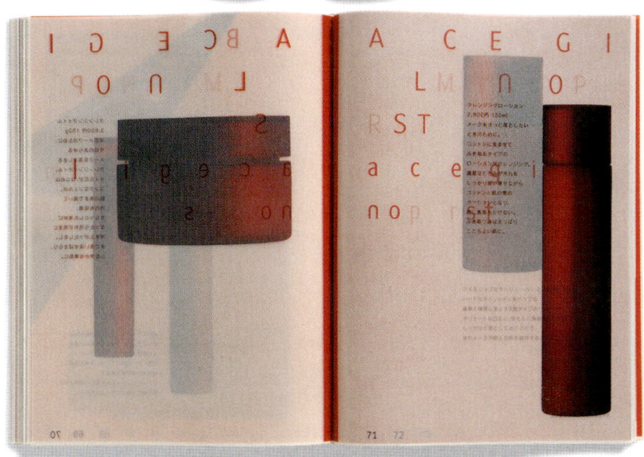

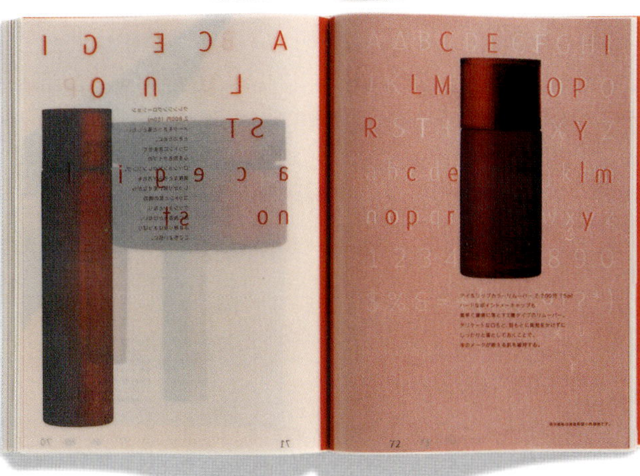

IPSA イプサ

肌の個性に合わせた豊富な商品バリエーションをデザインでアピール

Design promotes the rich variations of a product line

戦略を読み解く 3 key words

主役は一人ひとりの肌。個性に合わせた商品を提供

一人ひとりの肌に合う化粧品を提供し、肌自身が持つ力をすべて引きだそうと商品開発を続けているイプサ。2003年1月末に発売された化粧液・新メタボライザーも15種のラインアップで、今以上の力を持った最強の肌を作りだすことを目指している。

進化するのは中味。商品ボトルはイメージを保って

ボトルは商品の顔。人の顔がまったく変わってしまうことがないように、見た目を大きく変えることはしない。5代目となるメタボライザーも中味には大胆な進化を加えながら、ボトル自体は、以前からのシンプルな美しさを継承している。

豊富な商品ラインアップを色の美しさで表現

サンプルキットは新メタボライザー発表会に合わせて制作。3タイプ×5種類であることが一目でわかるセットとし、種類の豊富さを色の美しさを通して表現した。招待状はシンプルなデザインでまとめつつ、中面に銀の紙を使用。光り輝く華やかさを織り込んだ。

3 key words

Your skin is the star -- offering products for every individual

Ipsa offers makeup that fits the skin profile of every individual, continually developing products that bring out the strength of your skin. With a lineup of fifteen kinds of skin moisturizers, revitalizers and new metabolizers introduced in January, the company hopes to make everyone's skin stronger than it is now.

A bottle that contains progress -- and preserves its image

The bottle is the face of the product. Just as a person's face never changes completely, the appearance of the bottle does not greatly change. While the formula for the metabolizer has rapidly progressed to its fifth version, the bottle that contains it continues to have the same simple beauty as before.

Expressing product variety through the beauty of color

Create a sample kit to coincide with the product launch party for the new metabolizer. Design the set so that people understand from a glance that the line consists of three types of five products each, and express the variation of products with the beauty of color. Create invitations with simple design, foil-coated inside to incorporate light and brilliance.

Naming

「自ら」「・・・自身の」「自発的な」を意味するラテン語。

A Latin word that means "myself", "mine" or "of my own volition".

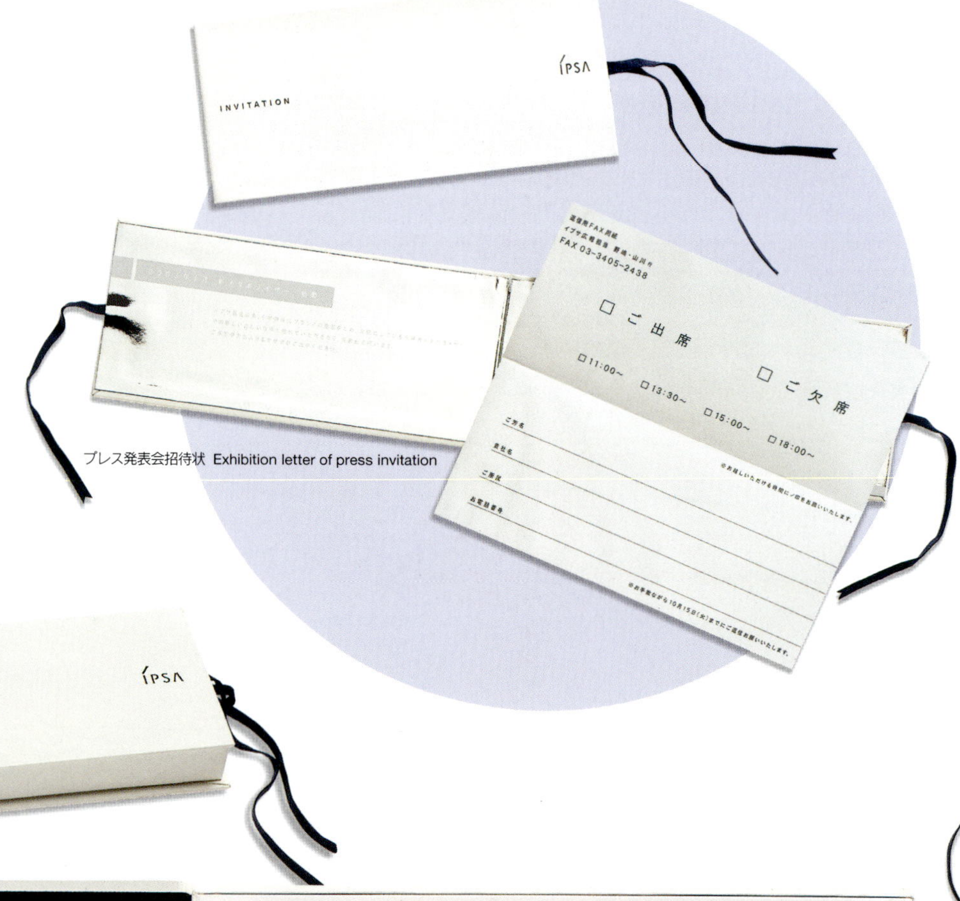

プレス発表会招待状 Exhibition letter of press invitation

メタボライザーサンプルキット New metabolizer sample set

■CL= イプサ IPSA
■AD= 日髙英輝 Eiki Hidaka ■CW= 藤城敦子 Atsuko Fujishiro ■D= 植杉 翠 Midori Uesugi ■D= 水野英樹 Hideki Mizuno ■P= 黒川隆広 Takahiro Kurokawa ■DF= グリッツデザイン gritz design
■S= グリッツデザイン gritz design

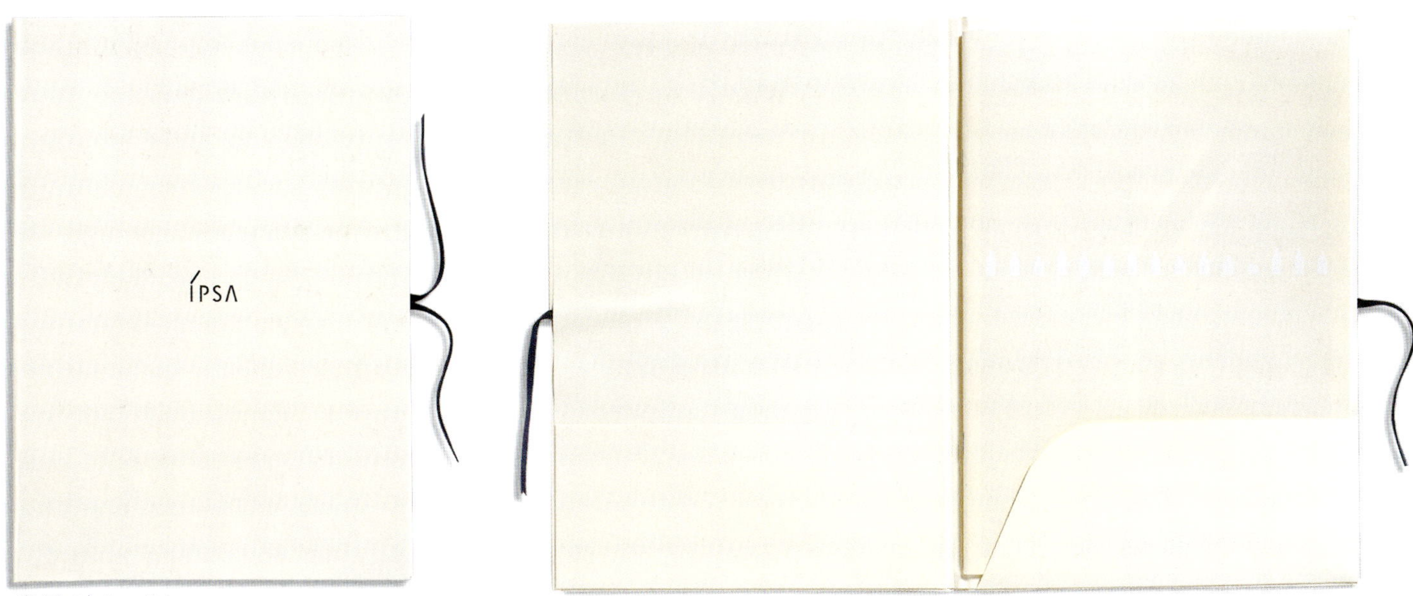

パンフレット Pamphlet

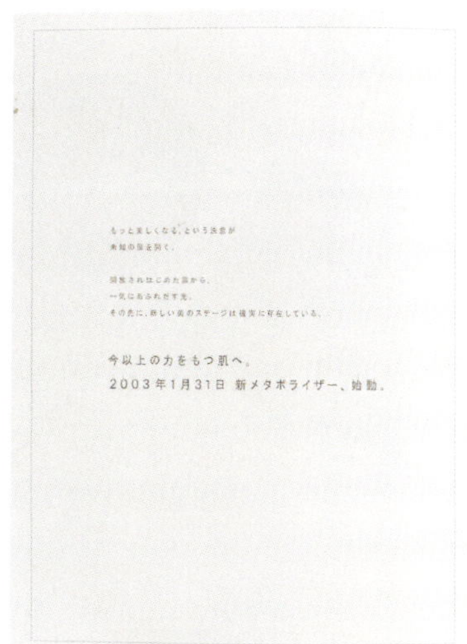

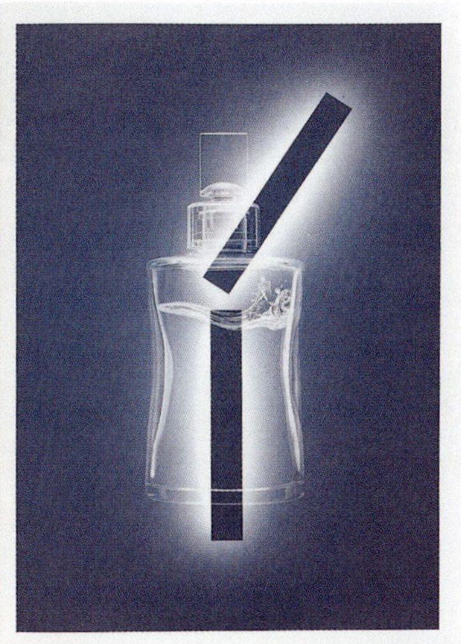

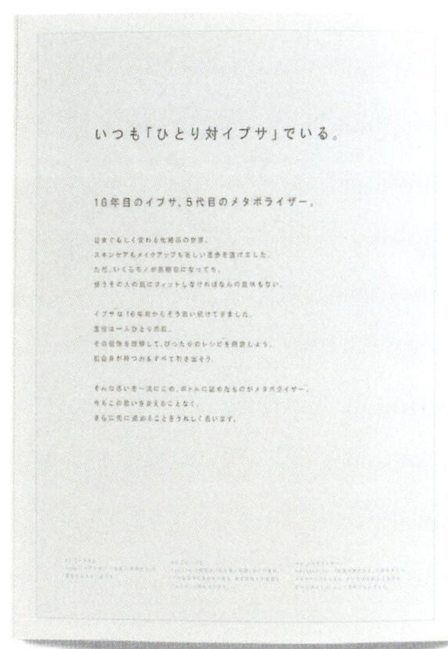

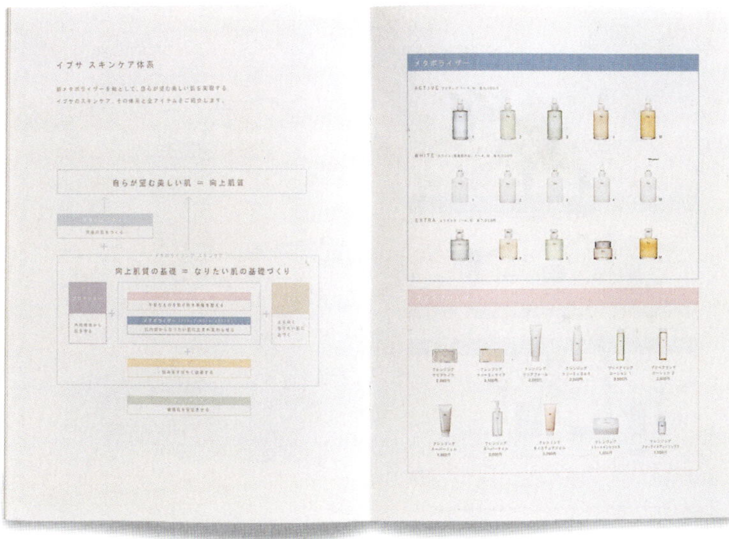

ANNA SUI COSMETICS アナ スイ コスメティックス

「アナ スイ」ワールド全開！ メイクがもっと楽しくなる！

Introducing the Anna Sui World, where make-up is more fun!

戦略を読み解く 3 key words

好き勝手に、楽しく自分だけの世界に浸ろう！

「もっと好き勝手に！ もっと楽しく！ ハジける気分のおまじない」をコンセプトに商品を企画。自分の好きなものを好きなだけチョイスし、自分だけの世界に浸ることが大切というメッセージを送り続けている。

テーマに添った「限定品」で商品価値をアップ

年4回のコレクション「BEACH」「 AUTUMN」「CHRISTMAS」「SPRING」を展開。各コレクションごとにテーマを設定し、限定色や限定品などを多用している。SPツールもコレクションテーマに添ったデザインでまとめている。

アナ スイらしさを大切に、使って楽しい化粧品を

バラ、ピオニー、バタフライをイメージキャラクターとし、パッケージデザインにも力を入れるなど、オリジナリティを大切にしている。メイクアップする楽しみはもちろんのこと、商品を使う楽しさも重要な要素と考え、デザインに反映している。

3 key words

What you like as you like it, in your own personal world of fun

The concept "More whimsical! More fun! Enchanting your spirit!" underlies the product line. Communicate the company's desire to let customers choose what they like and how they like it, so that they can immerse themselves in a world all their own.

Increasing product value with themed limited-edition goods

Introduce four collections, "Beach", "Autumn", "Christmas" and "Spring", give each a theme and promote limited-edition products and limited-edition colors. Design sales promotion tools in accordance with the collection theme.

Providing fun cosmetics worthy of Anna Sui

Focusing on originality, create image characters from a rose, a peony and a butterfly, and give particular effort to package design. Design reflects the fun of make-up and the fun of using Anna Sui products as important elements.

Naming

紫、黒、赤の3色が基本色。ブランド名は創設者本人（ANNA SUI）の名前を起用。

Purple, black and red are the three base colors. The brand name is the name of the founder of the company.

商品 Goods

■CL= アルビオン ALBION
■CD= アナ スイ ANNA SUI ■AD= 錦織章三 Syozo Nishigori ■AD= 小泉陽一 Yoichi Koizumi ■D= 中野 恵 Megumi Nakano ■S= アナ スイ コスメティックス ANNA SUI COSMETICS

ギフトパッケージ Gift package

ギフトボックス Gift Box

通常ペーパーバッグ Paper bag

限定ペーパーバッグ Limited paper bag

コレクションパンフレット
Collection pamphlet

<Collection pamphlet, DM, P.O.P.> ■CD= アナ スイ ANNA SUI ■AD + D + I= 水井智子 Tomoko Mizui ■CW= 桐生貴子 Takako Kiriu

NEWS!
ANNA SUI
ANNA SUI COSMETICS 2002 BEACH COLLECTION
NEW ITEMS 4.11.thu.in stores!
このマスカラ 過激につき ご注意あれ。
NEWS!
このマスカラ
過激につき
ご注意あれ。

NEWS!
ANNA SUI
NEW COLORS
1月23日(木)より新発売

DM

ANNA SUI COSMETICS
2001 BEACH COLLECTION
"SPLASH MERMAID"
ANNA SUI

ANNA SUI COSMETICS 2002 SPECIAL PROMOTION
DOUBLE FASTENER POUCH
PRESENT!
3.1 FRI. START

P.O.P.

ANNA SUI COSMETICS 2002 AUTUMN COLLECTION LIMITED COLORS
NEWS!
Rock'n'Roll Fairy Tale

1月23日(木)より新発売
2003 SPRING COLLECTION
NEWS!

ANNA SUI COSMETICS
SUMMER HOLIDAY PROMOTION 2002 LIMITED ITEMS
6. 6. thu. IN STORES!

ANNA SUI COSMETICS
2002 SPRING COLLECTION LIMITED COLORS 1.24.THU.IN STORES
NEWS!

le mieux　ル・ミュウ

心地良い手触りに込めた、敏感肌へのいたわりとホスピタリティー
Sympathy for sensitive skin feels good to the touch

戦略を読み解く 3 key words

敏感肌専門のコスメティックブランド

2001年7月、「敏感肌を美しくする革命」をコンセプトに誕生した敏感肌専門の化粧品ブランド。これまでメイクには消極的だった敏感肌の女性たちが臆することなく前向きに化粧を楽しめる、毎日の生活が明るくなるブランドを目指している。

「手触り」を重視した媒体でブランド姿勢を発信

敏感肌の人は触れるものに対しても敏感に反応するのではないかと考え、ブランドブックやポスターにガーゼを取り入れ、立体的に加工。ユーザーがじかに触れる媒体にアイデアを取り入れることで、ブランドの姿勢を感じ取ってもらおうとした。

ブランドテーマをガーゼと素の肌の質感で表現

敏感肌への「いたわり」と「ホスピタリティー」を表現するため、ポスターのモデルの顔には肌をやさしく守るイメージを持つ「ガーゼ」が半分かかっている。さらに、ナチュラルな使用感を表現するため、ほぼノーメイクで撮影し、素の肌の質感を大事にした。

3 key words

Cosmetics brand for sensitive skin

July 2001 saw the birth of a cosmetics brand developed exclusively for sensitive skin based on the concept "a revolution in beautifying sensitive skin". Women who previously shied away from "passive" makeup, can now enjoy "constructive" makeup. A brand that aims to make everyday living brighter.

Convey brand posture with tactile media

Based on the supposition that people with sensitive skin have a responsive sense of touch, brand books and posters incorporate gauze to create three-dimensionality.

Brand theme expressed with gauze and naked skin

To express the brand's "sympathy" and "hospitality" to sensitive skin, half of the poster model's face is protectively covered in gauze. And to express the natural feeling application, she was photographed with almost no makeup -- emphasizing the precious quality of bare skin.

Naming

「le mieux」は、フランス語で「最も良い（the best）」という意味。「お客さまに最良の化粧品を」という意志がこめられている。

Le mieux is French for "the best". It expresses the desire to offer customers "the best in cosmetics".

le mieux

le mieux

それは、敏感肌を美しくする革命。
『ル・ミュウ』発表会へのお誘い

プレス発表会招待状
商品の箱の内側に文面をシルク印刷。空箱がそのまま郵送されてくるインパクトをねらった。全6色。

Press exhibition letter of invitation
The inside of the product package is silkscreen printed in a total of six colors. Empty boxes were direct mailed to make an impactful impression.

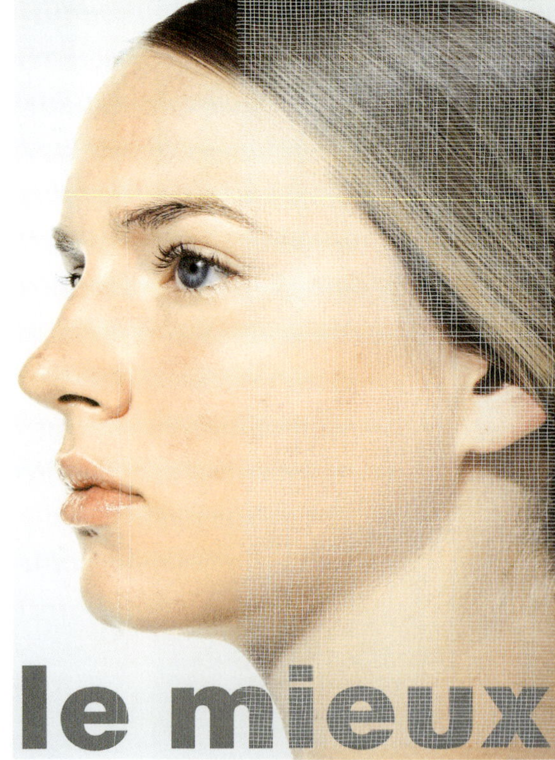

ポスター
顔にかかったガーゼ部分はUVコート印刷で手触り感を出した。

Poster
The gauze covering the face is UV coated to give it a tactile quality.

■CL= ル・ミュウ le mieux
＜All except for Sample kit, Bag＞ ■AD= 石井　原 Gen Ishii　＜Sample kit, Bag＞ ■AD= 信藤洋二 Yoji Nobuto　＜Sample kit, Products package＞ ■AD= 平戸絵里子 Eriko Hirato
＜All except for Sample kit, Products package＞ ■CD= 平戸絵里子 Eriko Hirato　＜Sample kit, Products package＞ ■CD=大智　恵 Megumi Oochi　＜Brand book, Poster＞ ■P= 小林　響 Hibiki Kobayashi
＜Brand book, Press exhibition letter of invitation＞ ■CW= 前田知巳 Tomomi Maeda　＜All except for Sample kit, Bag＞ ■D= 山口範久 Norihisa Yamaguchi　■D= 林　智徳 Tomonori Hayashi
＜Sample kit, Bag＞ ■D= 春田登紀雄 Tokio Haruta　＜Sample kit, Products package＞ ■D= 信藤洋二 Yoji Nobuto　■Project production= ル・ミュウ le mieux　■Project production= 資生堂 SHISEIDO
■Project production= 博報堂 HAKUHODO Inc.　■S= 博報堂 HAKUHODO Inc.

le mieux

le mieux

le mieux

le mieux
www.e-lemieux.com

ステーショナリー
紙も手触り感を大切にし、ロゴや住所等は活版印刷で仕上げた。

Stationery
Paper was chosen for its tactile quality as well, with the logo, address and other information letterpress printed.

le mieux
マーケティング部
久保井 一裕
株式会社 ル・ミュウ

le mieux
マーケティング部
高田 由美子
株式会社 ル・ミュウ

le mieux
取締役 営業本部長
竹山 茂樹
株式会社 ル・ミュウ

le mieux
取締役 営業部長
大月 章充
株式会社 ル・ミュウ

le mieux
営業部
石川 一美
株式会社 ル・ミュウ

le mieux
マーケティング部
柴田 京美
株式会社 ル・ミュウ

名刺
商品の箱に合わせた全６色。スタッフは自分の好きな色を選べる。文字は活版印刷、紙も手触り感のある紙を使用。

Business Card
The six product package colors. Staff can choose the colors they prefer. Type is letterpress printed. Paper has a distinct texture.

le mieux
www.e-lemieux.com

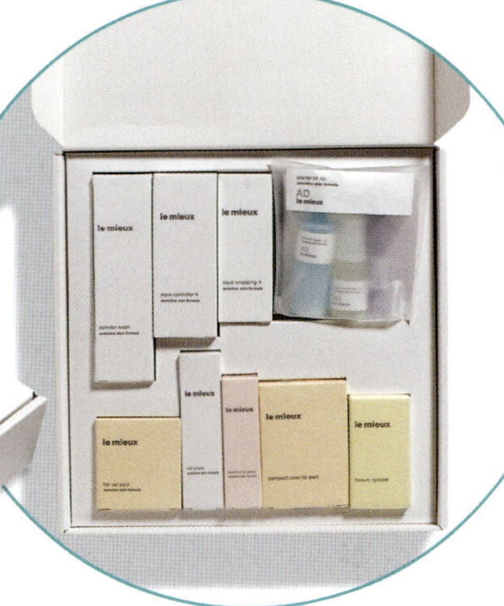

プレスキット
「ブランドブック」、「サンプルキット」のセット。ブランドブックのカバー表面は、本物のガーゼをスキャニングし、一本一本をトレース。さらにUVコートを使った特殊印刷で、手触り感を出した。専用のバッグも紙と布の中間のような微妙な手触り感。

Press kit
Brand book / sample kit set. The brand book cover was created by scanning a real piece of gauze and tracing each fiber. Finished with a special UV coating to give it a tactile quality. The custom bag is made of quasi- paper/fabric which too has a subtle tactility.

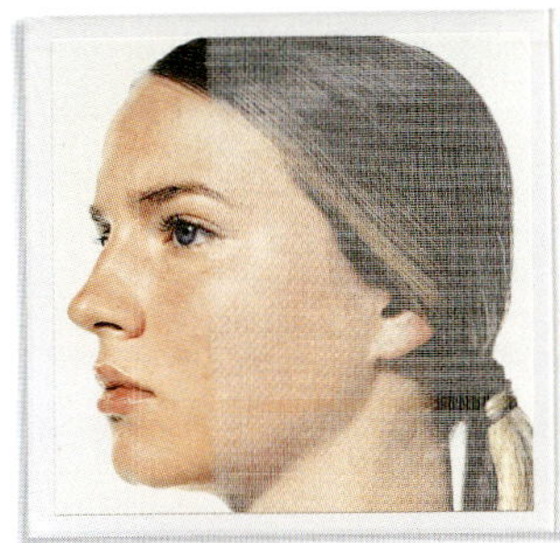

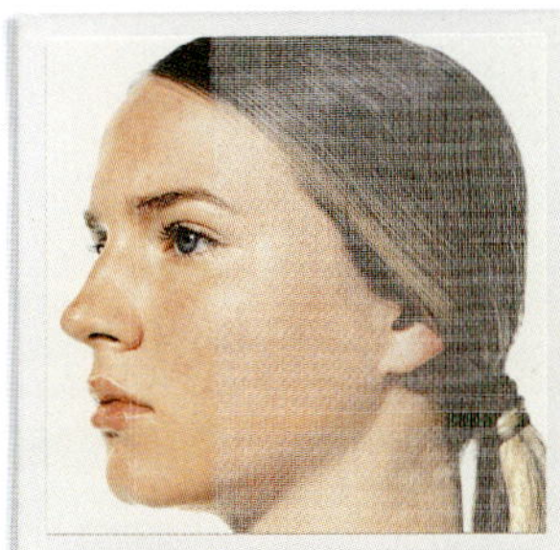

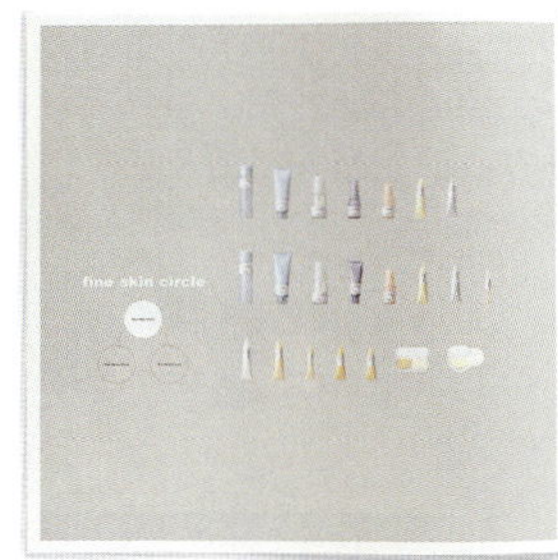

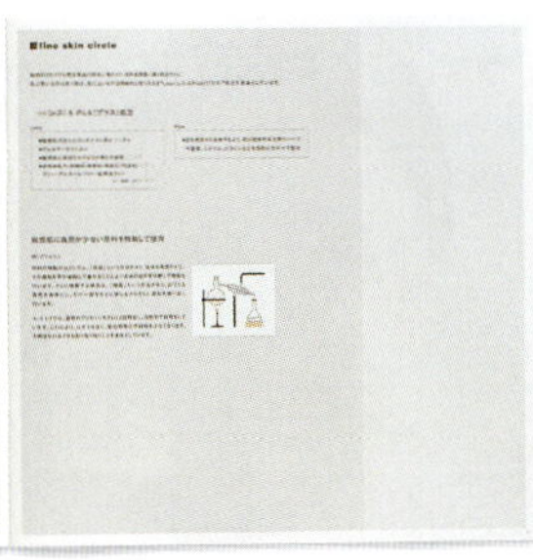

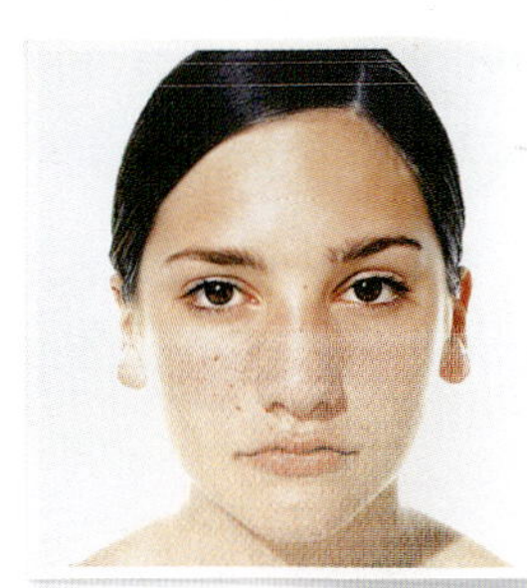

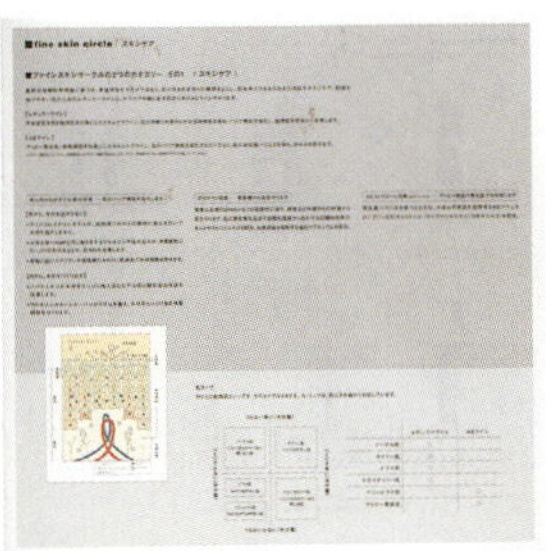

ET BOÎTE エ・ボワット

卸売をメインとするファッションブランドのプロモーション戦略
Promotional strategy for a wholesale-oriented fashion brand

戦略を読み解く 3 key words

ストリートシーンを意識したカジュアルブランド

10〜20代の女性をターゲットにしたジーンズ・カジュアルブランド。ストリートのトレンドを常に意識しながら、最新の素材と加工技術、デザインにプラスαを加え、ファッションに敏感な女の子たちが“今、着たい服”と感じるアイテムを提案する。

卸先の店頭でのプロモーションを目的にしたツール

シーズンごとに、ポスター・カタログと雑誌広告、店頭P.O.P.を使ったプロモーションを展開。レディースカジュアルショップへの卸売をメインにしているため、その店頭で使用してもらうポスター・カタログと店頭P.O.P.の制作に力を注ぐ。

商品のもつ“空気感”をイメージさせるイラスト

複数のブランドが並ぶ店頭でも目を引くビジュアルを目指す。商品のセールスポイントが風合いや素材感など、写真では伝えにくい部分であるためイラストを使用。実際にスタイリストが手がけたスタイルをもとに、ブランドと波長の合うアーティストがイラスト化。

3 key words

A "street scene"-conscious casual clothing brand

A casual clothing brand aimed at women in their teens and twenties. Staying conscious of street trends, using the latest materials and manufacturing techniques and designing clothes with "that extra something", the company offers fashion-conscious young women what they want to wear "now".

Promotional tools for wholesalers' distribution to stores

Seasonal promotion uses posters, catalogs, magazine advertisements and point-of-purchase displays. With wholesale sales to ladies' casual fashions shops being the main objective, efforts are focused on creating posters, catalogs and point-of-purchase displays the stores can use.

Illustrations that convey the "atmosphere" of the product

The goal is a visual display that will catch the customer's eye among all the brands lined up in a store. Illustrations are used to convey what photographs cannot -- textures, materials, &c. In practice, we have an artist turn an image designed by a professional stylist into illustrations that perfectly match the brand's wavelength.

Naming

ブランド名は英語の「and square」をフランス語に訳したもの。ブランドがスクエアなイメージをもつフレンチワークウェアからスタートしたことと、言葉の響きの良さから名付けた。

The brand name (which means "and square" in English) comes from the French work-wear with a very "square" image that formed the departure point for the brand, chosen as much for the sound as the meaning.

ポスター・カタログ Poster・Catalog

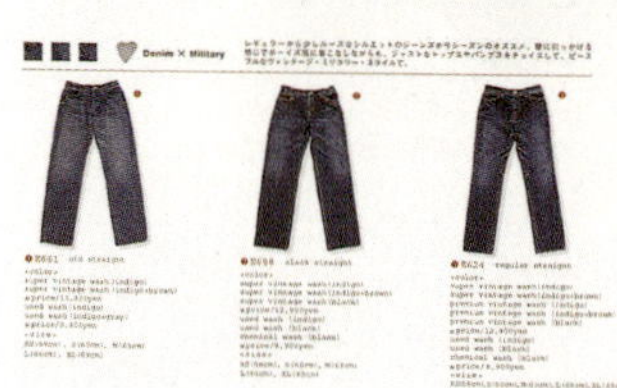

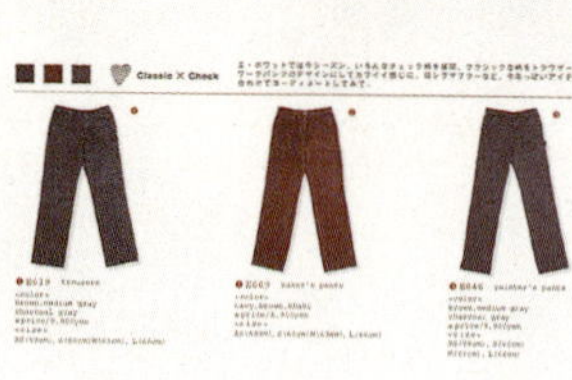

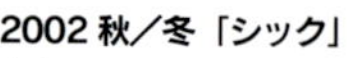

2002 秋／冬「シック」

大人っぽくシックに楽しむ、ジーンズを中心にしたスタイルを提案。

2002 A/W “chic”

A mature chic yet fun style centered around jeans.

P.O.P.

■CL= ブルーウェイ BLUE WAY COMPANY
■CD= 大島秀一 Shuichi Oshima ■AD= 林田佳子 Yoshiko Hayashida ■P= ヨンヨンプラス（ポスター・カタログ） 44+plus (Poster·Catalog) ■I= カンバラクニエ Kunie Kanbara ■Stylist= 大橋マリ Mari Ohashi
■Model= ユリエ（ポスター・カタログ） yurie (Poster·Catalog) ■Production= ヨンヨンプラス 44+plus ■S= ブルーウェイ BLUE WAY COMPANY

2003 春／夏「リゾート!!!」

"仲のいい友達と気軽に出かけよう！" というイメージで、リゾートで楽しむカジュアルスタイルを提案。

2003 S/S "resort!!!"

A casual resortwear style imaged after the idea of "taking a quick and easy trip with one's friends".

商品 Product

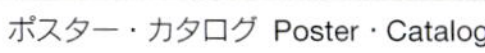

ポスター・カタログ Poster・Catalog

P.O.P.

NIKE presto ナイキ プレスト

アーティストとのコラボレーションで若者文化をリードする存在に

Collaborating with artists to lead youth culture

戦略を読み解く 3 key words

コンセプトは "Self-expression＝自己表現"

豊富なカラーバリエーションと斬新なデザイン、SMLのサイズ展開など、スポーツシューズのイメージを覆す革新的なモデルとして2000年に登場。発売時には "self expression＝自己表現" をコンセプトにしたキャンペーンを展開した。

コラボレーション企画を主軸にしたプロモーション

毎年、新商品の発売時期に合わせてキャンペーンを展開。ストリートカルチャーシーンで活躍する国内外の様々なアーティストとコラボレートし、そこで生まれた作品をユーザーに贈ったり、音楽・映像関係者などにゲリラサンプリングしてブランディングを強化。

革新性と創造性に満ちたビジュアルを目指す

各キャンペーンにおいて、ブランドの特性を "自由な表現方法" によってビジュアル化。アーティストとのコラボレーション作品そのものを広告ビジュアルとして使用するなど、常に先鋭的でクリエイティブなイメージを追求し続けている。

3 key words

Identifying the product with self-expression

A new model of sport shoe that revolutionizes the genre with novel styling and a wide variation of colors, the presto makes its debut in 2000 in small, medium and large sizes. The campaign focuses on identifying the product with self-expression.

Promotion centers on collaborations with artists

Coordinate a promotion to coincide with each year's product debut season. Collaborate with artists active in street culture in Japan and abroad, presenting the resulting works to customers, and place products with musicians and entertainers, resulting in stronger branding.

Visuals filled with innovation and creativity

Make every campaign involve a visual expression of the brand's defining characteristic: " a way to express yourself freely". Using the products of the artist collaborations as advertisement visuals, continually pursue an creative, always groundbreaking image.

Naming

ブランド名のprestoは、イタリア語で「急速に」という意味で主に音楽用語として使われる。"リズムよく飛び跳ねるような軽い履き心地" という商品特性を表し、"明るい、楽しい" という商品イメージを象徴する語感のよさから名付けた。

The brand name, "presto", is an Italian word for "very quickly" used in music. It expresses the product's main characteristic, "light shoes you can bound along in with a quick rhythm", and was also chosen for the connotations of lightness and fun it lends to the product.

2001年キャンペーン

キャッチコピーは「表現してる？」。クラブミュージックのシーンで世界的に活躍する、日本人DJ・サウンドクリエーター4人とコラボレーションを行った。

2001 Campaign

Catchcopy: "Expressing yourself?" A collaboration with four Japanese DJs and sound artists active in the club music scene.

ノベルティ

アナログ盤に収録した楽曲をまとめたコンピレーションDVD。DVDプレーヤーで音楽や映像によるVJが楽しめる「DVDJ」を搭載しており、まさにユーザーが "自己表現" できる仕掛け。更に、コラボレーションに参加した4人のDJ情報やブランド情報、映画界で活躍する気鋭のエディターHank Corwinによるイメージ映像を収録。キャンペーン期間中の商品購入者に抽選でプレゼントした。

Novelty

A compilation DVD of the analog recordings loaded with music and visuals for "DVDJs" to enjoy "VJing" as a form of self-expression. It also features information about the four participating DJs, the brand, and imagery by spirited film editor Hank Corwin. Presented to lottery-winning product purchasers during the campaign.

ノベルティ

4つの新商品それぞれから受けるインスピレーションを基に、4人のトップDJがオリジナル楽曲をクリエイトしたアナログ盤。iモードの「プレスト」サイトの会員に抽選でプレゼントした他、クラブDJなどにゲリラ的に配布した。

Novelty

Analog recordings of musical compositions by four top DJs each inspired by one of the four new products. Presented to lottery-winning members of the i-mode website "Presto" and sent to club DJs

■CL= ナイキジャパン NIKE JAPAN Co., Ltd.
■CD= John C Jay ■CD= 佐藤澄子 Sumiko Sato ■AD= Philip Lord (2001 Campaign) ■AD= Eric Cruz (2003 Campaign) ■Agency & Production= ワイデン・アンド・ケネディトウキョウ Wieden & Kennedy Tokyo
■S= ワイデン・アンド・ケネディトウキョウ Wieden & Kennedy Tokyo

2003年キャンペーン

テーマは「instant go」。"常にスイッチが入っていて、すぐに行動できること" を意味し、アクティブな若者文化を象徴するフレーズとして選んだ。"ポストグラフィティ" をテーマに、日本、アメリカ、香港のグラフィティ・アーティストたちとコラボレーションを行った。

2003 Campaign

Theme: "instant go", implying "always powered up and ready to go", symbolizing active youth culture. Collaborative works based on the subject "post-graffiti" by Japanese, American and Hong Kong graffiti artists.

ノベルティ
アメリカ、日本、香港のアーティストたちのコラボレーションによって創り出された、実写とアニメーションの合成によるDVD。ユーザーに抽選でプレゼントした。

Novelty
A DVD of composite filmed and animated imagery created as a collaboration between American, Japanese and Hong Kong artists. Presented to lottery-winning customers.

雑誌広告
DVDに収録された作品ビジュアルを使ったイメージ広告。一部の雑誌にはDVDを付録として付けた。

Magazine AD
Advertising images using visuals from the works recorded on the DVD. The DVD was offered as a giveaway in selected magazines.

Design News デザインニュース

“表紙が最強のメディアになる” ことを狙った、雑誌のプロモーション

The magazine cover as the strongest self-promotional medium

戦略を読み解く 3 key words

コンテンツのリニューアルと同時に表紙を一新

1975年の創刊という歴史あるインダストリアルデザイン誌が、総合デザイン誌として生まれ変わったのを機に表紙デザインをリニューアル。新たなコンセプトとして“Magazine for Brilliant Design Tomorrow” を掲げ、これを雑誌のサブタイトルとした。

“登場感” を強く打ち出した表紙デザイン

“雑誌の表紙がそのままメディアになる” ことを念頭に置き、華々しい登場感をもつ表紙となるようデザイン。また、あえて雑誌のイメージから離れ、展示スペースに何冊も並べたときに新たな視覚効果を生み出せるデザインを目指した。

購買層の更なる拡大を図ったプロモーション

新たな読者層として学生をターゲットに定め、書店やデザイン系大学などを中心にプロモーションを展開。表紙と同じグラデーションを用いて、ポスターはもちろんイベント時に使用するP.O.P.や紙袋なども制作した。

3 key words

Completely new cover design signals change in content

Redesign the cover of the industrial design journal first published in 1975 reborn as a comprehensive design magazine. Use the new magazine concept -- " Magazine for Brilliant Design Tomorrow" -- as the subtitle.

Cover design that makes an impressive entrance

Bearing in mind that the magazine cover is a form of media, design the cover to impart a dazzling sense of arrival. Intentionally depart from the image of the magazine, aim for design that creates a new visual effect when multiple issues are displayed side-by-side.

Promotion to reach a wider range of readership

Targeting students as a potential new readership group, develop promotions for use in bookstores and design-teaching colleges and institutions. Use the same gradation as on the magazine cover on posters as well as point of sales materials and paper bags for special events.

Naming

雑誌名に込められた “デザインに関わる実用情報を正確に伝える” という創刊以来の方針は、リニューアル後も変わらないため、そのまま踏襲している。

Retain the original magazine name which communicates the magazine's unchanging policy "to accurately convey practical design-related information".

DM

デザインニュースから、
うれしいニュース。

展示 Exhibition Photo= 松本理加 Rika Matsumoto

ブックスタンド Book stand

紙袋 Paper bag

■ CL= 日本産業デザイン振興会 Japan Industrial Design Promotion Organization
■ CD= 山田裕一 Yuichi Yamada ■ AD= 松下 計 Kei Matsushita ■ D= 田辺智子 Tomoko Tanabe ■ DF= 松下計デザイン室 KEI Matsushita Design Room Inc. ■ S= 松下計デザイン室 KEI Matsushita Design Room Inc.

カード Card

DM

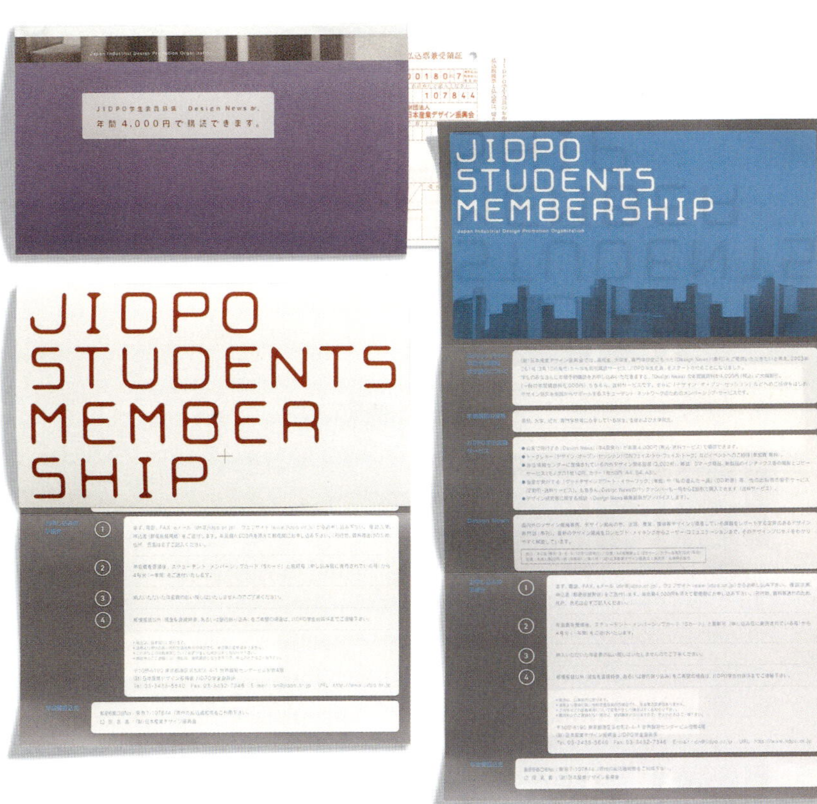

バナー Banner

HAKOJIN 箱人（ハコジン）

新種の占い「箱人」を複数企業がタイアップしてPR

Promoting a new kind of fortune-telling with tie-ins

戦略を読み解く 3 key words

「箱人」キャラクターが登場する新しい占い

生年月日をもとに性格を、「のびのび組」「きらきら組」など10通りのタイプに分類にした占い。各タイプの長所を組名にし、「箱人」というキャラクターで親しみやすさを出した。さらに、各箱人には、それぞれの特徴を示すポーズと伝統色を持たせている。

タイアップ企業が各キャンペーンを展開

「箱人」占いをPRするために、講談社、サントリー、EZweb、J-SKY、ディックカラー＆デザインなど複数企業が連携。雑誌での特集やサイトでの紹介、オリジナルグッズ制作など、各社独自の展開をしている。書籍発売に合わせたキャンペーンも開催。

120色のカラーで箱人の世界を表現

基本である10組に設定した10色を、さらに生まれ月によって分類し、合計120色ものバリエーションを展開。箱人の特徴である色をさらに強調した。この120色は、DICの「日本の伝統色」「フランスの伝統色」から選択している。

3 key words

Debut of the Hakojin character -- a new kind of fortune-telling

The fortune-telling system categorizes people by date of birth into ten types, each named after their best point, like "nobinobi-gumi (free-and-easy group)" or "kirakira-gumi (dazzling group)", and assigned a particular Hakojin, a friendly character. Each Hakojin has a different pose, representing the characteristics of its group.

Tying up with businesses for promotional campaigns

Tie up with a wide variety of companies, such as Kodansha, Suntory, EZweb, J-SKY and DIC Color & Design. Promote the uniqueness of the system through magazine special editions, a website and original goods. Also develop a campaign suited to tying in with publication releases.

The Hakojin world in 120 colors

The ten colors of the ten groups, when further divided according to birth month, make 120 variations. Emphasize the characteristic Hakojin colors, selected from DIC's traditional Japanese and traditional French color lines.

Naming

箱を渡されたら、人はどういうリアクションをとるのか。そのリアクションの違いからネーミング。箱＋人で箱人。

The fortune-telling system derives a person's personality type from what action they perform when handed a box. Thus, Hakojin (box man).

書籍「HAKOJIN占い」 Book

シールブック Sticker book

ストラップ Strap

■CL= ディックカラー＆デザイン DIC COLOR & DESIGN ■CL= 心本舗 COCOROHONPO
<Book> ■Project production= 講談社 Kodansha ■AD= スタジオ・ギブ Studio GIVE <Sticker book, Strap> ■Project production= ディックカラー＆デザイン DIC COLOR & DESIGN ■Project production= 心本舗 COCOROHONPO
<Magazine「FRaU」> ■Project production= 講談社 Kodansha <Official web site> ■CD= Kerog P. Suzuki ■AD= 北岡 陽 Akira Kitaoka ■Project production= ディックカラー＆デザイン DIC COLOR & DESIGN
■Project production= 心本舗 COCOROHONPO <SUNTORY HAKOJIN> ■CD= Kerog P. Suzuki ■AD= 北岡 陽 Akira Kitaoka ■Project production= サントリー SUNTORY
■Project production= ディックカラー＆デザイン DIC COLOR & DESIGN ■Project production= 心本舗 COCOROHONPO ■S= ディックカラー＆デザイン DIC COLOR & DESIGN

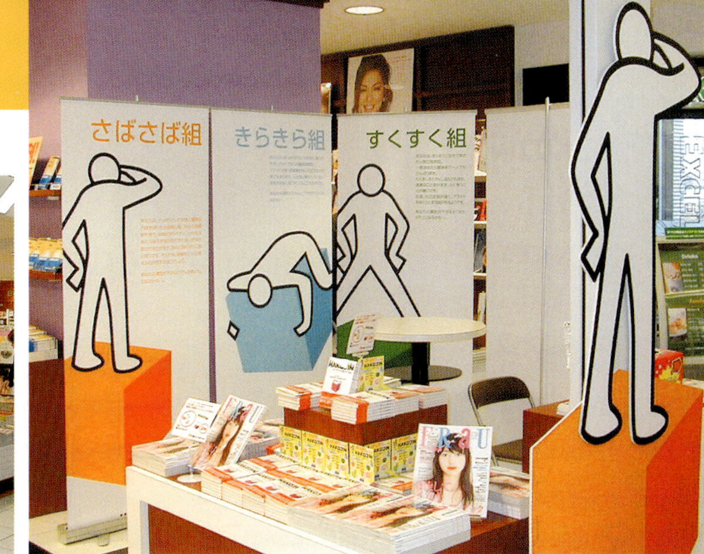

キャンペーン風景 Campaign scenery

雑誌「FRaU」(No.277／2002年11月26日号)
Magazine 「FRaU」(No.277 / 2002.11.26)

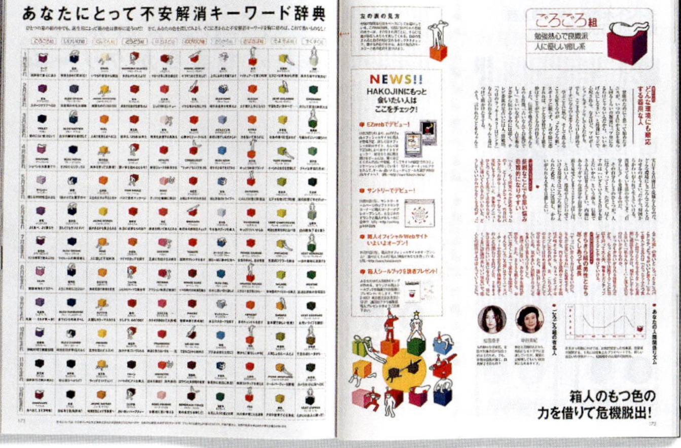

サントリー箱人 SUNTORY HAKOJIN

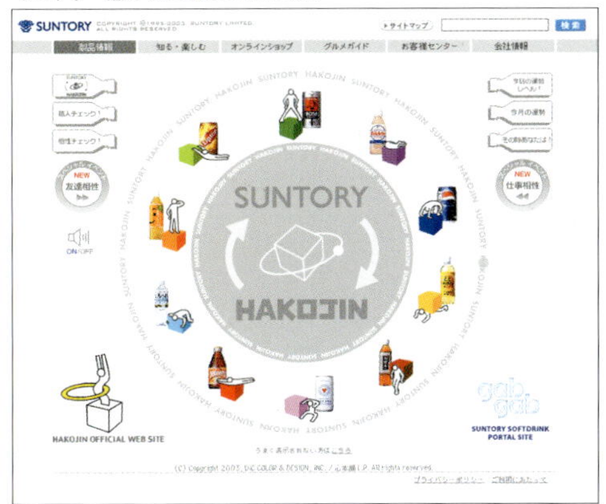

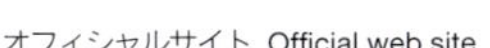
オフィシャルサイト Official web site

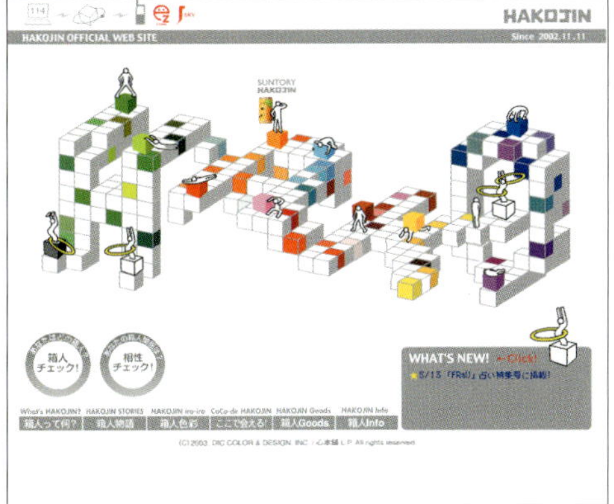

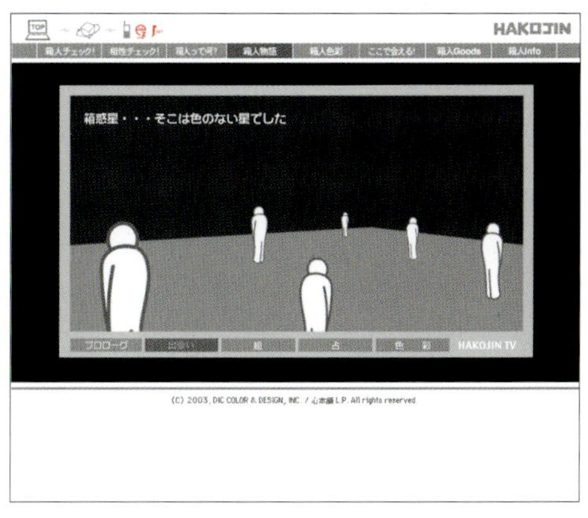

SLY COOPER 怪盗スライ・クーパー

標的は他企業ポスター。「怪盗」をキーワードにプロモーション展開

The target: other advertisements. The keyword: Phantom Thief

戦略を読み解く 3 key words

怪盗アライグマが大活躍の3Dアクションゲーム

先祖代々、義賊を生業としているアライグマが主人公のプレイステーション2用ゲームソフト。内容は、主人公のアライグマが悪党からお宝を盗み取るという3Dアクション。目的のお宝をちょうだいしたら、顔型のカードを置いていくストーリー。

他企業の広告を盗んで街行く人にアピール

キャラクターではなく、「怪盗」という内容自体を前面に出すことで、ゲームファンのみならず、より多くの人にアピールできると考え、他業種の企業に協力を依頼。企業ポスターの一番肝心な部分を盗まれたように切り抜き、その上にメッセージを残した。

ポスター&限定キット　アイテムを絞り込んで

限られた予算内で最大限に効果を発揮するためには、スピーディに、且つ、内容に合った媒体をピックアップすることが大切と考え、デザインツールはポスターとプレミアムキット（商品に添付されているカードを送ると貰える）のみに絞り込んだ。

3 key words

A phantom raccoon stars in an exciting 3D video game

This Playstation 2 action game has the descendant of a long line of honorable raccoon thieves on a quest to steal treasures from various villains. Each time the heroic raccoon makes it to one of his goals, he finds a face card with a new story.

"Stealing" advertisements appeals to people in the street

Emphasizing the "Phantom Thief" component of the game, rather than the character, appeals to a much wider market segment than just hardcore game fans. Tying up with other companies, create a promotion where the Phantom Thief "steals" the most valuable part of their poster and leaves behind a message.

Focusing resources on posters and a limited edition kit

In order to achieve the maximum effect with a limited budget, we placed importance on speed and appropriate selection of medium and confined our efforts to a poster campaign and a premium kit (which customers can receive by sending in a card included with the game).

Naming

元々はアメリカのゲーム。キャラクターの名前をゲーム名とした。

Originally an American game, it was named after the main character.

プレミアムキット
変装シールや変装マスク、水に溶ける紙を使ったメモ帳がセット。限定2000個。

Premium kit
A limited, 2000-set edition of disguise stickers and masks and memo pads with paper that disintegrates in water.

■CL= ソニー・コンピュータエンタテインメント Sony Computer Entertainment
■AD + D= 田中　元 Gen Tanaka　■CW= 水谷正輝 Masateru Mizutani　■D= 丸橋佳寿子 Kazuko Marubashi　■D= 大森　州 Shu Ohmori　■Creative producer= 仲田繁乃 Shigeno Nakada
■Advertising agent + Project production= 電通 DENTSU INC.　■Project production= アドブレーン ADBRAIN　■S= 電通 DENTSU INC.

ポスター
300枚以上にも及んだ企業ポスターの切り抜きはすべて手作業で行った。

Poster
The over 300 company posters were all torn out by hand.

rimococoron リモココロン

小さくて、かわいくって、毒気のあるキャラクターが街を席巻

Cute, tiny and malicious characters overwhelm a town

戦略を読み解く 3 key words

キャラクターにちょっかい出して人生を変えちゃおう

人間、動物、モノなど200種類もの多彩なキャラクターが登場するプレイステーション2用ソフト。家庭や商店街、遊園地にいる、かわいいけれど、ちょっと毒気のあるキャラクターたちにちょっかいを出し、人生を変えてしまうというストーリー。

女の子の目に止まる、かわいらしいキャラクターを

ターゲットとした「プレステ2をやってみたい」と思っている女の子たちに見てもらえるよう、ゲームソフトの広告にありがちな実写表現や、ゲームシーンの挿入はせず、リモココロンの世界観を、小さくてかわいらしく、毒気のあるキャラクターで表現した。

広告の掲出場所・企画に応じてキャラクターを配置

ビジュアルはキャラクターを中心に表現することで統一したが、掲出場所・企画に合わせて、各キャラクターを配置、演技させた。ラフォーレ原宿やマクドナルド、HMVなどさまざまな企業とタイアップして幅広く広告展開した。

3 key words

Meddle with your characters and change their lives

A PlayStation 2 game with over two hundred widely varying characters, including people, animals and things. The story takes the game player to a variety of settings -- a home, a shopping street, an amusement park -- where they meddle with the cute but slightly malicious characters and change their lives.

Catching young girls' eyes with cute characters

In order to draw the attention of the target audience, girls who would like to try the PlayStation 2, refrain from using the usual screen shots and game scenes and express the game world through its tiny, cute, slightly malicious characters.

Matching characters to location

The visuals are consistent in that they all focus on the characters, but the ads are carefully matched to their display location in terms of the character they feature and the action that character is performing. The high-profile department store LaForet Harajuku, McDonalds, HMV and other businesses become part of a wide-scale tie-up promotional campaign.

Naming

ココロ（心）をリモコンで自由に操るというゲームの特徴から造語した。

The game's name is a combination of "rimocon (remote control)" and "kokoro (heart)", referring to the game's main characteristic.

ポスター
JR高田馬場駅に掲出されたポスター。すべてゲーム内に登場する店の看板。

Poster
A poster hung in the JR Takadanobaba Station. The signs of all stores appearing in the games.

■CL= ソニー・コンピュータエンタテインメント Sony Computer Entertainment
■CD= 中野雅春 Masaharu Nakano ■AD + D + Project production= 田中 元 Gen Tanaka ■AD + D= 丸橋佳寿子 Kazuko Marubashi ■CW= 水谷正輝 Masateru Mizutani ■D= 保坂丈二 Joji Hosaka
■D= 大森 州 Shu Ohmori ■D= 河上 誠 Makoto Kawakami ■I= 中根ケンイチ Kenichi Nakane ■Creative producer= 仲田繁乃 Shigeno Nakada ■Advertising agent + Project production= 電通 DENTSU INC.
■Project production= アドブレーン ADBRAIN ■S= 電通 DENTSU INC.

ポスター & シール
シール付き2連ポスター。ペットボトルと同種の素材を用いてキャラクターのシールを制作。そのシールをポスター上にランダムに貼り付け、持ち帰ることもできるようになっている。

Poster & Sticker
A two-part poster with stickers made of PET bottle material randomly adhered to the surface, that passersby are free to take home.

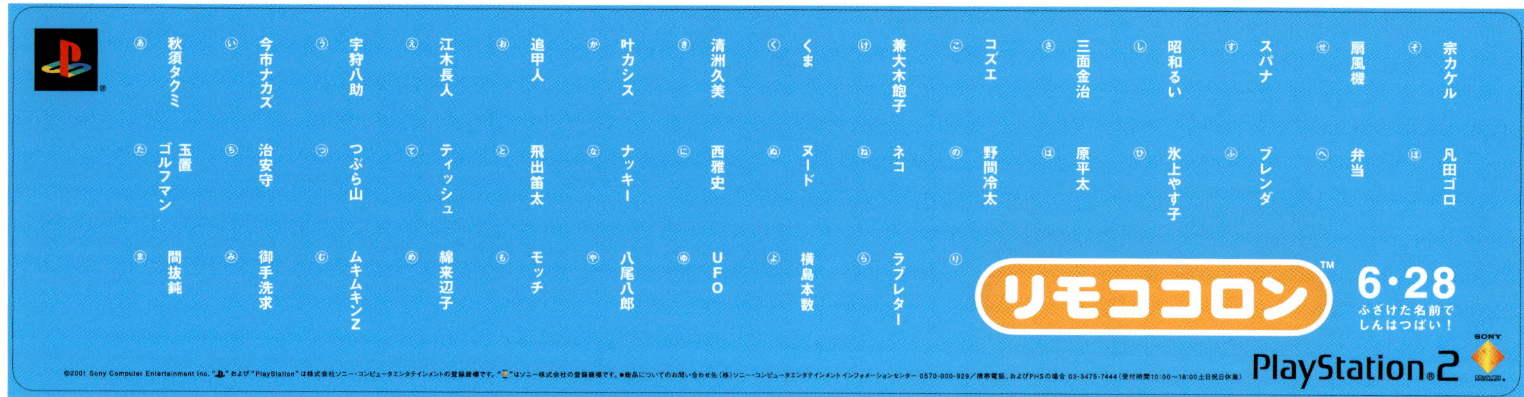

ステッカー
東京、大阪、名古屋の電車内に掲出したツインステッカー。上がキャラクターのビジュアル、下がその名前。

Sticker
Twin stickers hung in Tokyo, Osaka and Nagoya trains. Above, the character visual; below, their names.

ウォールメディア
新宿ミロード・モザイク通り沿いの壁に展開。ゲームステージが順に描かれ、ゲーム攻略のヒントも隠されている。

Wall media
Presented along the mosaic street of Shinjuku My Lord. The game stages are depicted in order, along with hidden game strategy hints.

ポスター（原宿駅） Poster

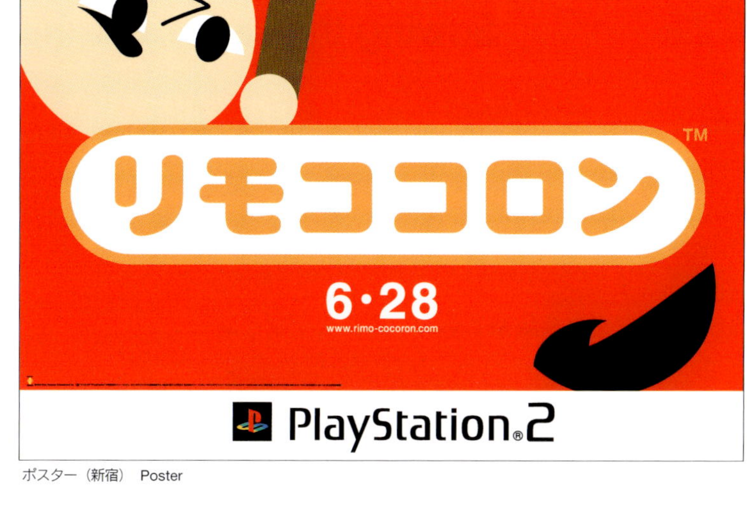

ポスター（新宿） Poster

なーんの罪もない小市民たちにちょっかいを出して彼らの人生をくるわせてみないかゲーム!!
リモココロン

アドマックス（音の出る電飾バス） AD MAX (Electric spectacular bus with sound)

シール Sticker

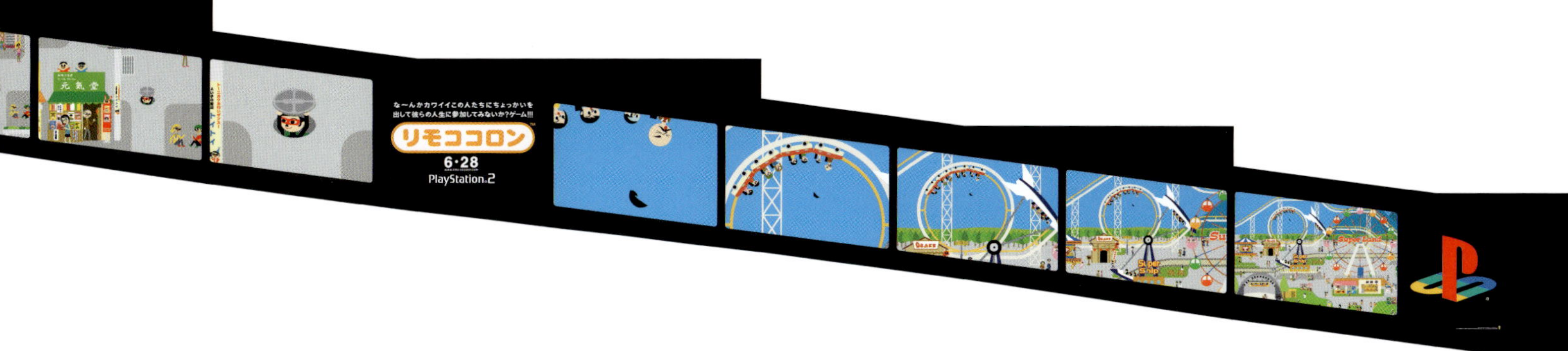

Màrm マーム

10年、20年後のブランドの成長を見据えた“種をまく”広告

Sowing the seeds of a ten, twenty year brand strategy

戦略を読み解く 3 key words

コンセプトは“人を優しい気持ちにする”こと

キャラクタービジネスを柱とするプロジェクトで、“人を優しい気持ちにする”をコンセプトに掲げる。しかし、単なるキャラクタービジネスには留まらず、将来は新しいエンタテイメントの形を生み出せるようなプロジェクトにまで成長したいと願う。

プロジェクトを象徴するシンボルをデザイン

ブランディングにあたり、まずはロゴとシンボルをデザイン。ピンク色の丸は“温かいもの”や“優しいもの”と、それらを誕生させる“love & peaceのもと”を象徴すると同時に“器の大きさ”を意味し、長期的ビジョンをもったブランドであることを示す。

徹底したイメージ戦略でブランド力を高める

プロジェクト設立時に大々的なプロモーションを展開。シンボルを効果的に使ったビジュアルで、プロジェクトのイメージ増幅と、それに賛同するクリエイターを集めるという相乗効果を狙った。また、広告自体が“人を優しい気持ちにする”ことを目指す。

3 key words

Giving people a tenderhearted feeling

A business built around promotional character design, its motto is "giving people a tenderhearted feeling". However, its future business plan calls for it to grow beyond character design to produce entirely new kinds of entertainment.

Designing a symbol for the project

The first step in branding is designing the logo and symbol. The pink circle symbolizes warmth and tenderness, as well as the source for both of those feelings, "love and peace". It also symbolizes a vessel of great volume, communicating the long-term vision of the brand.

Increasing brand strength with a comprehensive strategy

Run large-scale promotion at the beginning of the project. Visuals that make effective use of the brand symbol have the dual effect of amplifying the project image and attracting creators of like mind. The advertisements in themselves are designed to "give people a tenderhearted feeling".

Naming

「マーム」は“ママ”を優しい響きにした造語。プロジェクトのキーワードである“優しさ”を感じさせる名称として選んだ。

"Màrm" is a variation on "Mom", chosen because it expresses the project's keyword, "tenderheartedness", so well.

カレンダー Calendar

Tシャツ T-shirt

■CL= アクシヴ axev inc.
■CD + AD + D= 青木克憲 Katsunori Aoki ■CD + CW= サトウ哲康 Noriyasu Sato ■I= 寄藤文平 (ポスター1、新聞広告1) Bunpei Yorifuji (Poster 1, Newspaper 1) ■P= 小山裕良 (カレンダー) Hiroyoshi Koyama (Calendar)
■P= 長島有里枝 (出版物) Yurie Nagashima (Publication) ■Artist= 生意気 (カレンダー) Namaiki (Calendar) ■Agency & Production= バタフライ・ストローク butterfly·stroke inc. ■S= バタフライ・ストローク butterfly·stroke inc.

新聞広告1 Newspaper AD 1

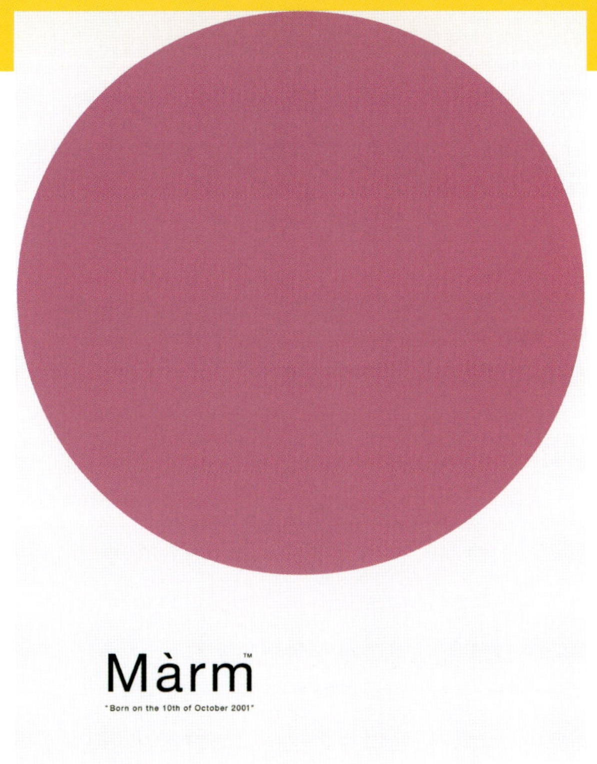

新聞広告 Newspaper AD

Màrm™

"Born on the 10th of October 2001"

ポスター Poster

出版物
プロジェクトの一環に出版物の制作もあり、その第一弾。“妊婦がトツキトウカの間に、お腹の赤ちゃんに贈った詩集”というコンセプト。

Publication
The first phase of product-related printed materials. A collection of poems written by mothers to their unborn babies during their pregnancy.

ポスター1 Poster 1

au

フライヤー＆クリアファイルが果たす「プチ・メディア」効果に注目

A flyer and clear folder -- the "petit media" effect

戦略を読み解く 3 key words

生活をより豊かにする携帯電話を追求

携帯電話をユビキタスネットワークの核として、人と人、人とモノ、モノとモノをつないでいく。KDDIが構築するトータルソリューションによって、人々の生活を豊かにしていくことを目指す。

おしゃれなクリアファイルが来店のきっかけ作る

2002年より、毎月違うデザインや企画でフライヤーを制作し、オリジナルファイルとともに店頭に設置。自由に持ち帰りできるようにしている。「ファイルを持ち帰る→携帯する→クチコミで広がる→ファイル目当ての来店者、リピーターが増える」というねらい。

遊び心＆仕掛け満載の個性派フライヤーを制作

フライヤーはデザインフォーマットを統一し、伝える情報をひとつに集約。そのなかに携帯電話の面白さ、楽しさを伝える遊び心のあるデザインを盛り込んでいる。フライヤーがシールやカレンダーになっていたり、組み立てると貯金箱になるなど仕掛けも満載。

3 key words

Mobile phones enrich life

The mobile phone is the nucleus of an ubiquitous network linking people to people, people to objects, and objects to objects. KDDI's total solutions aim to enhance people's lives.

A stylish file folder draws customers to stores

Flyers different in design and concept produced monthly since 2002 are available in retail outlets in an original folder free for the taking. The objective: take home file → mobile → word-of-mouth communication → visit to retail outlet to obtain a new file = increased repeat visitors.

Produce a playful, device-filled, individualistic flyer

Unify the design format and concentrate the information to be communicated singularly. Incorporate playfulness into the design to convey the interest and fun of mobile phones. Design the flyer using devices that make it into stickers, a calendar, assemble into a bank, etc.

Naming

KDDIが展開する移動体通信事業の方向性を象徴する数々のキーワード、Access、Always、Amenityなどの頭文字である、"A" と、Unique、Universal、Userなどの頭文字である "U" から構成された造語。Access to U（You）という意味も併せ持つ。

"A" and "U" are the initials of several key words -- access, always, amenity, unique, universal, user -- that symbolize KDDI's mobile unit communications business. They brand name also embraces the meaning "access to u (you)".

シール Sticker

コースター Coaster

クリアファイル＆フライヤー
Clear file & Flyer

■CL= KDDI
■CD= 佐々木　宏 Hiroshi Sasaki　■AD= 日高英輝 Eiki Hidaka　■CW= 小川英紀 Hidenori Ogawa　■D= 白須慎之 Noriyuki Shirasu　■D= ながしま　明 Akira Nagashima　■D= 杉山紘一 Koichi Sugiyama
■I= 山根茂樹 Shigeki Yamane　■Project production= 電通 DENTSU INC.　■Project production= グリッツデザイン gritz design　■Project production= Ogawa Pro.　■S= グリッツデザイン gritz design

クリアファイル＆フライヤー
Clear file & Flyer

DREAMS COME TRUE!

au MONEY BOX

LET'S BECOME RICH!

auで貯めるBOX

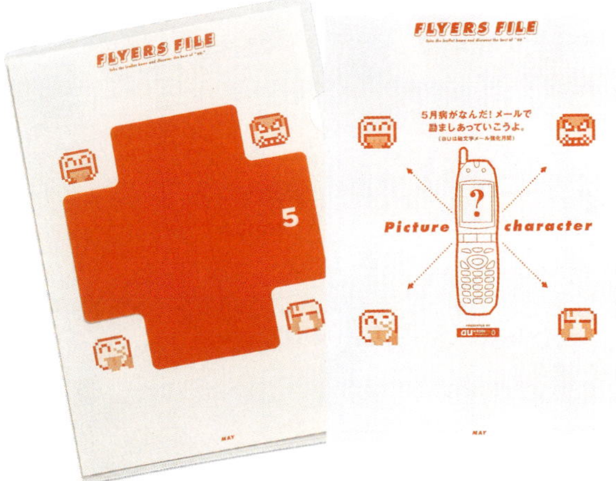

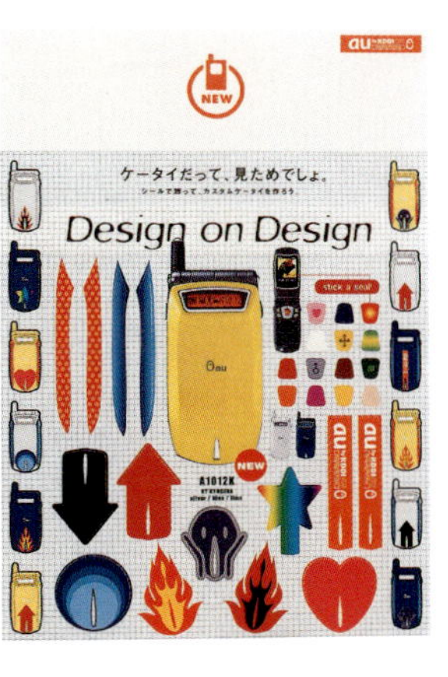

MONEY Kit マネーキット

店舗をもたないネットバンキングが挑む、ユーザーへのアプローチ
Promoting an Internet bank without physical branches

戦略を読み解く 3 key words

企業理念を具現化した資産運用ソフトウェア

ネットバンキングが提供する、web上で資産計画や資産運用が手軽にできるソフトウェア。"単なる金庫としてではなく、個人の視点に立って、お金とよりよく付き合うための道具を提供する"という企業理念の具体化のために開発された。

ブランド名の浸透を効果的にするツールを制作

店舗をもたないネットバンキングだからこそ、ソフトウェアを含めたあらゆるアイテムを重要なコミュニケーションツールとして認識。新規参入組であるため、ブランド名の認知度向上をプロモーションの主目的としている。

"楽しく使える道具"のイメージを増幅させる

各ツールのデザインにおいては、ブランドの顔であるロゴをアイコン的に使用。また、"感覚的に、そして楽しく使える身近な道具"としてのイメージを喚起させるビジュアルをテーマに制作している。

3 key words

Software that makes company principle reality

The software offers Internet banking that allows users easy financial planning and asset management. It was developed as a realization of an ideal -- "more than just a safety-deposit box, a tool created from the point of view of individual users that allows them to keep closer company with their money".

Creating tools to increase brand penetration

Precisely because Internet banking does not have a retail establishment, treat all materials including the software as important communication tools. As a new entry into the market, the main objective is to promote brand recognition.

Amplifying the product's image as "a fun, easy-to-use tool"

Incorporate the company logo in the design of the promotional tools in a way reminiscent of a computer icon. Create visuals that evoke an image of a "sensible but fun, easy-to-use, familiar tool".

Logo

ロゴそのものをアイコンのようにデザインし、カラフルに色づけすることで、商品のもつ堅いイメージをやわらげた。

Avoid a stiff, rigid product image by designing the company logo as a computer icon and making liberal use of color.

撮影用小物
ポスターのために制作した小物。あくまで撮影用なので実際に使われるアイテムではない。

Goods for poster
Items produced for the poster for photographic purposes only, not for use.

ポスター
ブランドを道具として認識して欲しいという考えから、"道具"を連想させる"パッケージ"をビジュアルのモチーフにした。

Poster
With the intention of getting the brand to be recognized as a tool, packaging associated with tools is used as a motif.

■CL= ソニー銀行 Sony Bank
■CD= 杓井一夫 Kazuo Shakui ■AD + D= 青木克憲 Katsunori Aoki ■D= 滝沢圭介 Keisuke Takizawa ■P= 小山裕良 Hiroyoshi Koyama ■Agency & Production= フロンテッジ FRONTAGE INC.
■DF= バタフライ・ストローク butterfly·stroke inc. ■S= バタフライ・ストローク butterfly·stroke inc.

パンフレット Pamphlet

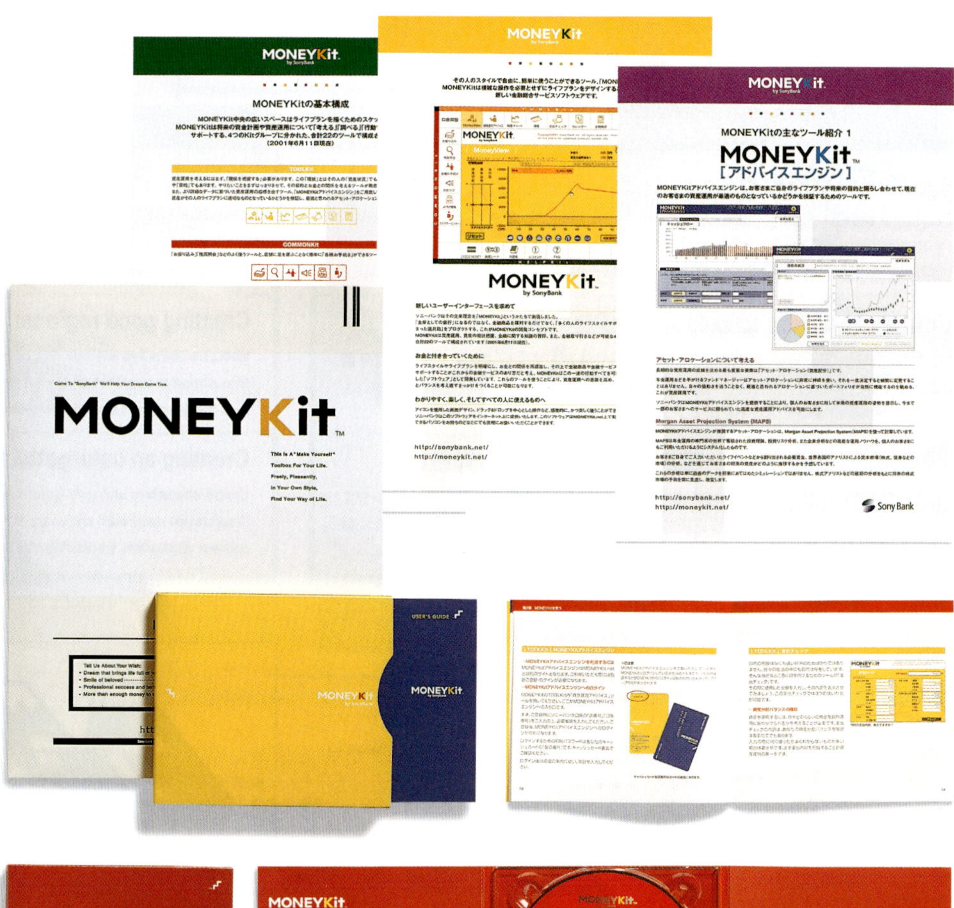

通帳ケース Passbook case

ポスター Poster

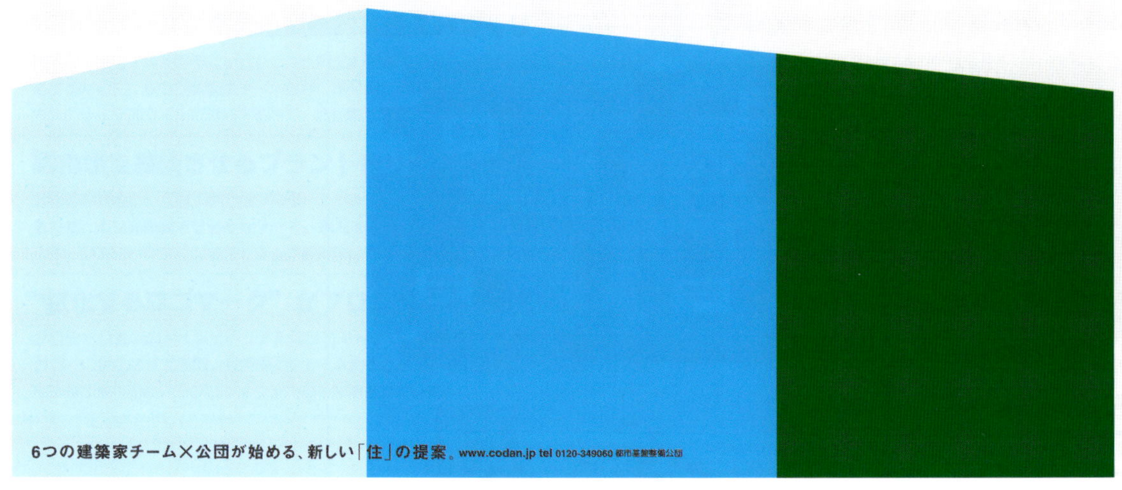

CODAN
Shinonome
1/6
6つの建築家チーム×公団が始める、新しい「住」の提案。www.codan.jp tel 0120-349060 都市基盤整備公団

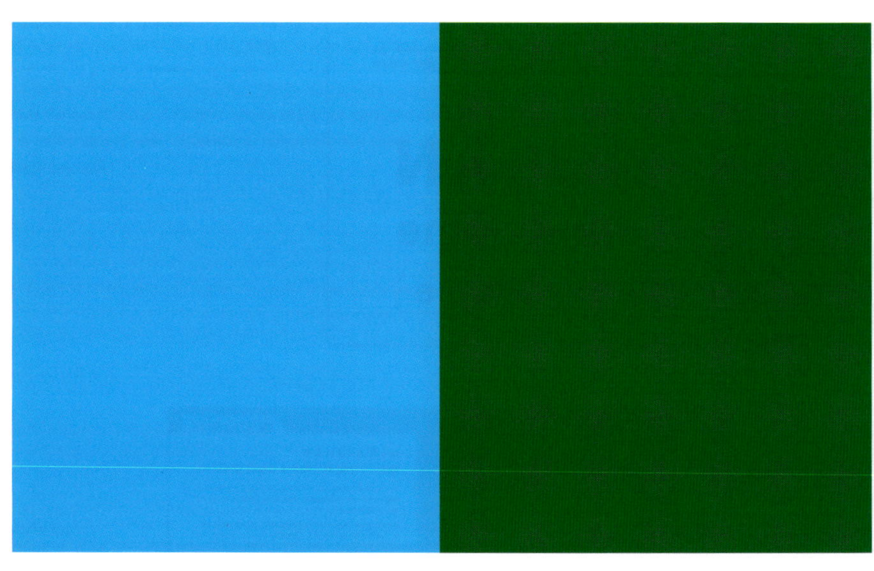

CODAN
Shinonome
1/6
1山本理顕、2伊東豊雄、3隈研吾+RIA、4山設計工房、5ADH/WORKSTATION設計共同体、6元倉眞琴・山本圭介・堀啓二設計共同体。www.codan.jp tel 0120-349060 都市基盤整備公団

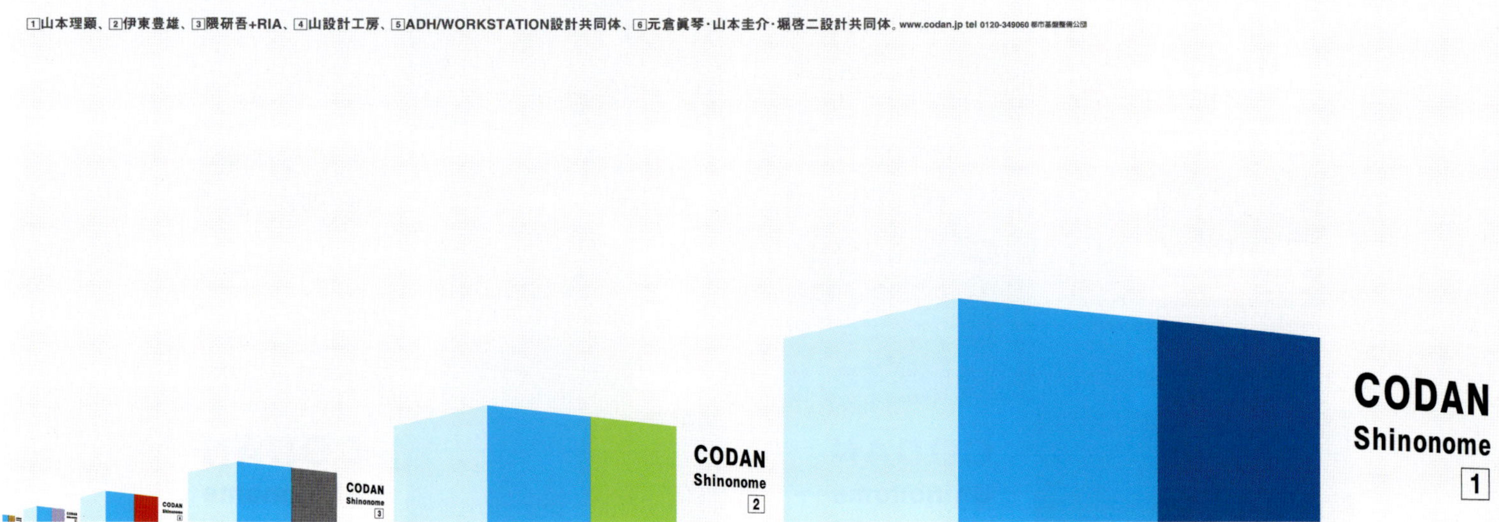

CODAN
Shinonome
3
CODAN
Shinonome
2
CODAN
Shinonome
1

コンセプトブック Concept book

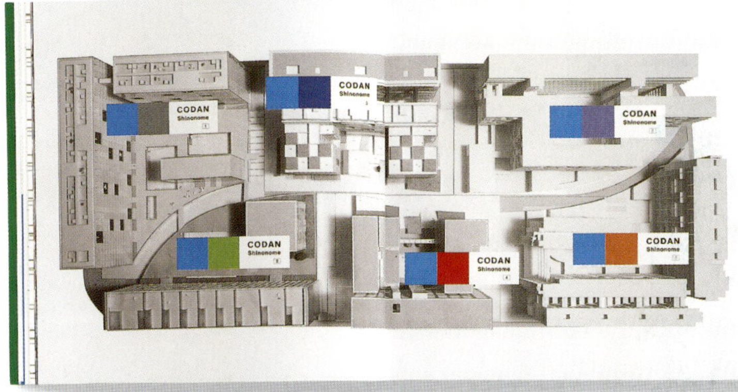

MARCH マーチ

「マーチアイ」がユーザーフレンドリーな車をアピール
Love March -- a campaign for a user-friendly car

戦略を読み解く 3 key words

「ユーザーフレンドリー」なクルマをコンセプトに

乗る人の気持ちを念頭におき、設計された車。単なる道具ではなく、パートナーというコンセプトのもとに開発された。コンパクトカー市場において不動のポジションを固めることを目指している。

皆に愛される使い勝手のいいキャラクターを創造

ヘッドライトを少し上から見ると、眼球らしいフォルムが浮かび上がる。これがマーチアイのモチーフに。子どもっぽくないこと、ポップアートのレベルに達していること、広告、Web、グッズなど媒体を問わず使いやすいデザインであることを配慮した。

愛らしい「マーチアイ」を全ツールに展開

「マーチアイ」キャラクターを全ツールに使用。メディア、街、店頭といった場所を問わず、自然に目が合う、一体感を持たせた展開にした。この愛らしい目がユーザーフレンドリーな車であることを素早く効果的に伝える役目を果たしている。

3 key words

The user-friendly car as concept

A car designed with the comfort and feelings of the passengers in mind, and developed along the concept of being a partner, not just a tool. The company's goal is to solidify their position in the compact car segment.

Conceiving a lovable, helpful character

If you look at the headline from just above, a pair of eyes pops out at you. This is the Love March motif. Care was taken to make the icon pop art, not childish, and easy to use in any medium, from conventional advertising to the Internet to promotional goods.

Making full use of the lovable Love March

Use the Love March character on all promotional tools. Develop a campaign that customers encounter naturally and that delivers a consistent message no matter the location -- in the media, on the street, and in showrooms. The lovable eyes fill the role of quickly and effectively transmitting the user-friendly quality of the automobile.

Character

「マーチアイ」および車のデザイン自体がキャッチコピー的な役割りを果たす。

The Love March name and the design of the car itself act as effective "advertising copy".

Shop

■CL= 日産自動車 NISSAN MOTOR
■CD= 八幡功一 Koichi Yahata ■CD= 永見浩之 Hiroyuki Nagami ■AD= 金子 敦 Atsushi Kaneko ■P= 児島孝宏 Takahiro Kojima ■P= Simon Harper ■CW= 菅野 忍 Shinobu Kanno ■Director= 田内健弥 Kenya Tauchi
■Planner= 清田小牧 Komaki Seida ■Planner= 菊川直子 Naoko Kikukawa ■D= 持永信也 Nobuya Mochinaga ■Advertising agent= 博報堂イン・プログレス hakuhodo in progress ■Advertising agent= 太陽企画 Taiyo kikaku
■DF= 水野デザインハウス mizuno design house ■S= 博報堂イン・プロブレス hakuhodo in progress

カタログ Catalog

DM

紙袋 Paper bag

new MARCH

ポスター Poster

雑誌広告 Magazine AD

新聞広告 Newspaper AD

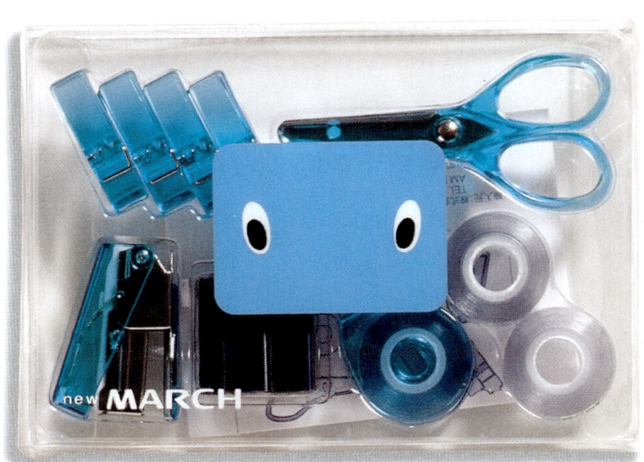

ノベルティー（ソーイングセット） Novelty (Sewing set)

ノベルティー（ストラップ）
Novelty (Strap)

ノベルティー（バスエッセンス） Novelty (Bath essence)

ノベルティー（Tシャツ） Novelty (T-shirt)

スクリーンセイバー
Screen saver

ノベルティー（マウスパット） Novelty (Mouse pad)

MOBILIO Spike　モビリオスパイク

遊び心と楽しさを感じさせるデザインでターゲット層の心をつかむ
Reaching the target demographic with fun and playful design

戦略を読み解く 3 key words

多様化する若者の好みに応えるマルチ・ワゴン

商品コンセプトのキーワードは“HOBBY × CAR”で、ターゲットは10代・20代の若者。様々なライフスタイルや趣味に対応できるよう、車体後部のスペースを大きくとり、コンパクトワゴンでありながらも活用度の高さを備えている。

2段階プロモーションで期待感を増幅させる

ブランドの認知度アップのためにインパクトを与えることとイメージの統一に留意しつつ、発売前と発売時の2段階にわたってプロモーションを展開。どちらもDMで期待感を膨らませ、ディーラーへの集客効果を図った。

ブランドのもつ遊び心を若者にアピール

若者に目新しさを感じさせると同時に“これは自分のための車だ！”と思ってもらえるよう、遊び心や楽しい雰囲気を感じさせるデザインを目指した。また、キーカラーの黄色を効果的に使ってイメージを統一した。

3 key words

A "multi-wagon" that appeals to a diversifying new generation

The product concept is "Hobby x Car", targeting young people in their teens and twenties. Designed to adapt to a wide variety of lifestyles and interests with a roomy cargo area, it is a concept car with great practical utility.

Sowing anticipation with a two-stage promotion

Develop a promotion to improve brand awareness, focusing on impact and image consistency, in two stages, pre-launch and post-launch. Both utilize direct mail to build anticipation and drive customers to dealerships.

Appealing to youth with playfulness

Brand design aimed for a playful and fun image, getting young people to feel the newness of the brand and think "this car was made for me!". As well, using yellow as the key color was effective in maintaining a consistent image.

Logo

車名を象徴するスパイク型のマークを添えてデザイン。「若さ」をイメージさせ、目に飛び込んでくる色として黄色をキーカラーに選んだ。

The car emblem integrates a spike shape into its design (playing off the car name). Yellow was chosen as the key color for its youthful connotation and its ability to catch the eye.

ポスター　Poster

雑誌広告　Magazine AD

■CL＝本田技研工業　HONDA MORTORS
■Agency＝博報堂＋原宿サン・アド　HAKUHODO Inc. + HARAJUKU SUN-AD　■CD＝横道浩明　Hiroaki Yokomichi　■AD＝佐野研二郎　Kenjiro Sano　■D＝杉山ユキ　Yuki Sugiyama　■D＝後藤　大　Dai Goto
■CW＝曽原　剛　Go Sohara　■S＝博報堂　HAKUHODO Inc.

READER'S CARD

Thank you for purchasing a fine PIE Books publication. We would appreciate it very much if you would take a moment to complete the following questionnaire and return it to us so that we can keep you up to date on our latest releases. We will use the information you provide as our inspiration for future projects.

BOOK TITLE: **Brand Strategy and Design**

1. Let us know what you think of this particular book. Tell us what themes you would like us to handle in future.

How I liked this book:

Themes I am interested in:

2. How did you discover this book?

A. Heard about it from a friend

B. Saw it in the bookstore (name of the store)

C. Read about it in another P·I·E publication

D. Received notice by direct mail E. Other ( )

3. Have you ever returned a reader's card to P·I·E before?

A. Yes B. No

NAME

OCCUPATION AGE

COMPANY

STREET

CITY

STATE ZIP COUNTRY

TEL. FAX.

e-mail

POSTCARD

Please
affix
postage

PIE BOOKS

2-32-4 Minami-Otsuka, Toshima-ku
Tokyo 170-0005
Japan

REQUEST FOR ENTRIES

We are planning to issue our Collection Series with the following contents. If you would like your work to be included, please circle each applicable category. We will contact you at a later date with specifics about a planned book when your work is to be included.

A. Postcard Graphics
B. Advertising Greeting Cards (DM)
C. Brochure & Pamphlet Collection
D. Poster Graphics
E. Book Cover & Editorial Designs
F. Corporate Image Logo Designs
G. Business Card & Letterhead Graphics
H. Calendar Graphics
I. Package & Wrapping Graphics

ポスター　Poster

雑誌広告　Magazine AD

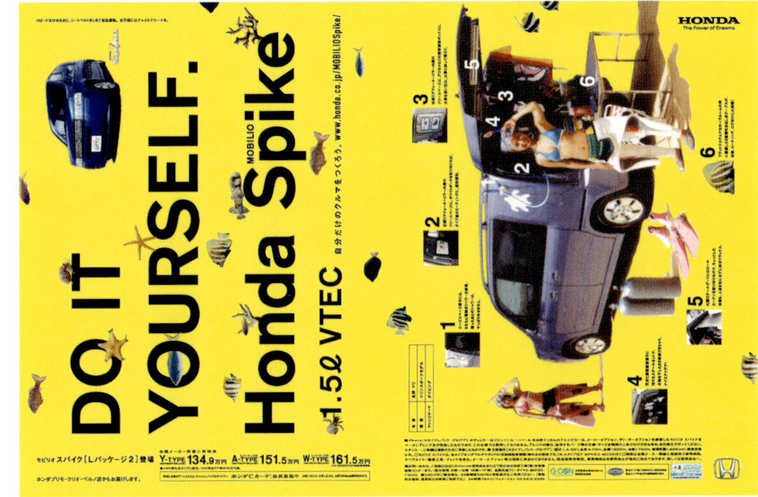

ティーザープロモーション用ツール

ペーパークラフト入りのDMと、店頭配布用のフリスビー付きカタログを制作。発売前のため車名などは出せなかったが、ロゴに使われる黄色を使ってイメージの定着を図った。

Promotional teasers

Direct mail containing papercrafts, and catalog with frisbee distributed at dealerships. In the pre-launch phase, the name of the car was consciously not revealed, so the yellow color of the logo is emphasized to build recognition.

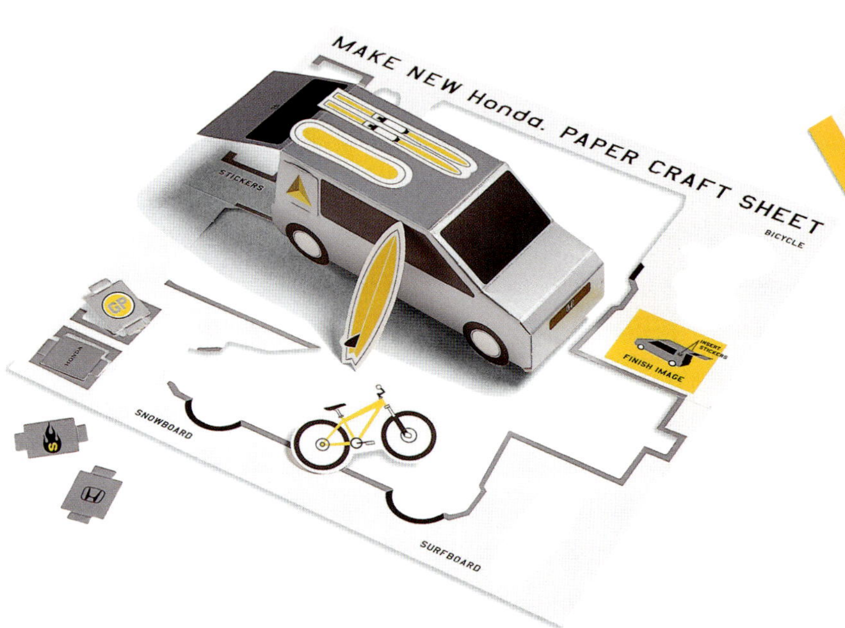

DM

フリスビー Frisbee

カタログ Catalog

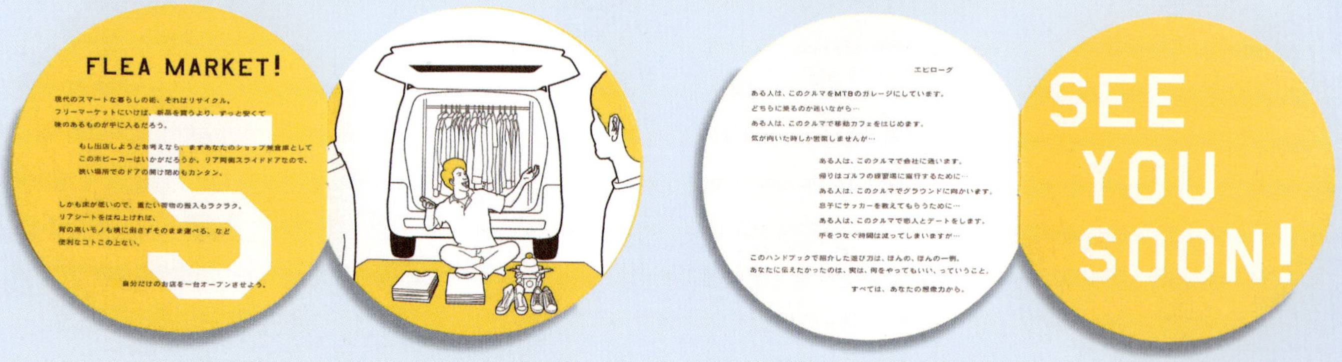

発売時のプロモーションツール
DMと店頭配布用のカタログを制作。カタログは車の顔を強調する設計にし、中面のデザインはポスターなどと連動させた。

Post-launch promotional tools
Direct mail and catalog for distribution at dealerships. The catalog emphasizes the face of the car, the inside pages relate to posters and other promotions.

DM

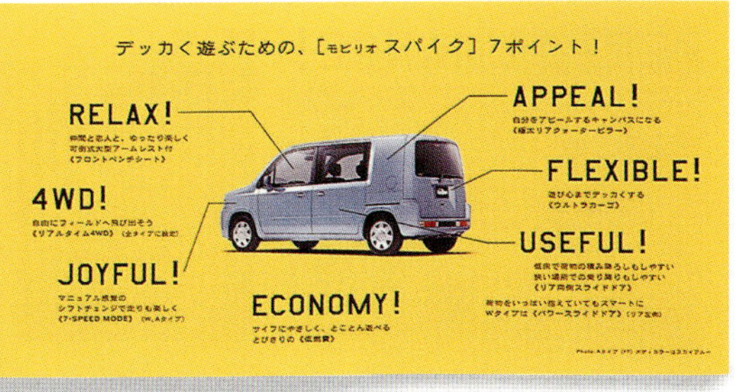

カタログ Catalog

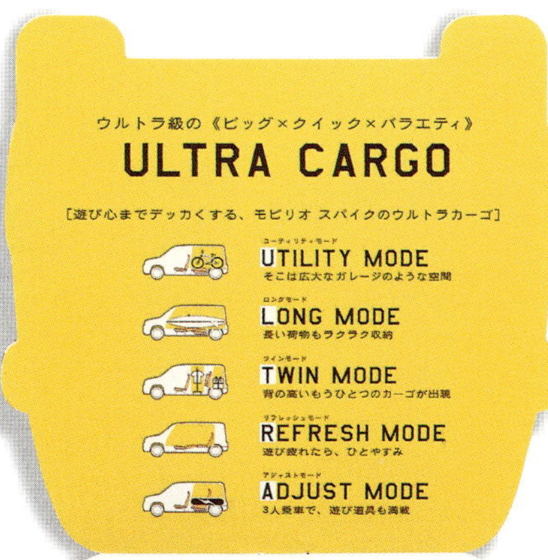

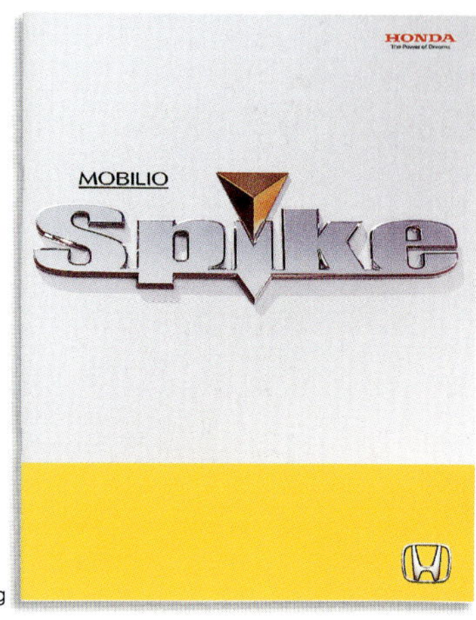

カタログ Catalog

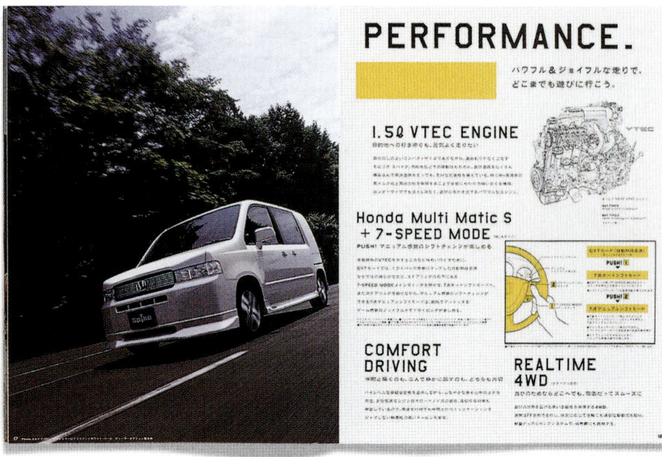

SHOP

TSUTAYA TOKYO ROPPONGI

ブランドがもつ従来の印象をワンステージ引き上げるビジュアル戦略

A visual strategy for quickly up-scaling a brand image

戦略を読み解く 3 key words

六本木ヒルズ内にオープンしたコンセプトショップ

1階はスターバックスを併設したブック＆カフェ形式の書籍販売、2階は映像・音楽ソフトのレンタル・販売コーナー。"様々な文化コンテンツの提供を通して生活提案をしていきたい"という企業理念を具現化した、フラッグシップ的な存在としてオープンした。

新たなイメージ作りを図ってサインを一新

フラッグシップ的役割を強化するために、レンタルビデオ店としての従来の印象を一度リセットしたいと考え、新たなサインを考案。ツタヤがもつメジャー感を"青と黄色"の配色に残しつつ、六本木という立地に合うワンステージ上のイメージを追求した。

ユーザーとの接点を重視したプロモーション

SPツールは、新たなサインをモチーフにしてビジュアルイメージを統一。ユーザーに一番近いところでのブランディングを大切にするため、ブックカバーやリボン、テープ、返却ボックスといったショップツールのデザインは特にこだわった。

3 key words

Concept shop opened in Roppongi Hills

The first floor bookstore-cafe, annexed to a Starbucks, sells books, while the second floor is a rental/retail corner for videos and music. The branch was opened as a flagship store that would embody the company's business philosophy of "a lifestyle, offered through a variety of cultural contents".

Revising signage to renew brand image

In order to emphasize the flagship store role, we create new signage that breaks with the previous "video rental store" image. The goal is a one-stage upward revision of brand image to match the store's Roppongi surroundings, while retaining the overall blue-and-yellow TSUTAYA feel.

Promotion that focuses on customer interaction

Sales promotion tools are designed consistent with the new signage. To concentrate branding efforts as close to the consumer as possible, the design of store items such as book covers, ribbon, tape and return boxes is paid particular attention.

Logo

六本木という場所柄外国人客も多い。そこで日本発のブランドであることを強調したいと考え、サインは"家紋"のような感覚でデザインして頭文字の"T"を引き立たせた。

Many non-Japanese customers visit Roppongi. In order to emphasize the Japanese origin of the brand, the new signage emphasizes the "T" that begins the brand name in reference to Japanese family crests.

ショップバッグ Shop bag

ショップバッグ Shop bag

■CL=カルチュア・コンビニエンス・クラブ Culture Convenience Club Co., Ltd.
■Agency & Production= フロンテッジ+サムライ FRONTAGE INC.+SAMURAI ■CD + AD= 佐藤可士和 Kashiwa Sato ■D= 奥瀬義樹 Yoshiki Okuse ■Creative Supervisor= 中上寛基 Hiroki Nakagami
■Account Planner= 町田 靖 Yasushi Machida ■S= サムライ SAMURAI

ラッピング&リボン Wrapping & Ribbon

シール Sticker

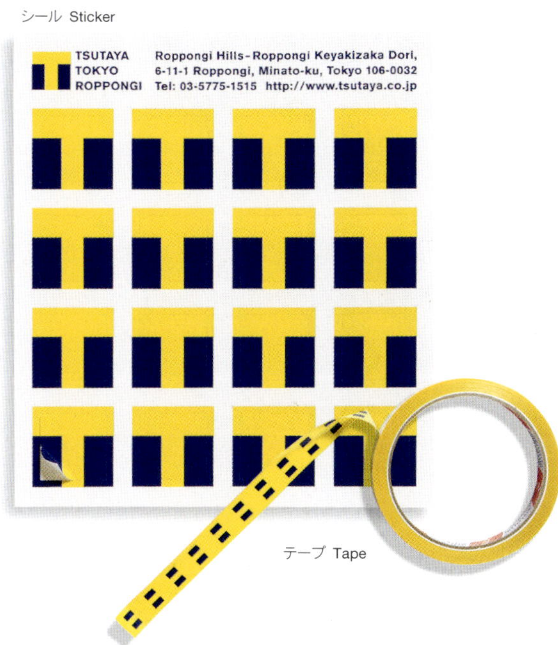

テープ Tape

名札 Nameplate

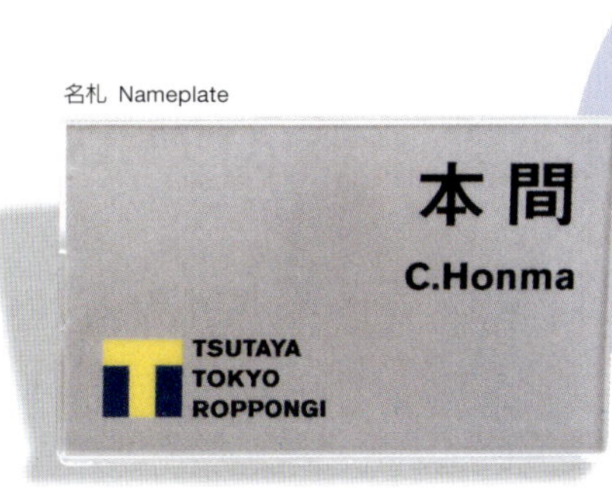

社章 Staff sign

シヨップカード Shop card

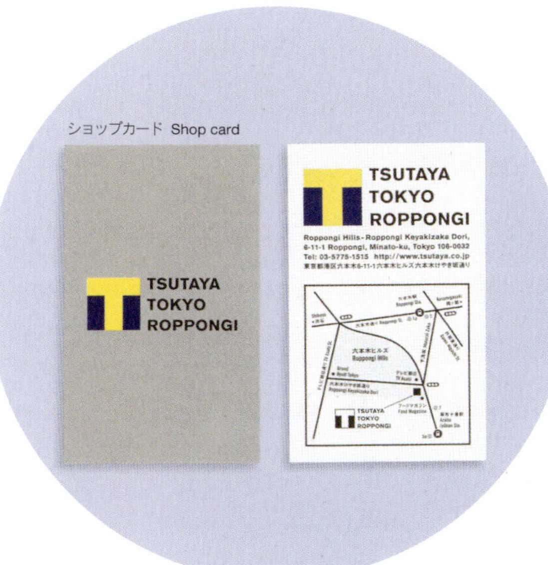

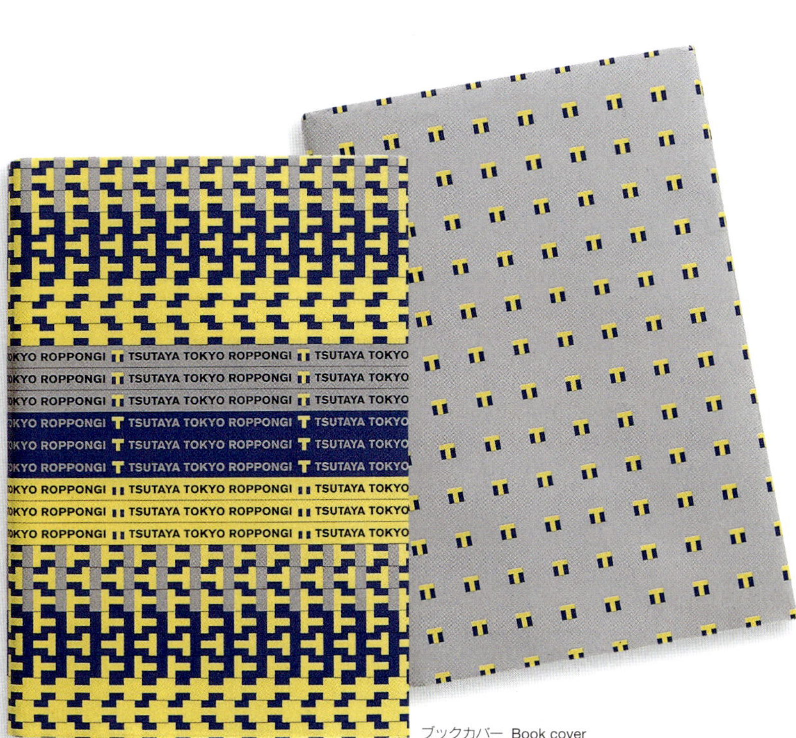

ブックカバー Book cover

フリーペーパー
オープン当日の折り込み広告として、港・渋谷区の周辺エリアで配布した。

Free paper
Distributed as a newspaper insert in the Minato and Shibuya Ward areas on opening day.

TSUTAYA
TOKYO
ROPPONGI

TSUTAYA TOKYO ROPPONGI

4.25! Grand Open.

1F: BOOK & COFFEE
2F: DVD,CD,VIDEO [Sell & Rental]
GAME [Sell Only]

TSUTAYA TOKYO ROPPONGI
Roppongi Hills-
Roppongi Keyakizaka Dori,
6-11-1 Roppongi, Minato-ku,
Tokyo 106-0032
Tel: 03-5775-1515
http://www.tsutaya.co.jp

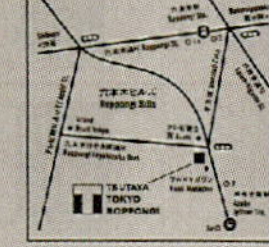

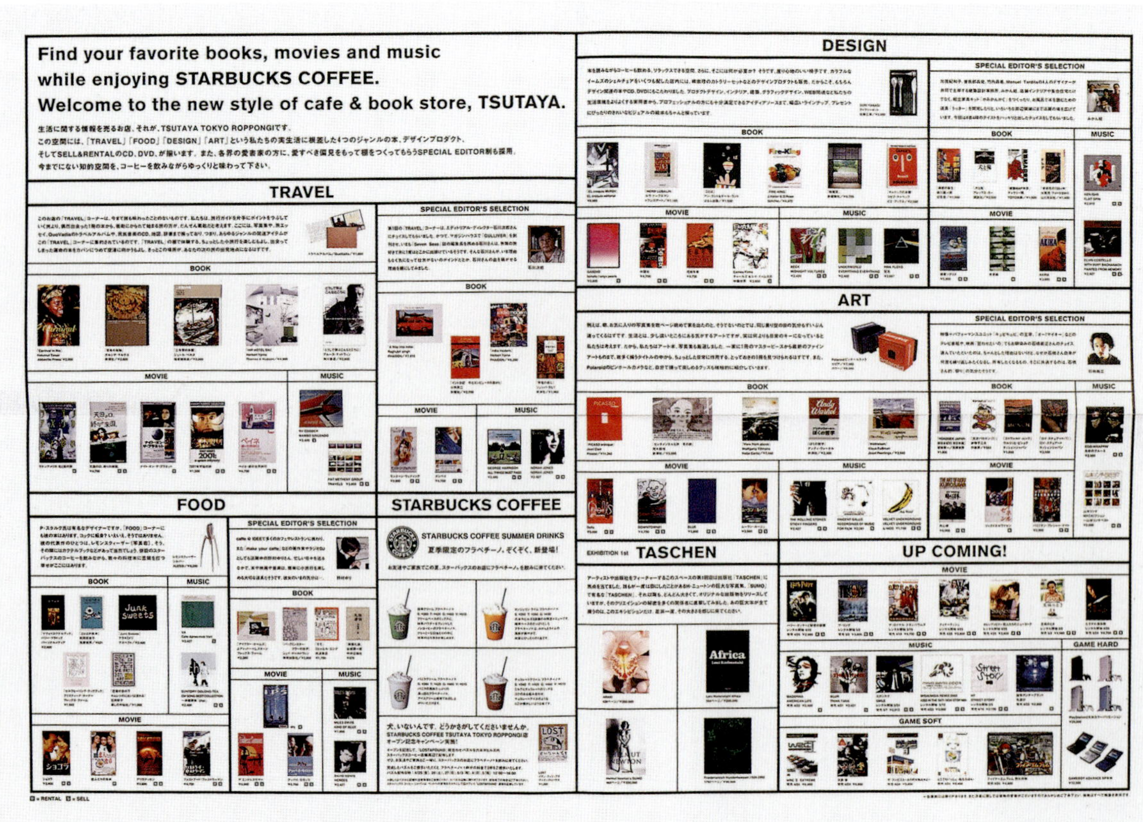
Find your favorite books, movies and music
while enjoying STARBUCKS COFFEE.
Welcome to the new style of cafe & book store, TSUTAYA.

TRAVEL

FOOD

STARBUCKS COFFEE

DESIGN

ART

TASCHEN

UP COMING!

招待状 Invitation

4.23! Press Conference Invitation

TSUTAYA TOKYO ROPPONGI
Roppongi Hills-Roppongi Keyakizaka Dori,
6-11-1 Roppongi, Minato-ku, Tokyo 106-0032
Tel: 03-5775-1515 http://www.tsutaya.co.jp

Press Conference
Invitation
4.23!
TSUTAYA
TOKYO
ROPPONGI

プレスキット Press kit

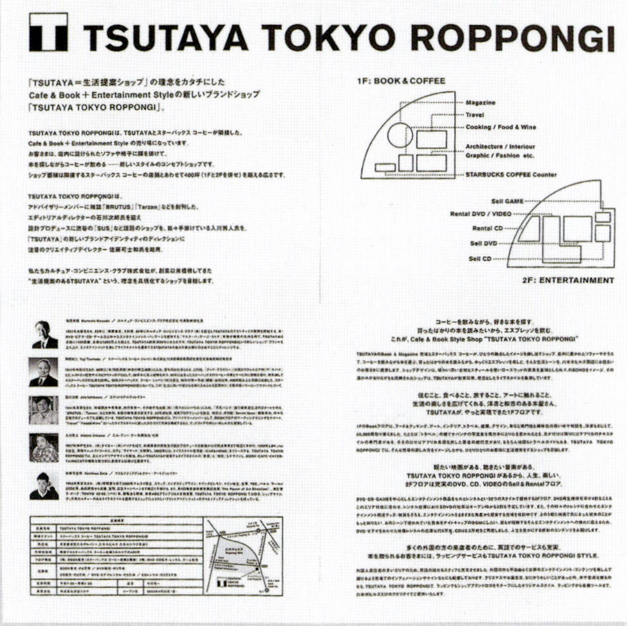

ノベルティ（ティッシュボックス）
Novelty (Tissue box)

ポスター Poster

会員証 Membership card

ノベルティ（ガイドブック） Novelty (Guide book)

Cinema Handbook 2003
TSUTAYA TOKYO ROPPONGI
Roppongi Hills-
Roppongi Keyakizaka Dori,
6-11-1 Roppongi, Minato-ku,
Tokyo 106-0032
Tel: 03-5775-1515
http://www.tsutaya.co.jp
Not For Sale.
Cinema Handbook 2003
Cinema
Handbook
2003
TSUTAYA
TOKYO
ROPPONGI

ノベルティ（CD-ROM） Novelty (CD-ROM)

返却ボックス Return box

Shop

EX'REALM エクスレルム

老舗企業の新たな可能性とイメージを創り出す実験的スペース

Experimental space with a new image and new possibilities for an old firm

戦略を読み解く 3 key words

企業のフィールドワークを兼ねた実験的スペース

バイクメーカーのヤマハ発動機が運営するコンセプトスペースで、カフェとイベントスペースで構成されている。気鋭の若手アーティストとのコラボーレーション企画を行うなど、新たなトレンドの発信基地を目指しながら、ヤマハの新しい可能性を探る。

企業名はあえて出さずにイメージアップを狙う

プロモーションではあえてヤマハの名前は前面に出さず、「実はヤマハがやっている」と後から知ることでの驚きを演出。戦略の柱にイベントを据えながら、それに付随するグッズや店舗内で使用するツールまで、トータルにブランディングを図っている。

ブランドのスタンスを投影したビジュアルを目指す

ビジュアルのコンセプトは、ヤマハという企業の“まじめさ＝シンプルなデザイン”＋新しいことをやっていこうとする“とんがり感＝ユーモアやスパイスを効かせたデザイン”の具現化。ツール全体を俯瞰したときのイメージの統一に努めている。

3 key words

Industrial fieldwork in an avant-garde space

This combination cafe and event hall is an experimental space run by motorcycle manufacturer YAMAHA. Through collaborations with energetic young artists the company hopes to create a spawning point for new trends, and discover new possibilities for the company.

Improve brand image without mentioning the company name

Keeping the use of YAMAHA's name to a minimum in promotion produces a surprise, after-the-fact realization of YAMAHA's involvement. While the main thrust of the strategy focuses on events, every aspect of the whole is planned down to the related merchandise and the promotional items used in the facility.

Visuals that project the brand's attitude

The concept behind the visuals combines the traditional YAMAHA "serious, simple design" and the new, adventurous "sharp, funny -- spicy! -- design". Particular heed was given to the overall image consistency of the promotional tools.

Naming

ブランド名は、EXPANDやEXTEND（ともに“広げる”の意味）の“EX”と、REALM（領土）を合わせた造語。ヤマハの新しい可能性を開拓していきたいという思いを込めた。

The brand name takes the "ex" from "expand" and "extend" and combines it with "realm" to symbolize the discovery of new possibilities for YAMAHA.

Shop

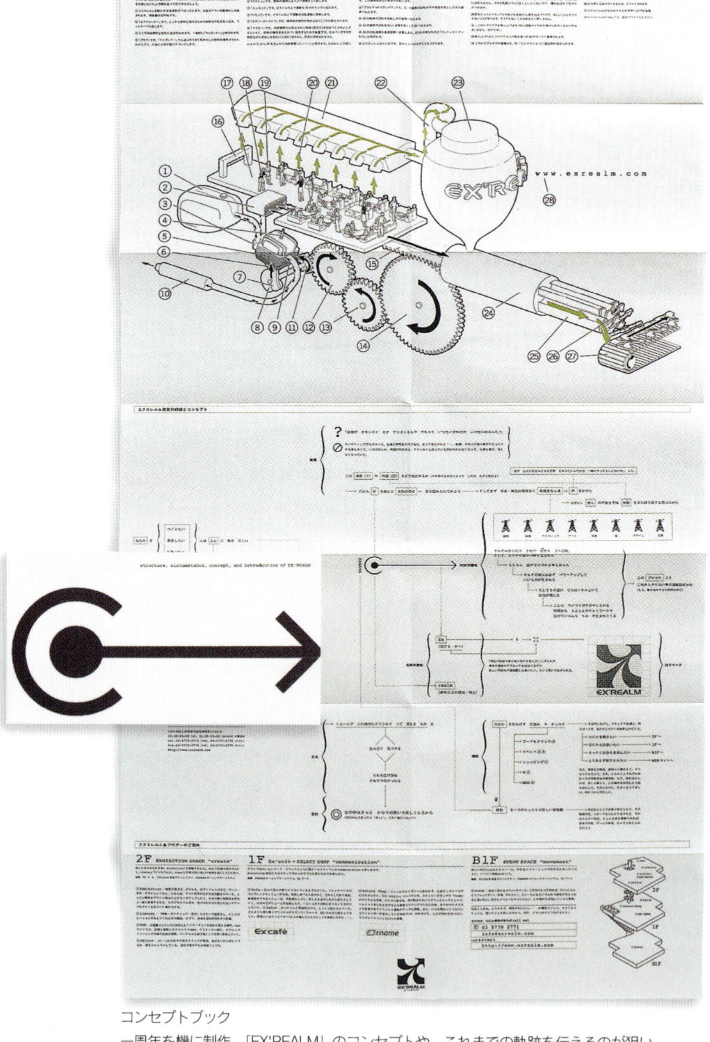

コンセプトブック
一周年を機に制作。「EX'REALM」のコンセプトや、これまでの軌跡を伝えるのが狙い。

Concept book
Produced for the brand's one-year anniversary to convey the EX'REALM concept and milestones to date.

■CL= ヤマハ発動機 YAMAHA ■Planning= エクスレルム EX'REALM ■S= エクスレルム EX'REALM
<Promotion of EX'REALM> ■D= 三木俊一 Shun-ichi Miki ■D= Name card, Shop card / 河野牧子 Makiko Kawano ■CW= Concept book / 伊勢華子 (ASOBOT) Hanako Ise (ASOBOT) ■DF= 文京図案室 Bunkyo-Zuan-Shitsu
<Promotion of Passol> ■D= A / 河野牧子 Makiko Kawano ■D= B / 荒木千絵 Chie Araki ■I= A / 川口澄子 Sumico Kawaguchi ■Direction= B / フランフラン Franc franc

Shop

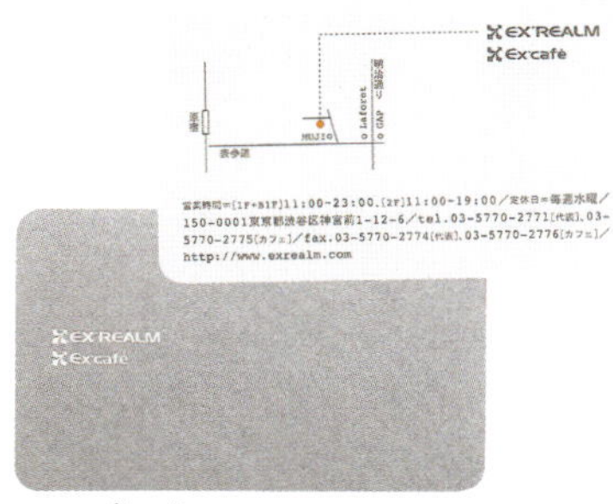

ショップカード Shop card

タグ Tag

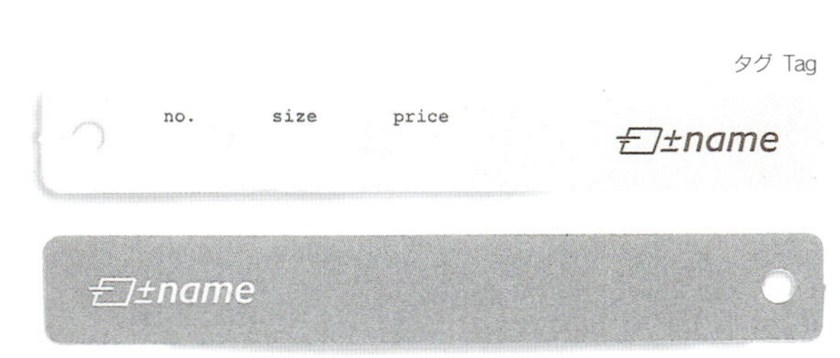

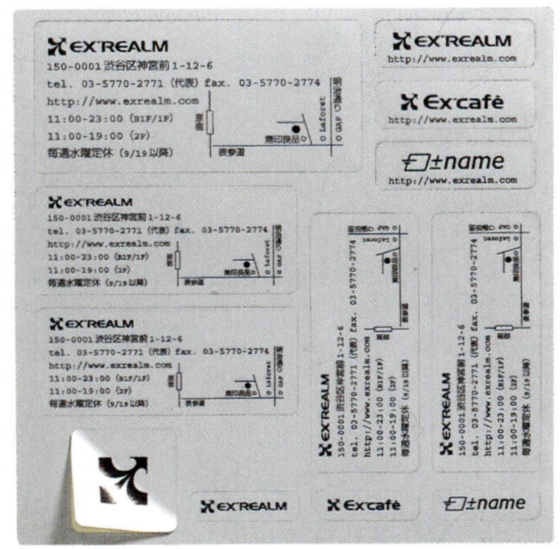

ステッカー Sticker

ショップカード Shop card

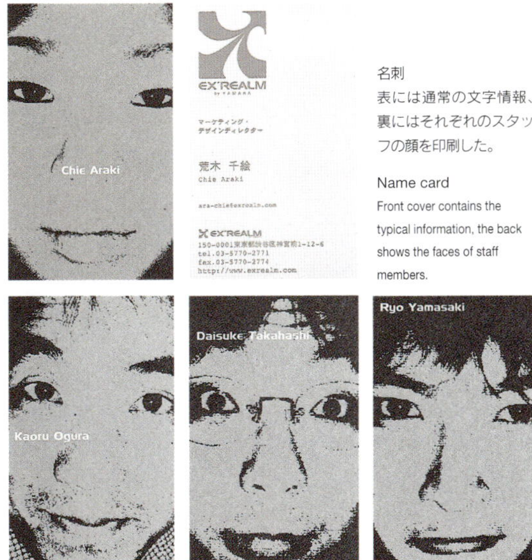

名刺
表には通常の文字情報、裏にはそれぞれのスタッフの顔を印刷した。

Name card
Front cover contains the typical information, the back shows the faces of staff members.

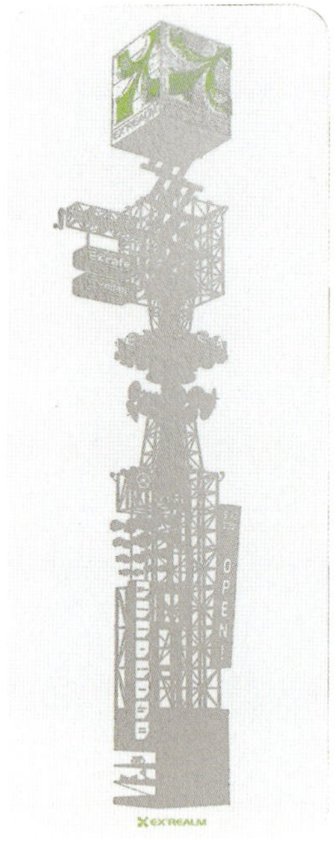

オープニングエキシビジョンの招待状
Opening exhibition invitation

オープニングパーティの招待状
"ありえない建築" をモチーフにして、面白いことが始まりそうな期待感を演出した。

Opening party invitation
"Impossible architecture" as a motif suggests that something interesting is about begin.

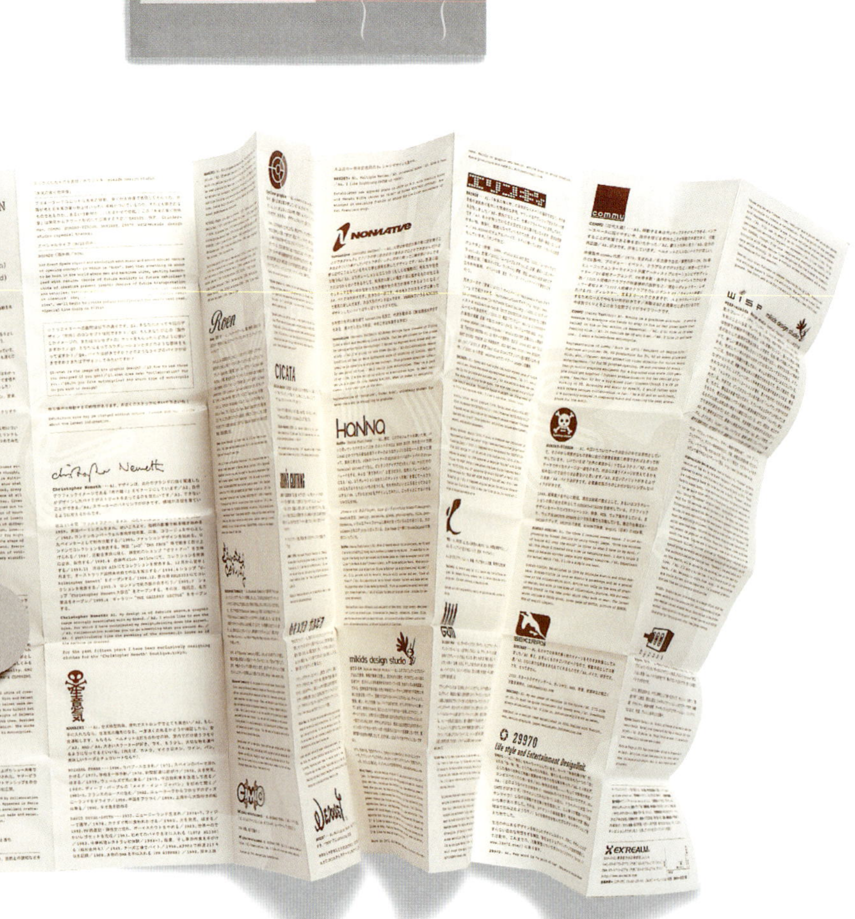

ノベルティ
オープニングエキシビジョンのパンフレットと、参加アーティストの各作品をモチーフにしたビジュアルブックをセットにしたもの。ブックの形は、バイクのチェーンをイメージして設計した。

Novelty
An two-piece set opening exhibition pamphlet and visual book featuring the works of each participating artist as a motif. The book is designed in the form of a motorcycle chain.

招待状
一周年記念パーティの招待状。「EX'REALM」そのものを立体的に表現できる仕組みになっている。

Invitation
Invitation to the brand's one year anniversary part, a three-dimensional rendition of the brand name.

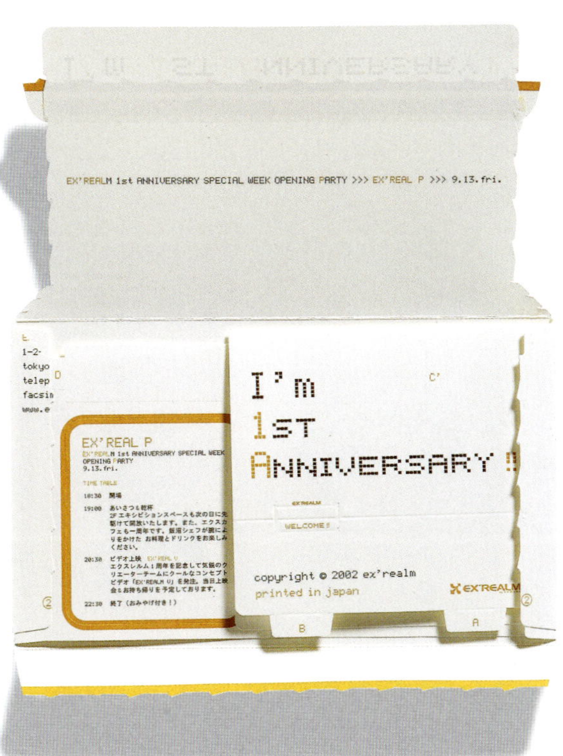

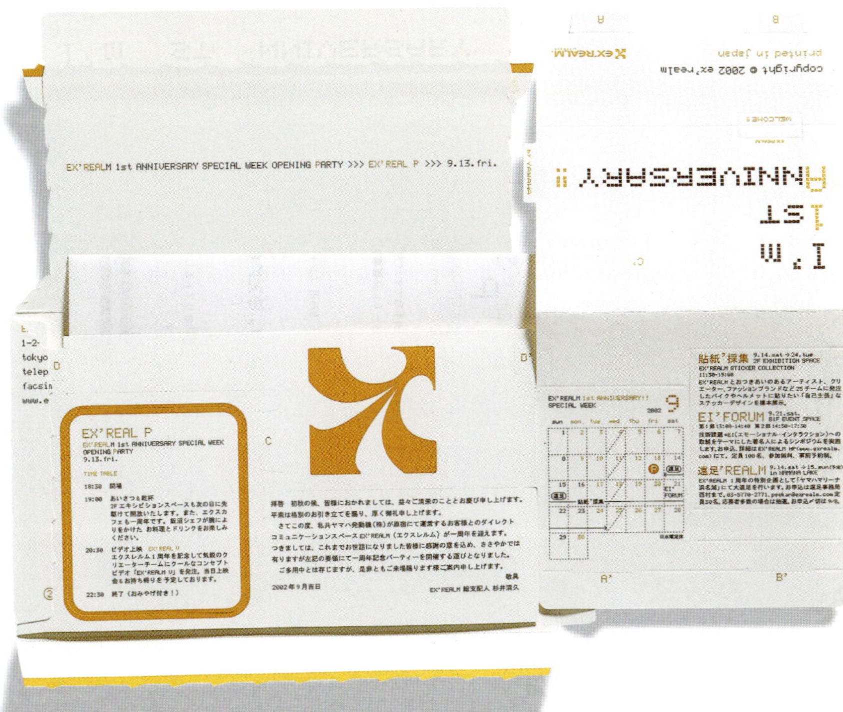

「パッソル」のプロモーション

ヤマハの電動コミューター「パッソル」のプロモーションを展開。エクスレルム独自で企画する他、異業種とのコラボレーションによって局地的にプロモーションを実施する。若い女性をターゲットにした商品であることを意識して、企画・デザインを行っている。

Promotion of "Passol"

Promotions developed for YAMAHA's electrically powered scooter. The campaign combines EX'REALM exclusive promotional materials and localized promotions conducted in collaboration with companies in other fields. Planning and design refelects consciousness for the product's target user: young women.

Shop

A.「エクスレルム」のオリジナル企画

エクスレルムのみで展開したプロモーション。イラストレーターに川口澄子氏を起用し、オシャレで現代的な女性の生活をイメージしたイラストで「パッソル」の世界観を表現した。

A. "EX'REALM" original promotion

Illustrator Sumico Kawaguchi's renditions of the fashionable and contemporary woman's lifestyle express Passol's world view.

DM

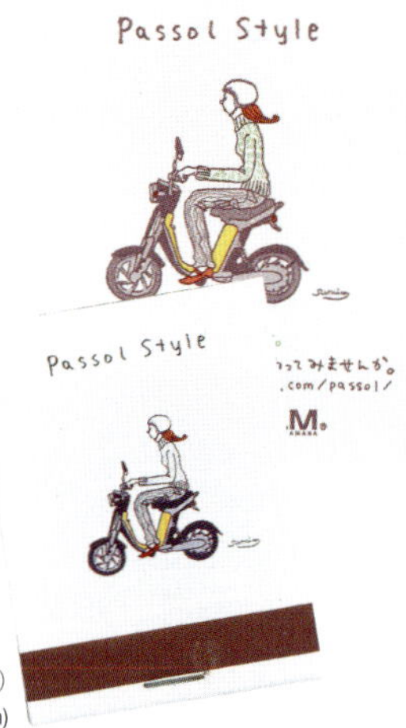

ノベルティ（コースター）
Novelty (Coaster)

ノベルティ（マッチ）
Novelty (Match)

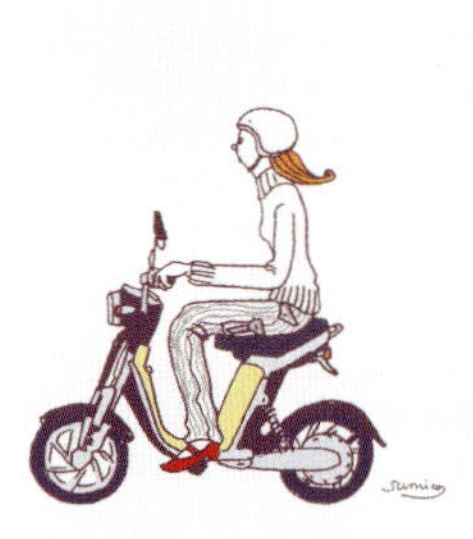

ノベルティ（ポストカード）
Novelty (Postcard)

B.「フランフラン」とのコラボレーション企画

若い女性に人気のインテリアショップ「フランフラン」とコラボレートしたイベントのツール。"Witch（魔女）"をテーマに、ちょっと毒のある魅力的な女の子をイメージして制作した。

B.Collaborate promotion with "Franc franc"

Event tools developed for a collaborative event with Franc franc, the interior shop popular with young women. A "witch" theme projects an attractive, less than innocent image of women.

リーフレット Leaflet

Tシャツ
商品として販売したほか、イベント期間中のスタッフTシャツとして使用した。

T-shirt
T shirts sold both as a product and worn by staff members during events.

canvas　キャンバス

200メートルのキャンバス地で1軒のレストランを形成
A restaurant build with 200 meters of canvas

戦略を読み解く 3 key words

本格フレンチをカジュアルな雰囲気で楽しむ

本格的なフランス料理をカジュアルな雰囲気のなかで楽しんでもらおうと、2階建ての住居をレストランへ改装。費用を抑えながらイメージを一新するため、建物全体、外側から内装までをキャンバス地で覆い、新たな表情を出した。

素材を一括発注し、ローコストを実現

内外装、インテリア、CIまでをトータルに企画。キャンバス地を一括発注することでローコストを実現した。また、建物の外側と内側（カーテン）の間に照明を入れ、ライトアップ。キャンバスを透過した柔らかな光が独特の雰囲気を醸し出している。

キャンバスをあますところなく使用・アピール

キャンバス地をふんだんに使用した内外装を前面に押し出すため、メニューやショップカード、マッチ箱などにも同様の素材を使用。また、200メートルにも及んだ使用量をイラストにし、DMに記載した。

3 key words

Genuine French dining in a causal atmosphere

Convert a two-storey house into a restaurant, and have customers enjoy genuine French dining in a causal atmosphere. Cover the entire building in canvas -- inside and out -- to create a revolutionary new image with minimal cost.

Ordering material in bulk cuts costs

Comprehensive planning for exterior, interior and store identity. Ordering the canvas in bulk resulted in lower costs. Install lighting between the exterior and interior curtain walls to light up the building. The soft-glow of the translucent canvas creates a unique atmosphere.

Extensive use of canvas as a form of appeal

Exploit the generous use of canvas for the restaurant exterior and interior by using the same material for menus, shop guides, match boxes and other peripheral items. Illustrate the use of over 200 meters of fabric and print it on direct mail.

Naming

まっさらなキャンバスで作った店に、料理、お客様がそろって初めて一枚の絵になるという意味をこめたネーミング。

The name supports the image of the food and customers transforming a white canvas into a painting.

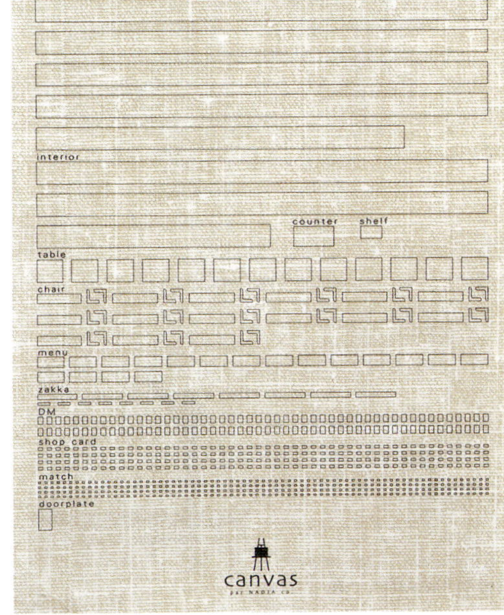

DM

Restaurant

マッチ、ショップカード Match, Shop card

■CL= キャンバス canvas
■P= 佐藤かな子 Kanako Sato　■DF= nendo　■S= nendo

Choko Choko 猪口猪口

料理から連想されるキーワードやイメージをビジュアル化
Turning a cuisine's connotations into visual imagery

戦略を読み解く 3 key words

旨い肴に旨い酒、そして絶品そばが自慢の和食店

"喰うにも呑むにも勝手良し。指三本でちょいと持つ。粋で手軽なそば猪口で、ちょこちょこやってほしいのよ"。そんなユニークなキャッチフレーズを掲げ、そばを中心に旨い酒と肴や珍味、飯物などのメニューを取り揃える和食居酒屋。

小型グラフィックで開店告知とイメージ浸透を図る

まずはDMやチラシでオープン告知を行い、来店した人に満足感を与えて常連客となってもらうべく、店で使うグラフィックツールの制作も重視した。全てのツールを通して、"粋な和食居酒屋" というイメージ作りを心がけている。

"粋な江戸文化" をモチーフにしたデザイン

デザイン面では "そば" "粋" という言葉から連想するイメージとして "江戸の庶民文化" をテーマとした。ロゴマークは、江戸時代に通貨や器物の品質保証印として使われた "極印" をモチーフにしたもので、"旨さの保証印" という意味を与えている。

3 key words

Boasting good food, good sake and world-famous soba

"Ideal for both eating and drinking. Held lightly with three fingers. The stylishly informal soba choko (cup) -- bottoms up". True to its unique catchphrase, the izakaya offers its excellent soba along with a variety of drinks and a wide-ranging menu of sweet and savory dishes.

Small-format graphics announce opening and promote image

Promote the restaurant opening with direct mail and flyers, and follow up by creating promotional tools for use in the restaurant to aid in satisfying customers and creating regulars. Appeal to customers with a "stylish Japanese izakaya" image throughout all the promotional tools.

Design follows a "stylish Edo culture" motif

The design is inspired by the "Edo-period popular culture" connotations of soba and "iki (stylish)". The brand logo is reminiscent of the hallmarks used in the Edo period to authenticate currency and properties, serving as a "hallmark of quality" for customers.

Naming

店名は "そば" がメイン料理であることをストレートに表現したもの。"ちょこちょこ来てほしい" という気持ちと語感のよさから「猪口猪口」と名付けた。

The store name is a straight expression that the store's speciality is soba. The double use of the word choko (referring to a sake cup or soba cup) is also a play on the mimetic word, here implying "come often", chosen as much for the sound as the meaning.

メニュー Menu

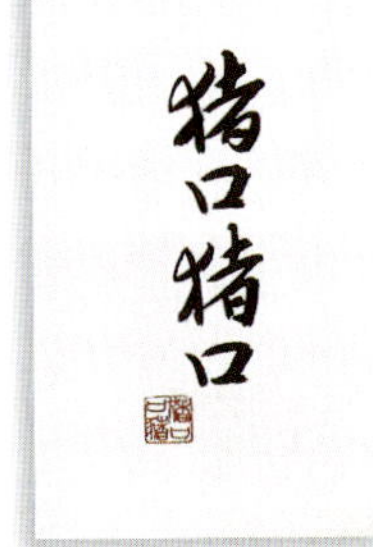

ショップカード
Shop card

Restaurant

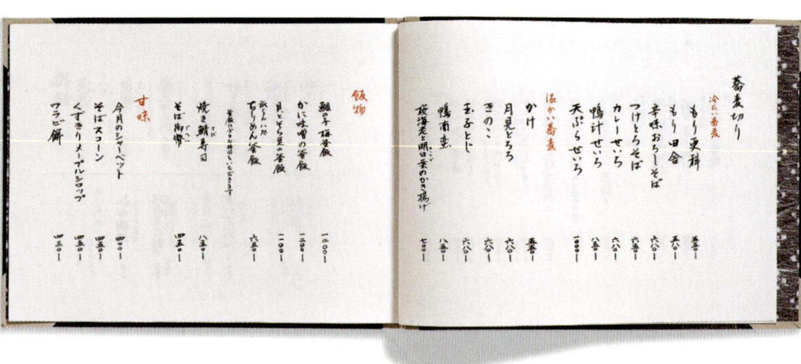

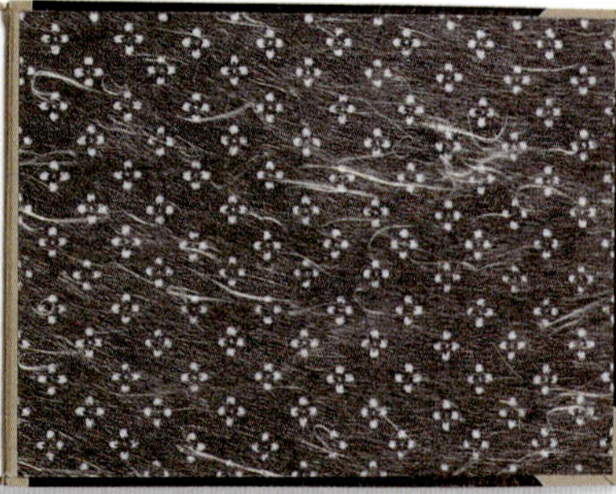

■ CL= ゼットン ZETTON Inc.
■ S= ゼットン ZETTON Inc.

ノベルティ（そば猪口）
Novelty (SOBA cup)

ノベルティ（あぶらとり紙）
Novelty (Skin care sheet)

はし袋 Chopsticks case

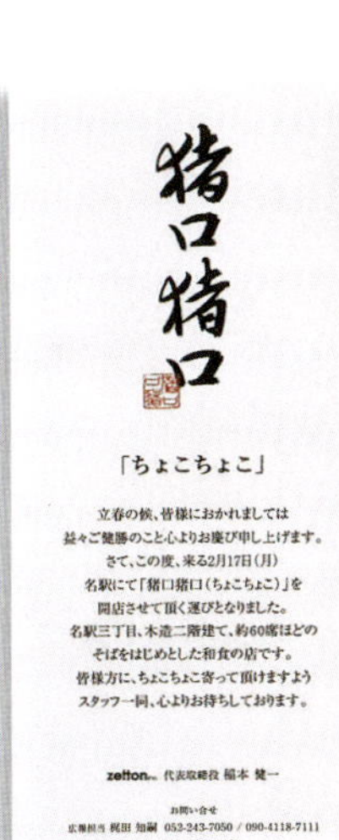

オープンDM Open DM

DM

フライヤー Flyer

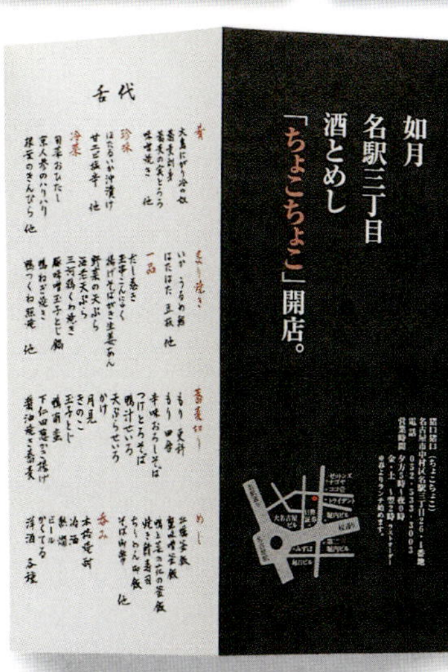

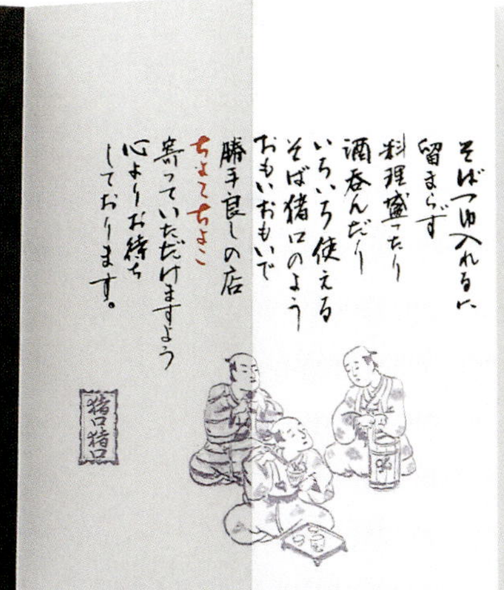

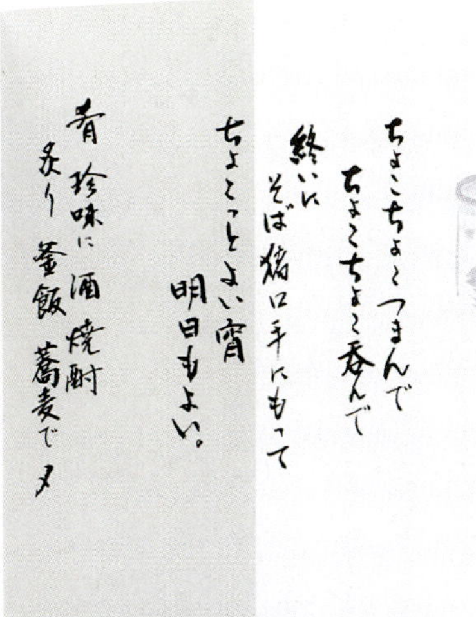

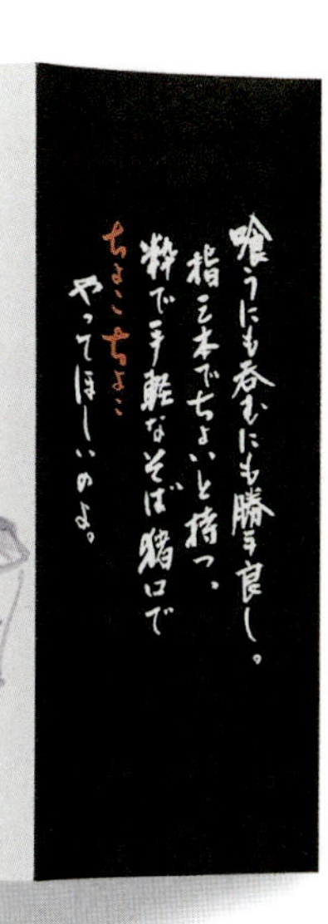

sumibi-yakiniku UMAMITEI　炭火焼肉 うまみ亭

“食べたい！” という欲求をダイレクトに刺激するデザイン効果

Aggressive design sparks consumer appetites

戦略を読み解く 3 key words

“上質と健康” をテーマに厳選素材を使用

飼育方法まで把握した肉や有機栽培の野菜など、生産者の顔が見えるスローフードに徹底的にこだわり、更に無添加の調味料のみを使用。また、現状に満足せず、常に新たなメニューの創作に努めている。

旨い食べ物屋にはデザイン要素が不可欠

“美味しいものを食べるときには、周りに楽しいツールがあった方がいい” という考えから、店内ツールの制作に力を入れている。何度店を訪れても新鮮な気持ちになってもらえるように、チラシや店内貼りのポスターは季節ごとに制作。

シズル感溢れるデザインで、見る人の食欲を刺激

各種のグラフィックツールの制作で心がけていることは、“品よく、かつダイナミック” に感じるデザイン。特にチラシや小冊子、ポスターでは、シズル感を大切にしたイラストとコピーで構成し、臨場感を演出している。

3 key words

Ingredients carefully selected for healthiness and quality

Avoiding at all costs the image of "commercially produced" food, the company uses organic vegetables and farm-raised meat as well as additive-free seasonings. In addition, it continually develops new menu items, never satisfied with the status quo.

Design an essential element in a good restaurant

Design fun in-store promotional tools that customers can enjoy as they are enjoying their food. Create new brochures and posters for the restaurant each season so that no matter how many times customers visit the restaurant it will always have a fresh feeling to it.

Sizzling design stokes viewers' appetites

Design any and all graphics with a "refined yet dynamic" feel. Illustrations and copy in brochures, pamphlets and posters "sizzle", announcing their presence.

Logo

店名、マークともに手描き。“おいしい” という文字で作った顔や、炭火の煙を連想させるシンボルをプラスすることで臨場感を強調した。

The store name and logo are hand-drawn. A face composed of the letters for the word "delicious" and a symbol that recalls smoke from a charcoal fire give the design a strong presence.

Restaurant

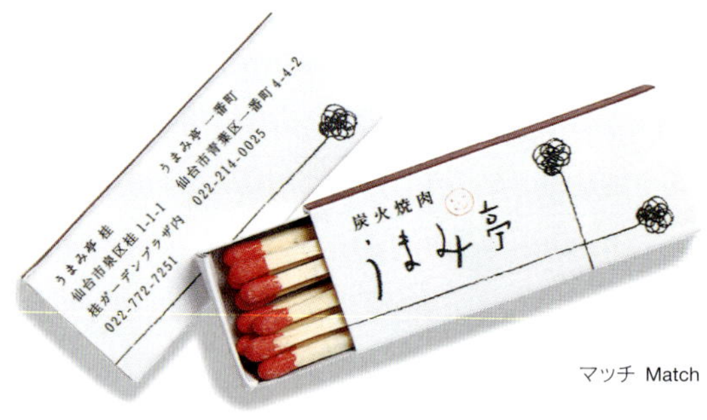

マッチ Match

ショップカード Shop card

■CL= エクスプレッション EXPRESSION Co.,Ltd.
■AD + D= 内藤 昇 Noboru Naito　■D= 宮田大史（ロゴの煙） Daishi Miyata (Smoke of Logo)　■Producer= 宮田大史 Daishi Miyata　■DF= ドラフト DRAFT　■S= ドラフト DRAFT

食器 Tableware

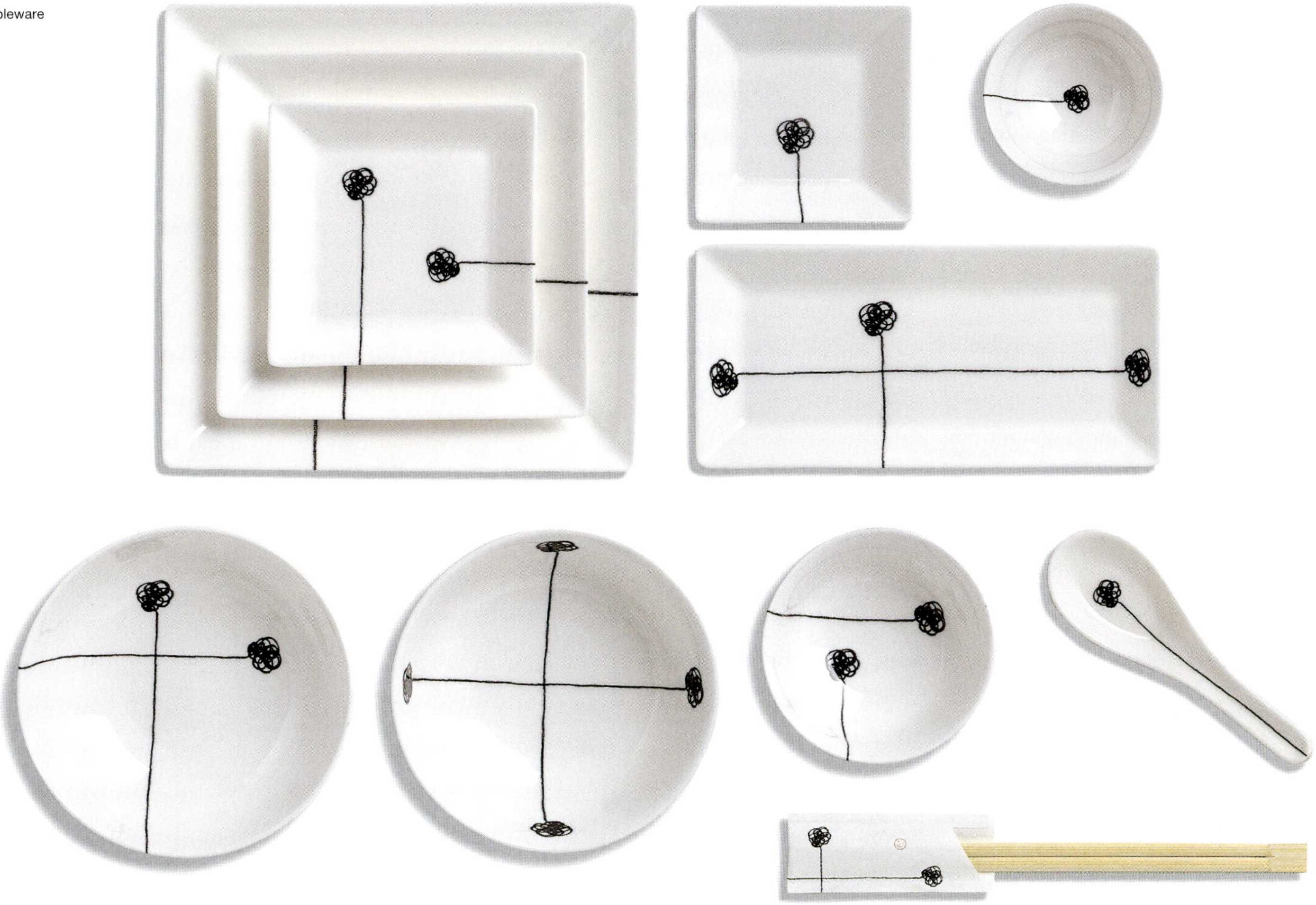

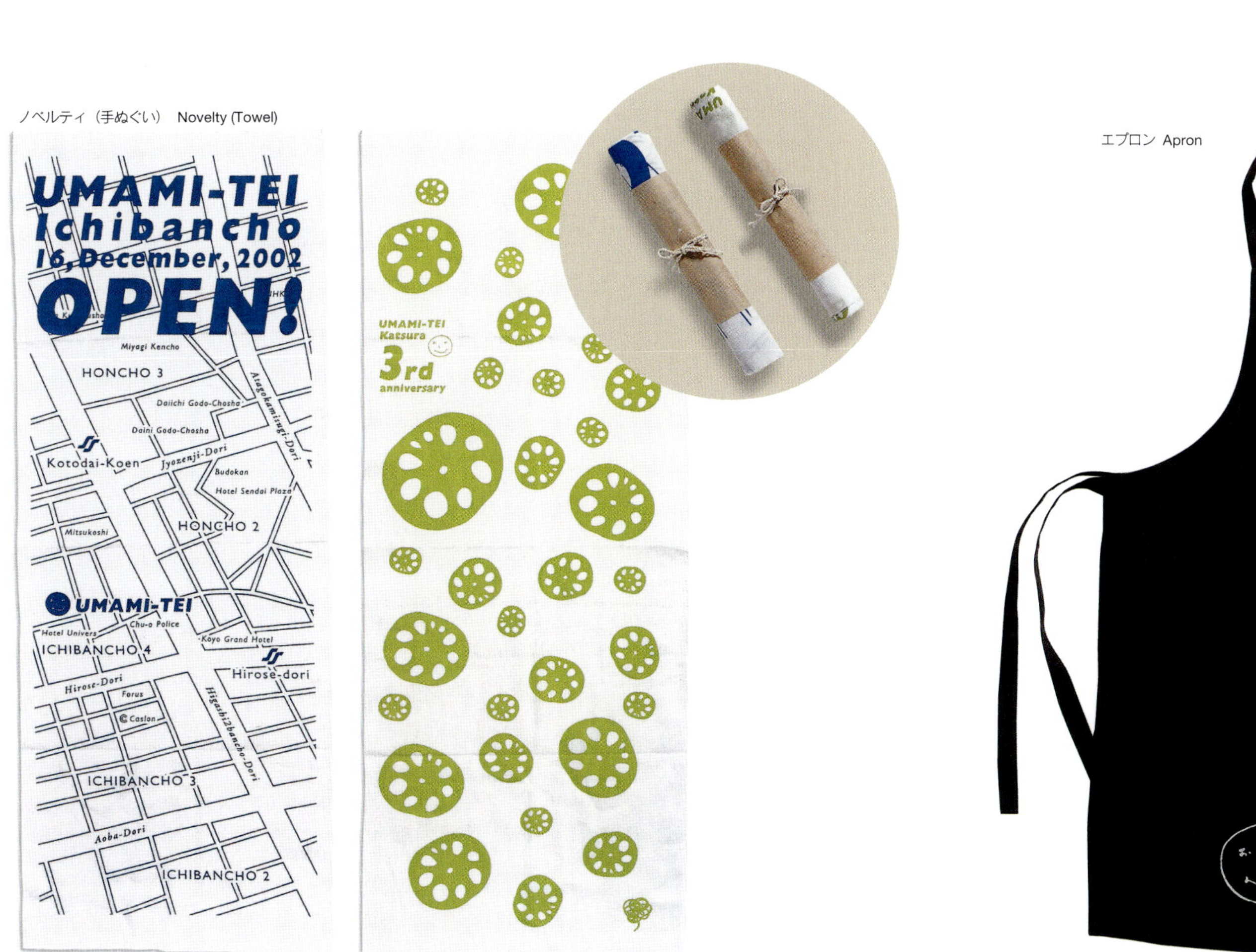

ノベルティ（手ぬぐい） Novelty (Towel)

エプロン Apron

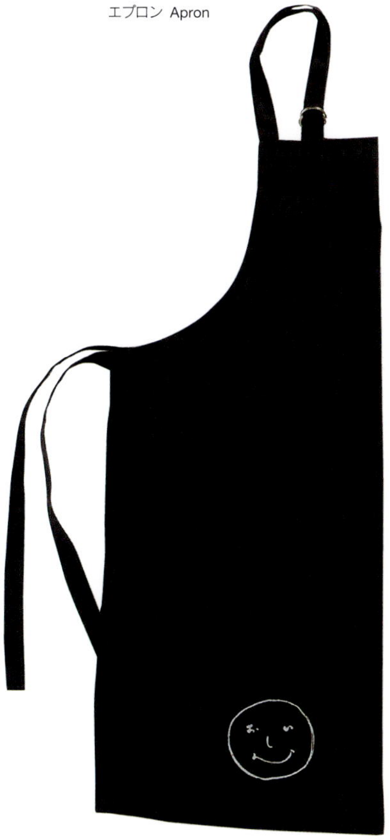

コースター
レンコンをモチーフにしたコースター。デザイナーはこのアイデアを思い付いたとき、レンコンを使ったサラダのメニューも提案して実際に採用された。

Coaster
Coasters with a lotus root motif. During design development, the designer presented a lotus root salad recipe which was adopted in the menu.

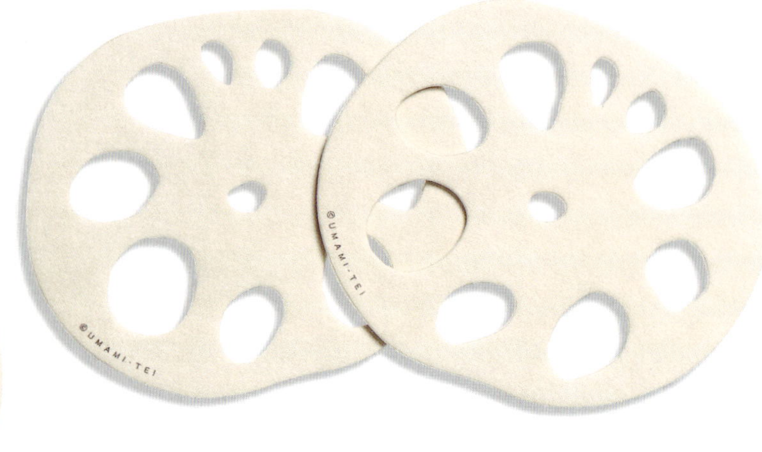

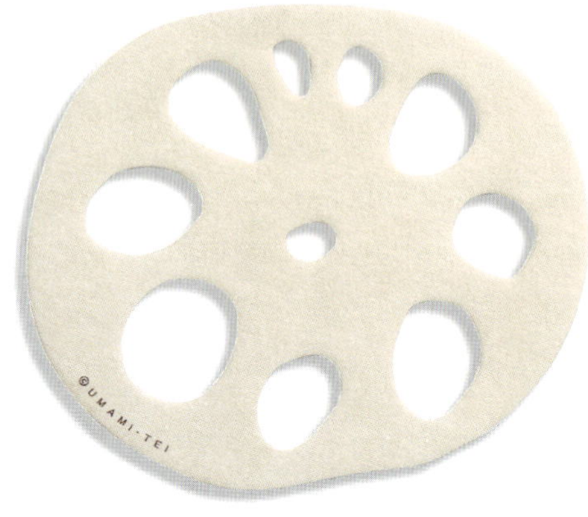

チラシ
低予算で新規の客を呼び込めるツールとして重視し、シーズンごとに制作している。

Flyer
Low-budget promotional tools targeting new customers are produced seasonally.

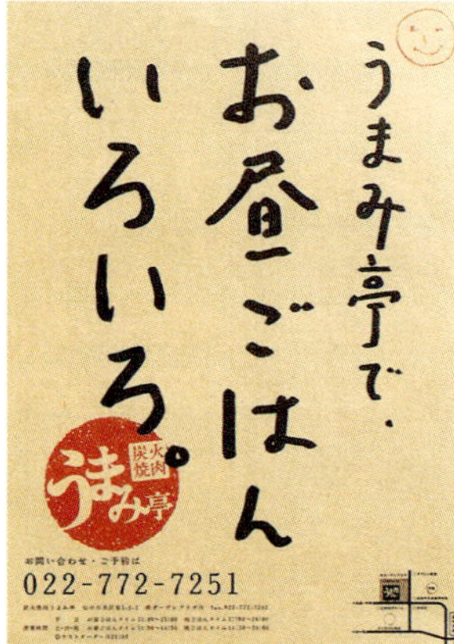

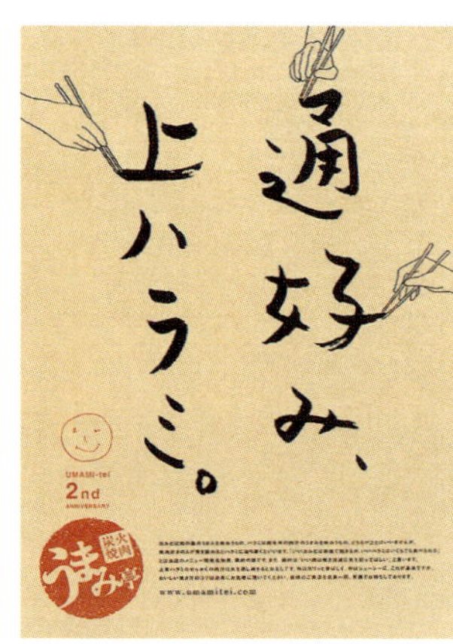

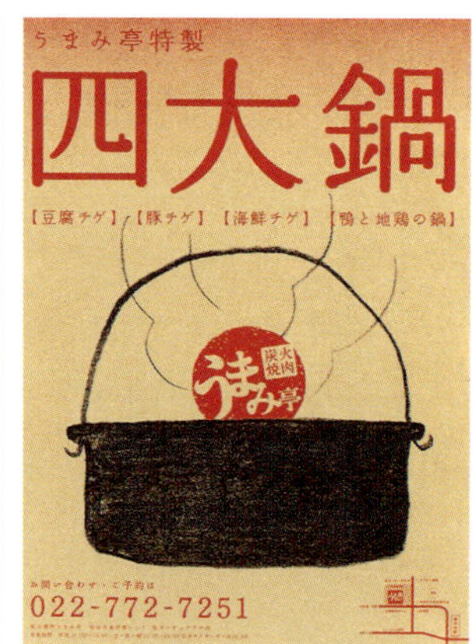

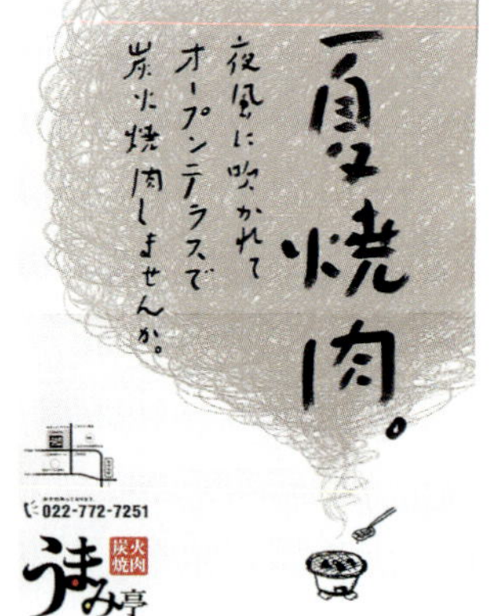

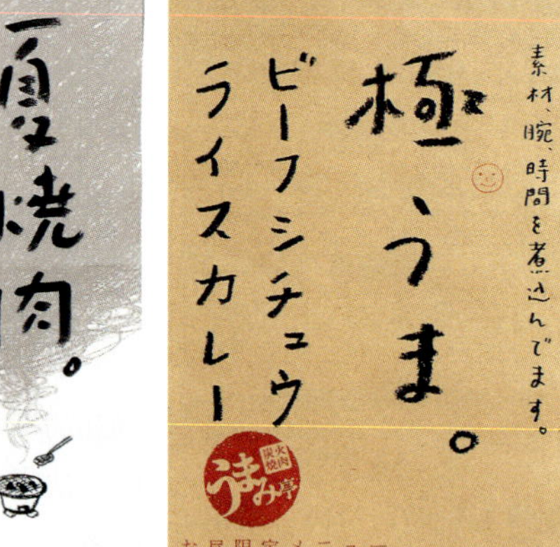

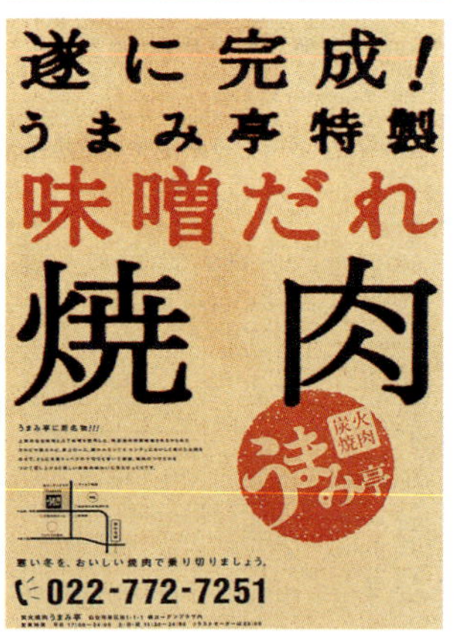

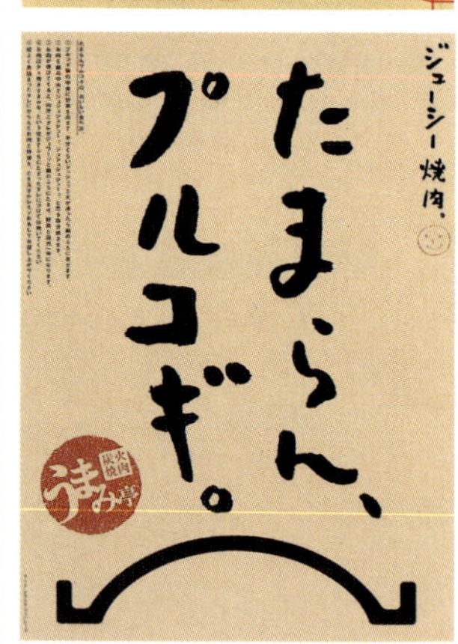

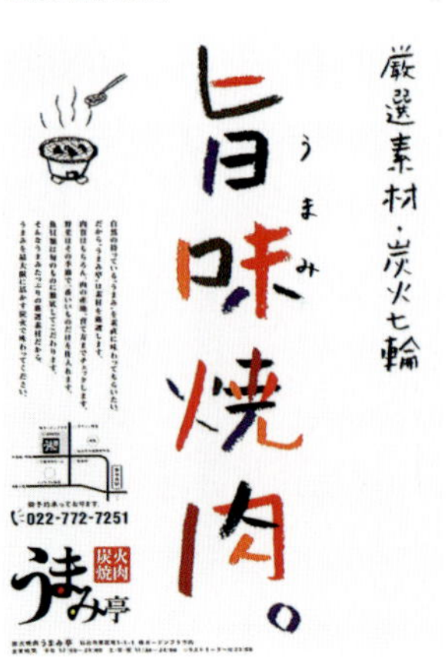

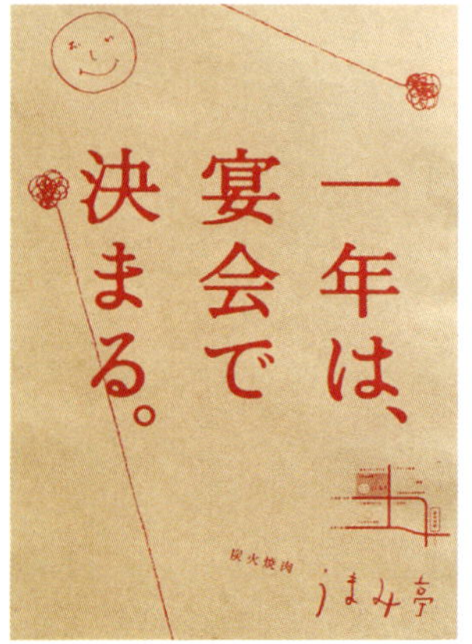

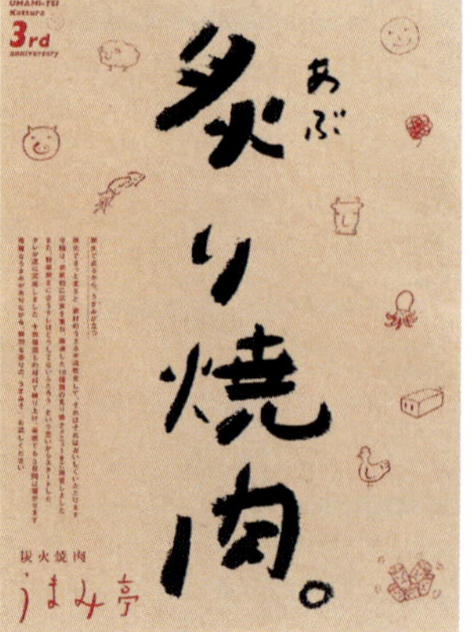

小冊子 Pamphlet

Restaurant

躍るエビ、
焦るイカ。

実はうまみ亭は、魚介類もスゴいんです。
オホーツク海や三陸沖の旬の新鮮な
ものから、日本全国を探して手に
入れた干物まで、どれも自信満々です。
ちょっと低人気なのが気になりますが、
知る人ぞ知るメニューの逸品です。

炭が真っ赤になることを、
"おこる"といいます。
カンカンのブンブンに
おこったほうが、お肉はもっと
おいしくなるんです。

炭火で焼くから、"うまみ"がたつ。
遠赤外線の効果により、表面はカリッと、
中はジューシーに焼きあがります。
お肉をいちばんおいしく食べる焼き方なんです。

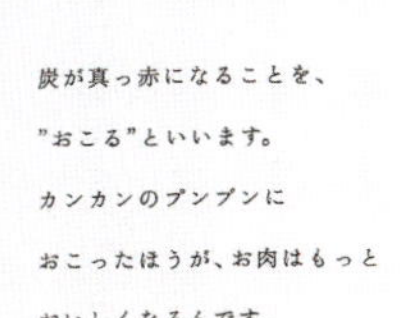

食べるものは、おいしくなくちゃ。
食べるものは、安心でなくちゃ。
食べるときは、笑顔でなくちゃ。
食べることは、幸せでなくちゃ。
食べることは、楽しくなくちゃ。
食べることは、健康でなくちゃ。
食べることで、成長しなくちゃ。

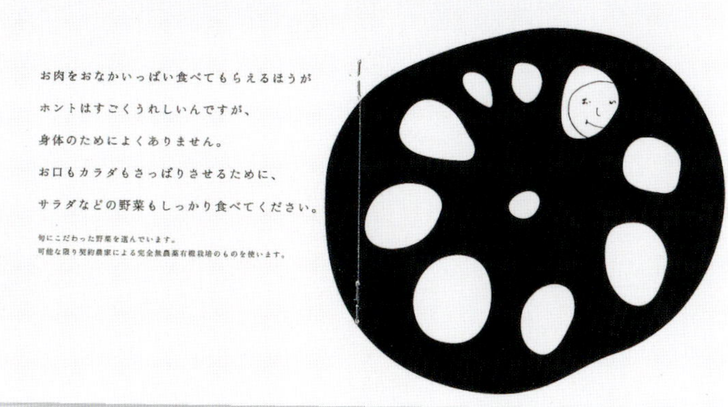

うまみ亭の豚肉は三元豚と
蔵王ハーブポーク。
やわらかい肉質と
香り高い脂の"うまみ"を
味わってください。

one's ワンズ

自分らしいライフスタイルをデザインする楽しさを喚起
Evoke the fun of designing your own lifestyle

戦略を読み解く 3 key words

日本の新しいライフスタイルを提案
“ウェルネス”をテーマに、素材やデザイン、機能、品質、価格を吟味した商品開発と情報発信を展開。ライフスタイルのトータル提案によって、単なる住空間のコーディネートだけでなく“生活全体を自分らしくデザインする楽しさ”を提唱し続ける。

テーマ性のあるショップツールを制作
ブランドコンセプトを反映させるものとしてショップまわりのツールを重視。常備ツールの他に、シーズンやライフイベントをテーマにしたツールを制作することで、“生活を楽しむ”ことを常にアピールする。

ユーザーにとって等身大のライフスタイルを描く
ブランドカラーであるオレンジを基本に展開。見る人に“生活の質の向上やホームファッションについての目覚め”を喚起することを目指し、季節感やストーリー性が感じられるビジュアルを心がけている。

3 key words

Promote a Japanese new lifestyle
On the theme "wellness", promote information distribution and product development based on careful consideration of materials, design, function, quality and price. Offering a total lifestyle rather than just coordinating a living space, advocate the "fun of designing your own lifestyle".

Create theme-based in-store promotional tools
Promotional tools in and near the store that reflect the brand concept are regarded with great importance. Season- and life event-themed materials go beyond common promotions to constantly promote the appeal of "enjoying your lifestyle".

Illustrate a lifestyle sized to each customer
Color schemes are developed primarily with orange, the brand color. Visuals built around seasonal feelings and vignettes inspire viewers to "improve their lifestyle and open their eyes to home fashion".

Naming
ショップ名は「自分の」「自分らしい」という意味。この基本ロゴを発展させた家の形のロゴを「one's home」と名付け、ブランドイメージの広がりを図っている。

The shop name evokes phrases such as "one's own" and "one's style". A house-shaped logo was developed from the main one's logo and named "one's home", seeking to expand brand image.

DM

リーフレット Leaflet

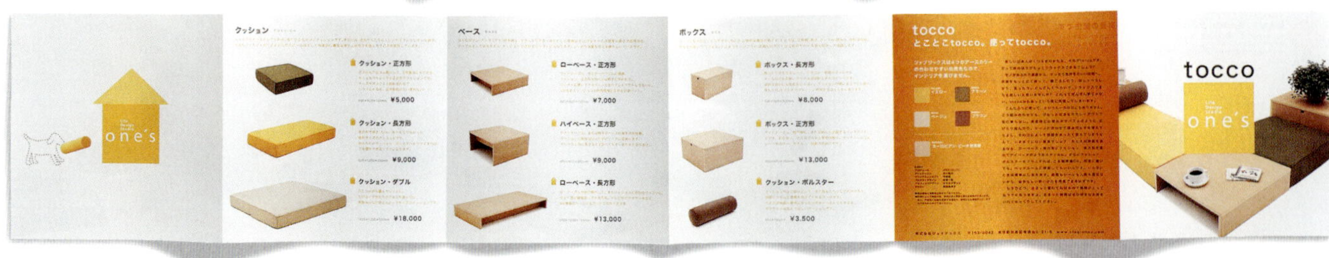

■CL= ジェイテックス JTEX CO.,LTD.
■D= 髙橋正実 Masami Takahashi ■P= 藤井 真（リーフレット） Makoto Fujii (Leaflet) ■S= MASAMI DESIGN

タグ Tag

ギフトボックス Gift box

Shop

CD

商品（カレンダー） Product (Calendar)

CD

MrMax ミスターマックス

平凡を豊かに美しく
Filling the ordinary with beauty

戦略を読み解く 3 key words

日常生活を豊かに、便利に、楽しく

日常生活をより豊かに、便利に、楽しくする商品やサービスを提供する総合ディスカウントストア。毎日の暮らしのなかで盲点になりがちな平凡なアイテムを、もっとチャーミングに美しくすることを目指している。

見やすい、分かりやすい、快適な売場を構成

広い通路と高い天井を備えた店内に、ほしいものが一目で分かる構成と、見やすく・買いやすい価格表示で、ゆったり快適に買物を楽しめるよう配慮している。また、「SELF STYLE」「Make a Good Choice!」など、プライベートブランドも展開。

安い、高品質、豊富な品揃えをストレートに表現

安いけれど質は良い商品が幅広く豊富にそろう店であることを、わかりやすくストレートに、ときにはユーモアを盛り込みながら表現。安さを重要なコンセプトとしながら、安っぽく見せない、且つ、お高く止まっているようにも見せない工夫をしている。

3 key words

Making everyday life richer, easier and more fun

A discount store that offers products and services that make everyday life richer, easier and more fun. The goal is to make the mundane items we tend to take for granted in everyday living more charming and beautiful.

A comfortable retail space, easy on the eyes and brain

Create a store where customers can enjoy shopping calmly and comfortably, with wide aisles and high ceilings, and price tags that are easy to read and easy on the wallet. Offer private brands, such as "SELF STYLE" and "Make a Good Choice!"

A straight pitch: low price, high quality, wide variety

Express the basic concept behind the store, i.e. a wide variety of high-quality products at affordable prices, directly and clearly with an occasional touch of humor. Affordability is a key concept -- but carefully construct the image to avoid making the goods look cheap or the store haughty.

Naming

英語のマキシマムに由来した社名。マキシマム＝極限に挑戦することをポリシーに、止まることなく、安んじることなく、さらに前進する。

The store takes its name from the English "maximum", referring to its policy of pursuing challenges to the extreme, never ceasing, continually improving.

ポスター（店内） Poster

■CL= ミスターマックス MrMax
■CD= 植原政信 Masanobu Uehara ■AD + CW= 伊藤敬生 Takao Ito ■P= 知識たかし Takashi Chishiki ■CW= 永野弥生 Yayoi Nagano ■D= 秋安淳一 Junichi Akiyasu ■D= 鈴木理恵子 Rieko Suzuki
■Advertising agent= 電通九州 DENTSU KYUSHU INC. ■DF= アド・パスカル AD PASCAL ■S= 電通九州 DENTSU KYUSHU INC.

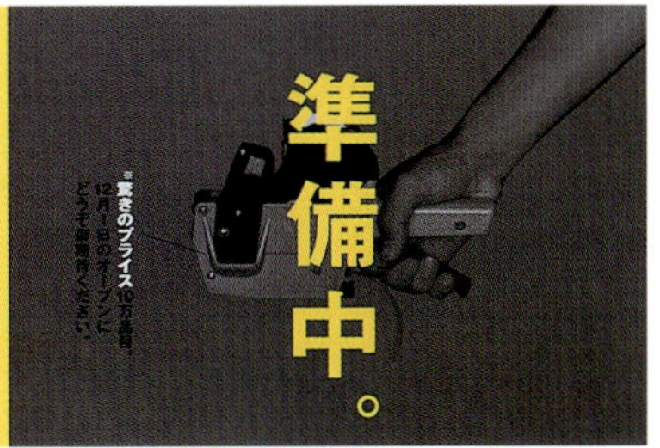

ポスター（車内） Poster

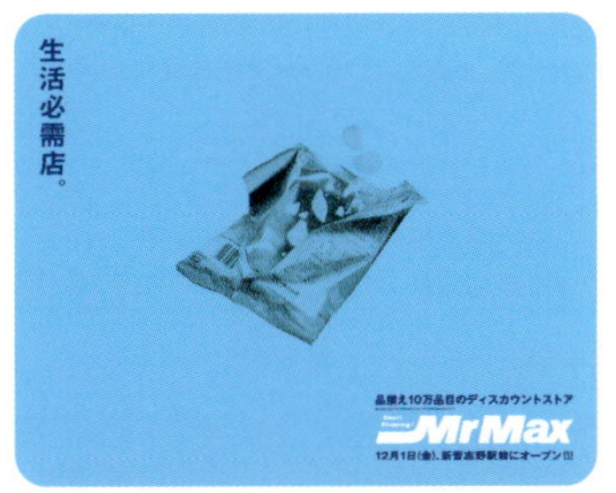

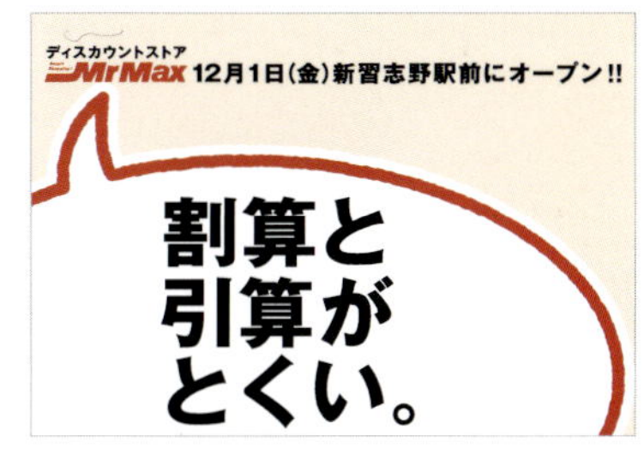

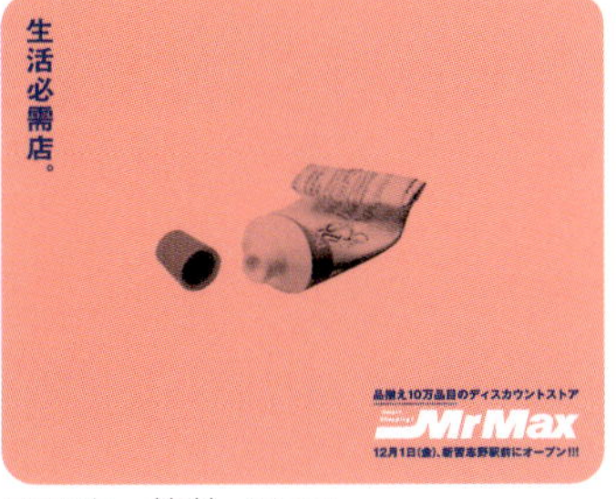

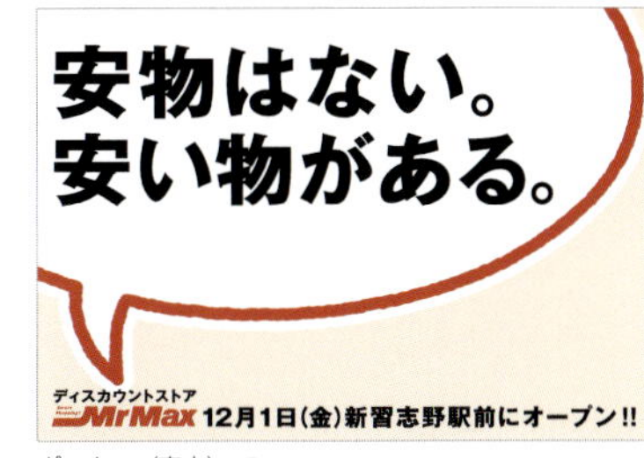

ステッカー（車内） Sticker

ポスター（車内） Poster

Smart Shopping! MrMax

鈴木家
予算委員会。

鈴木家も吉田家も伊藤家にとっても、我が家の予算審議は真剣そのもの。家族ひとりひとり欲しいものが違うし、言い分だってさまざまです。そこで、我が家の総理大臣・大蔵大臣のお耳にぜひとも入れておきたいのはミスターマックス。家族生活における物価全般を下げ、予算審議を円満に可決できるよう、日夜企業努力を続けております。すべては家族生活の幸福化のためにある。さあ、今すぐミスターマックスでスマートな予算通過をいたしましょう。

ポスター（駅貼り） Poster

Shop

店内サイン In the store, autograph

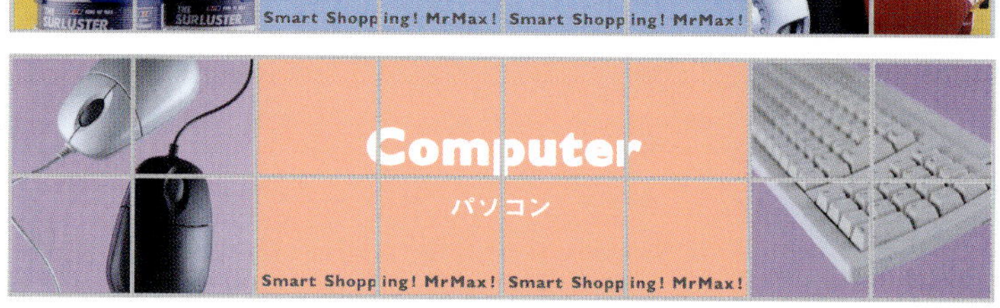

ポスター（店内） Poster

プライベートブランド「SELF STYLE」
カジュアル＆ベーシックなライフスタイルを応援するブランドとして開発。流行に左右されない、決して飽きないをスローガンとして掲げている。

Private brand 「SELF STYLE」
Developed as a brand that supports casual, basic lifestyles. Upholds as its slogan not being swayed by fad, neither become tiresome.

商品 Goods

ポスター（店内） Poster

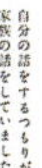

店内サイン
（ペット売場「PET'S MAX」）

In the store, autograph
(Pet counter 「PET'S MAX」)

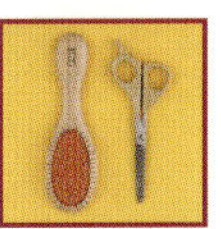

Yellow Hat イエローハット

「ハットさんファミリー」がユーモラスに店舗アピール
The Hat Family --creating store appeal humorously

戦略を読み解く 3 key words

「感動を与える接客」をモットーに

1962年に設立されたカー用品の総合商社。「カーライフを通じて感動を与える接客」をモットーに、消費者の求めるカー用品を幅広くそろえ、カーライフをより豊かにするために、質の高いサービスを追求している。

「ハットさんファミリー」が店の広告塔

店の認知度アップを狙い、2001年11月に「ハットさんファミリー」が誕生。それまでタレントを起用して展開していた広告をキャラクターに切り替え、親しみやすさを前面に押し出した。ポップなキャラクターは店内を楽しく彩るアクセントにもなっている。

シンプルでおもちゃ感覚のキャラクターを創造

パパは元走り屋の車好き、ママはお金にシビアと、店を訪れる家族と重なり合いそうなキャラクター設定で、親しみやすさを強調。ブランドカラーの黄色をメインに据えながら、シンプルなパーツを組み合わせ、おもちゃ感覚のキャラクターを作り出した。

3 key words

"Impression-making customer service" as a motto

An automotive goods trading company established in 1962, offering the wide variety of automotive goods consumers desire. As its policy, the store pursues high-quality service to enrich its customer's driving life.

The Hat Family form the store billboard

The Hat Family was developed in November 2001 to help increase store recognition. The switch from TV-personality-based advertising to cartoon characters represent an emphasis on friendliness. The pop feeling of the characters give the store interior a fun-filled, colorful accent.

Creating simple, toy-like cartoon characters

Papa is a former hotrodder/car freak, Mama is tight about money -- all have characters that are easy for families visiting the store to identify with, thus emphasizing a sense of intimacy. With principal use of the brand color yellow, parts are assembled to create characters with a toy-like feeling.

Character

子どもが通学時にかぶる黄色い帽子・イエローハットは「安心」「安全」の象徴。ハットさんファミリーも黄色い帽子をかぶって買い物に訪れる。

The yellow hat, which Japanese children wear to and from school, symbolizes security and safety. The Hat Family also wears yellow hats to go off shopping.

新聞広告 Newspaper AD

1億円山わけしてくださーい☆

みんなで来てね☆
1億円山わけキャンペーン
12/16(SUN)マデ!

☆いま3,000円以上(税込み)のお買物をすると➡イエローハットお買物券がアタリます➡1等:1万円ぶん 2等:5千円ぶん 3等:千円ぶん 総額1億円➡あなたのクルマに幸運が舞いこむ(かも)☆ご来店のお客様にハットさんファミリー特製シールをプレゼントいたします➡お店で「シールください」と言ってね!!

■CL= イエローハット Yellow Hat
■CD= 古川裕也 Yuya Furukawa ■AD + D + Character design= 田中 元 Gen Tanaka ■CW= 赤石正人 Masato Akaishi ■D= 村野崇行 Takayuki Murano ■D= 折田笑子 Emiko Orita ■Creative producer= 仲田繁乃 Shigeno Nakada
■Project production= 電通 DENTSU ■Project production= アドブレーン ADBRAIN ■Project production= 電通テック DENTSU TEC ■S= 電通 DENTSU INC.

新聞広告 Newspaper AD

ノベルティ（マグカップ、弁当箱、トースター、ティッシュペーパー、ホットボトル、うちわ、ランチョンマット）
Novelty (Mag cup, Lunch box, Toaster, Tissue paper, Hot bottle, Japanese fun, Place mat)

新聞広告 Newspaper AD

新聞広告 Newspaper AD

愛人はいません。愛車がいますから☆

ドライバーズ・マーケット
Yellow Hat
www.yellowhat.co.jp/

©ハットさんファミリー／ハットパパ

OZOC オゾック

ショップという建築物をメディアの中心として機能させる実験的試み
Using shop architecture as a promotional medium

戦略を読み解く 3 key words

ショップの立地条件を活かしたプロジェクト

原宿にオープンする旗艦店のプロモーションにあたり、今までにない斬新な試みを展開。「HAAP(HARAJUKU ADVERTISEMENT ARCHITECTURE PROJECT)」というプロジェクト名が示す通り、ショップという建築物自体を基幹メディアとした。

通りを歩くターゲットへ強烈にアピールする建築物

ショップそのものが広告として機能することを図り、インパクトのあるビジュアルとして外観を赤いキューブのように設計。ファッションがシーズンによって変化するように建物を着替えさせたいと考え、外壁パネルは取り外しができる仕組みになっている。

プロジェクトの過程を広告のビジュアルで再生

SPツールではショップの外観をモチーフにしたビジュアルを徹底。プレゼン用に制作したツールを使うなど、プロジェクトのプロセス自体を広告に反映させた。また、原宿周辺で駅のビジュアルジャックなどを行い、プロジェクトの更なる強化を図った。

3 key words

Exploiting store location

Promote the never-before-seen aspects of the company's Harajuku-located flagship store. The "HAAP (Harajuku Advertisement Architecture Project)", true to its name, made the architecture of the store itself its main promotional medium.

Architecture that appeals strongly to passersby

Design the exterior of the store as a red cube for maximum visual impact, planning to use the shop as an advertisement for itself. With exterior walls designed as removable panels, just as fashion changes with the seasons so will the building.

Relive the project through visuals

Sales promotion tools make thorough use of the store exterior as a motif, and tools created for presentation purposes are used to reflect the process of the project itself. OZOC exclusive campaigns occupying all available advertising space in the Harajuku station area reemphasized the project.

Logo

ロゴは小さなキューブの集合体になっている。ショップの外観のビジュアルに合わせてデザインした。

The logo is an aggregate of small cubes, designed to match the external appearance of the store.

ショップバッグ Shop bag

■CL= ワールド WORLD CO., LTD.
■Agency & Production= サムライ+タグボート SAMURAI + TAGBOAT ■CD + AD= 佐藤可士和 Kashiwa Sato ■CD= 多田 琢 Taku Tada ■P= 皆川 聡 Satoshi Minakawa ■D= 奥瀬義樹 Yoshiki Okuse
■Architect= 荒木信雄 Nobuo Araki ■S= サムライ SAMURAI

Shop

ピンバッジ Pinbadge

シール Sticker

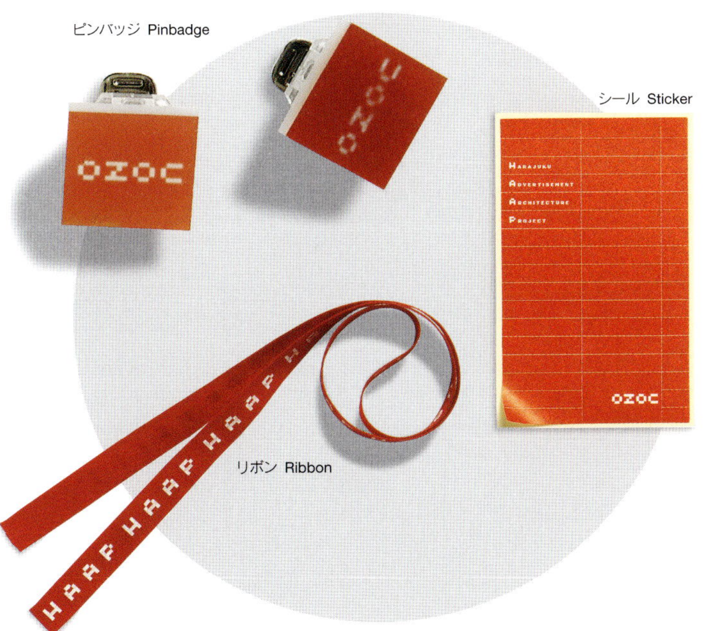

リボン Ribbon

ショップカード Shop card

ショップバッグ Shop bag

プレスキット
オープニングの招待状と便せん、コンセプトブックをセットにした。

Press kit
Opening invitation, letterhead and concept book designed as a set.

コンセプトブック
「HAAP」プロジェクトのコンセプトやプロセスをまとめたもの。

Concept book
Documents the HAAP project concept and design process.

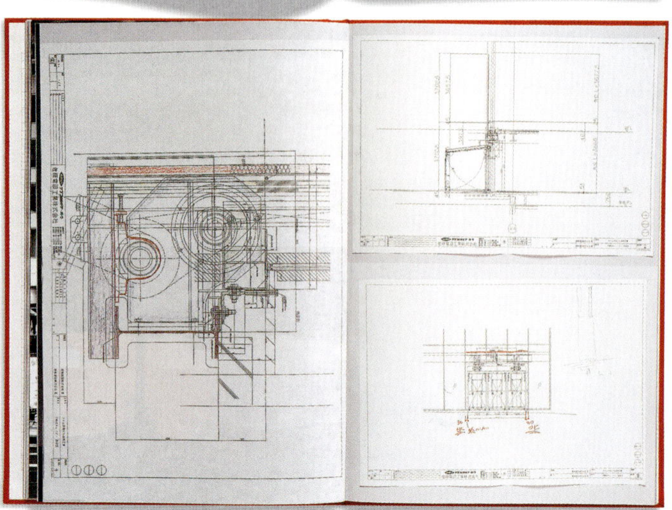

ノベルティ（携帯用灰皿）
Novelty (Portable ashtray)

レセプションの招待状 Reception invitation

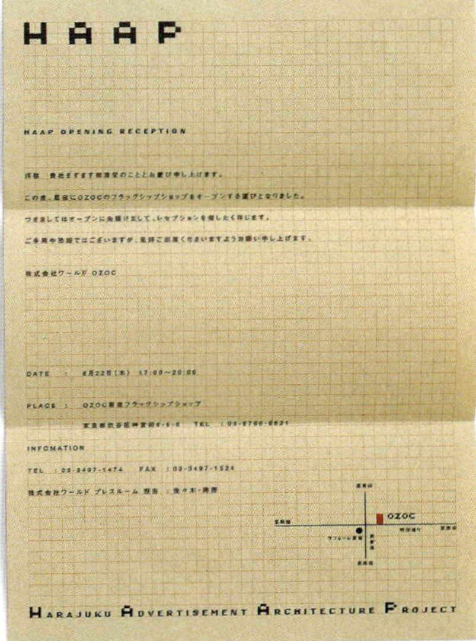

招待状 Invitation

ポスターの駅貼り風景

渋谷駅のプラットホームに掲出した巨大ポスター。何枚ものポスターを連貼りしている。

Promotion in Shibuya Station

Giant poster, composed of multiple sheets pasted edge to edge, hung on the Shibuya Station train platform.

ポスター Poster

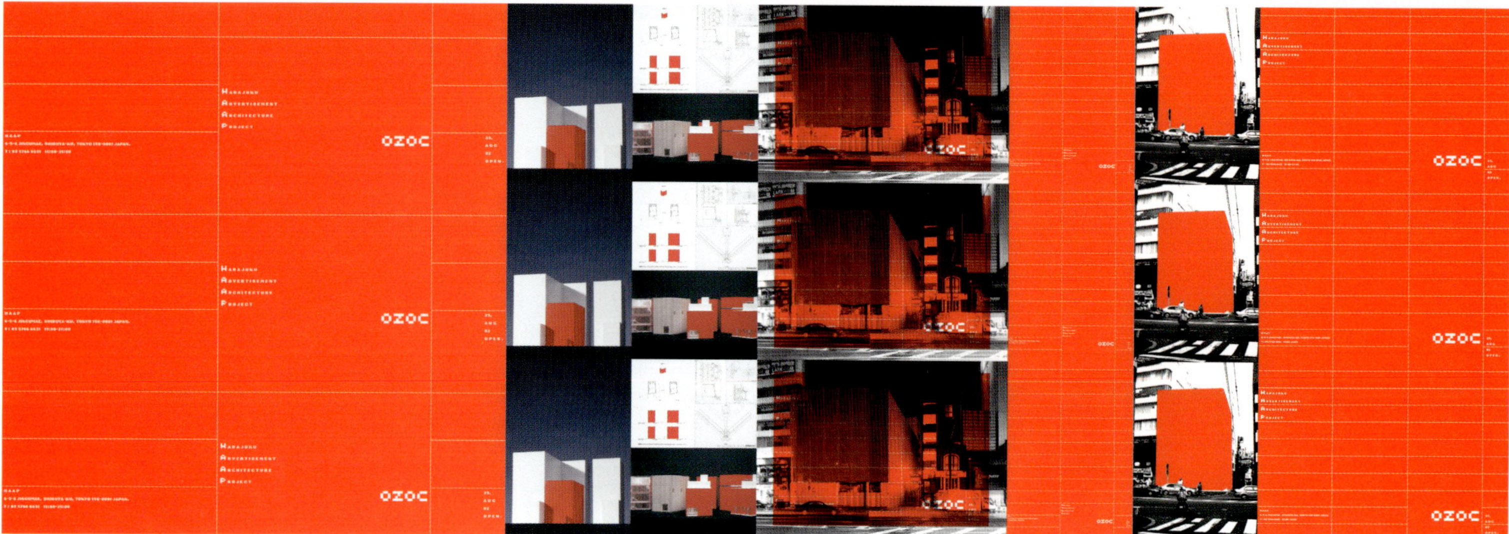

原宿駅でのビジュアルジャック

"駅というスペースを使った展示会" をイメージして行った。

Promotion in Harajuku Station

Conceived as "an exhibition incorporating railroad station space"

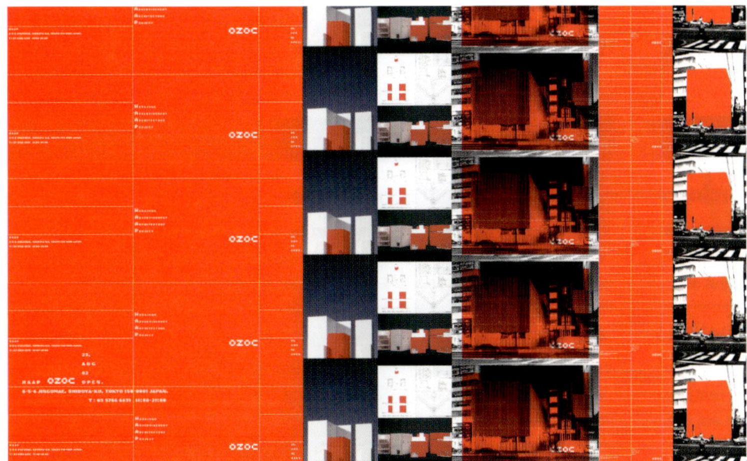

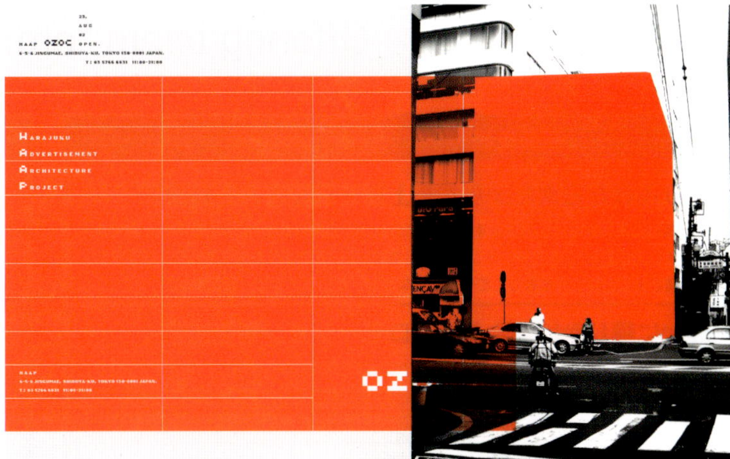

雑誌広告 Magazine AD

新聞広告 Newspaper AD

Abahouse Devinette アバハウス・ドゥヴィネット

服の素材を打ち出した販促物でシーズンテーマを発信
Clothing materials become seasonal promotional goods

戦略を読み解く 3 key words

大人の女性たちへ軽妙で開放されたスタイルを提案

無垢で透明な視線を持ち、媚びることのない意志を秘めた女性たちに向けて、素材やディテールにこだわったアイテムを提案。ファッションビルや百貨店など全国に店舗展開している。

ノベルティにメッセージと仕掛けをしのばせて

春夏、秋冬のシーズンに合わせて実施する5回の展示会を中心にプロモーションを展開。カタログを兼ねたノベルティには、ドゥヴィネットのスタイルに合わせた発信性の高いアクセサリーを入れ、シーズンテーマ及びブランドイメージの浸透を図っている。

シーズンテーマを各媒体でリアルに表現

ショップバッグや下げ札など通年使用するツールはシンプルで洗練されたイメージで統一。DMやポスター、カタログ兼ノベルティでシーズンテーマを表現している。DMには洋服の素材を使用するなど、細部までテーマを盛り込んだツールがそろう。

3 key words

Offering women smart and clever style

The company offers items carefully made from high-quality materials to women with the lucid gaze of purity and the will to resist flattery. Its product line is sold in fashion shops and department stores throughout Japan.

Concealing message and intent in novelty

Design a promotion centered around five exhibitions to be held in conjunction with the spring-summer and fall-winter seasons. Include a Devinette-styled, highly communicative accessory with the catalog and novelties to propagate the season theme and brand image.

Expressing the season theme through every medium

Give year-round items, such as shopping bags and hang tags, a simple, elegant, consistent image. Use direct mail, posters and the catalog/novelty gift to express the season theme. With touches like samples of clothing materials in the direct mail, assemble a set of promotional tools that reflect the theme down to the smallest details.

Naming

Devinetteとはフランス語で「なぞなぞ」の意味。

"Devinette", in French, means "enigma".

Abahouse Devinette

Shop

ショップバッグ Shop Bag

タグ Tag

ショップカード Shop Card

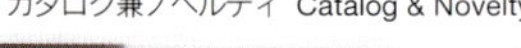

カタログ兼ノベルティ Catalog & Novelty

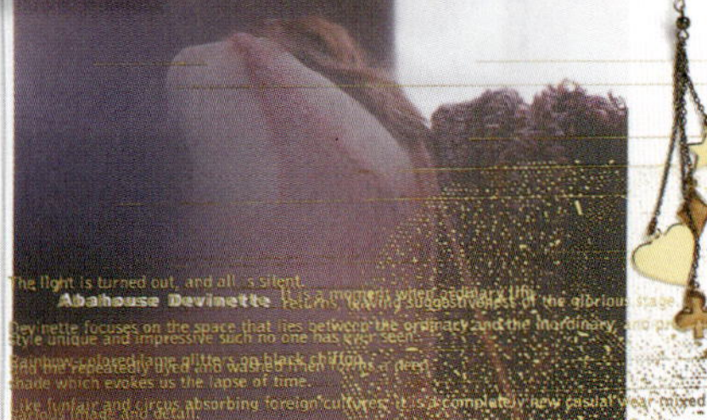

2002-2003 秋／冬「After the show time」

移動遊園地やサーカス一座が華々しいステージから日常生活へと戻る瞬間など、日常と非日常の狭間に視点を置き、印象的なバランスや深い色合いのアイテムを展開。

2002-2003 Autumn/winter 「After the show time」

A series of items with striking balance and deep coloration poised between the everyday and special -- like coming home from the spectacular stages of a traveling circus or bazaar.

■CL= アバハウスインターナショナル Abahouse International
■S= アバハウスインターナショナル Abahouse International

カタログ兼ノベルティ
カタログは袋とじになっている。

Catalog & Novelty
Catalog is fukuro-toji (pouch) bound.

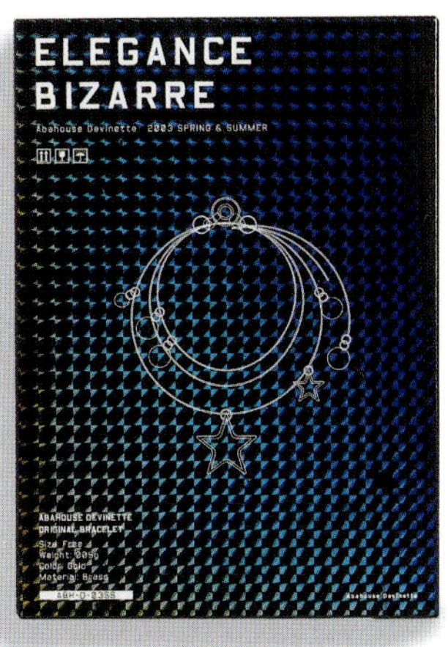

DM

2003 春／夏「エレガンス・ビザール」
素朴さを一歩抜け出した、光と色気のあるエレガンスを提案。

2003 Spring/summer 「ELEGANCE BIZARRE」
Proposes a light-filled, sexy elegance breaking one-step away from simplicity.

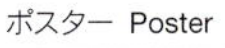

ポスター Poster

Pinceau par adam et ropé パンソー パーアダムエロペ

“可愛らしさ”と色にこだわった店頭グラフィックで女性の心を掴む

Store graphics based around pretty colors capture women's hearts

戦略を読み解く 3 key words

ライフスタイルというキャンバスに彩りを添えたい

ユーザーそれぞれの“ライフスタイルというキャンバスに、色をつけるお手伝いをしていきたい”と願い、30代からの大人の女性に向けて、“新しいものと古き良きものを融合させた、遊び心のあるコーディネイト”を提案する。

“色”を大切にした小型グラフィックに力を入れる

店頭でのプロモーションを重視して、大々的な広告は行わず小型グラフィックに力を入れる。まずは“色”を大切にしたいと考え、“上品な可愛らしさ”をテーマに、DICのフランス伝統色の2色（F39とF264）の組み合わせをブランドカラーに選んだ。

女性のハートをくすぐる“可愛らしさ”をテーマに

グラフィックツールでは、ブランドのベースカラーを大切にしながら“可愛らしさ”や“ノスタルジック”をキーワードにデザイン。商品構成も含めたトータルなブランディングに成功し、設立から約2年で6店舗をもつまでに成長した。

3 key words

Adding color to life's canvas

Offer to help every customer "add color to their lifestyle canvas", providing women in their 30's up "fun-loving fashion coordination that merges the classic with the new".

Focus on small graphics with carefully selected colors

Abandoning large-scale advertising for more effective in-store promotion, we focus our strength in small-scale graphics. Making color the starting point for our theme of "elegant prettiness", we combine two of Dainippon Ink & Chemical's (DIC) traditional French colors to create the brand color.

"Prettiness" to tickle women's hearts

Design graphics around the themes "prettiness" and "nostalgia", keeping the brand color central. Successfully incorporate the company's product line in a total branding effort as the chain expands to include six locations within two years of establishment.

Naming

Pinceauはフランス語で「絵筆」の意味。“生活に彩りを”というブランドコンセプトを象徴させるネーミング。

"Pinceau" means "paintbrush" in French. The name refers to the company's desire to add color to customers' lifestyles.

ショップカード Shop card

ショップバッグ Shop bag

リボン Ribbon

タグ Tag

シール Sticker

ショップバッグ Shop bag

■ CL= ジュン JUN CO., Ltd.
■ CD= 福島達代 Tatsuyo Fukushima
■ S= ジュン JUN CO., Ltd.
■ AD + D + I + CW= 舟山明男 Akio Funayama
■ D + I= 秀島由里 Yuri Hidejima
■ P= FANTA
■ P= 小木曽 博 Hiroshi Ogiso
■ DF= パンダグラフィックス PANDA GRAPHICS

フライヤー Flyer

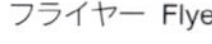

フライヤー Flyer

カタログ Catalog

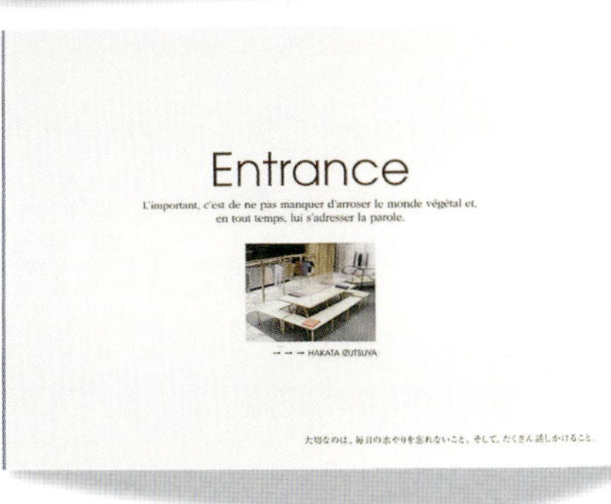

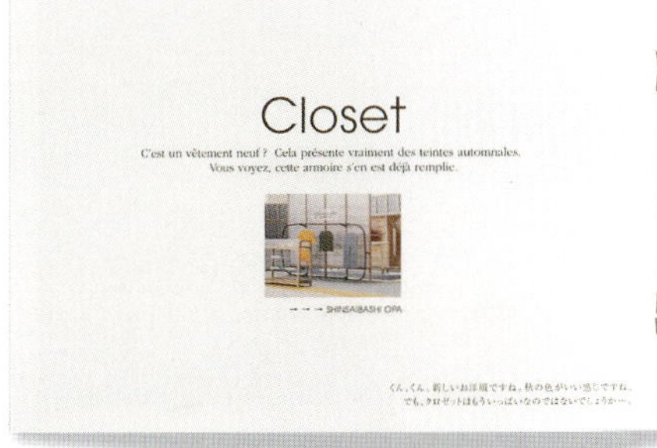

DM

JOURNAL STANDARD ジャーナルスタンダード

テーマ性のあるカタログ作りでブランドのポテンシャルを訴求
Expand brand potential with a theme-based catalog

戦略を読み解く 3 key words

ユーザーが"今"を体感するブランドを目指す

ノーエイジ、ユニセックスをコンセプトにしたセレクトショップ。国内外の気鋭のクリエイターによる最新アイテム、ベーシックライン、ワーク&ミリタリースタイルという3つのカテゴリーのラインナップで、"今"を表現するショップブランドを目指す。

独創的なツール作りでブランドの存在価値を高める

ブランドの"顔"である商品構成に付加価値を与えるものとして、カタログやノベルティをはじめとするSPツールの制作を重視。とくにカタログではシーズンごとにテーマ性をもたせ、ビジュアルブックとしての鑑賞にも堪えうるクオリティを追求している。

テーマは"シンプルさに遊びを加味したデザイン"

グラフィック全体のテーマは"素材と質感"と、"ベーシックなものに新しさを加えた、遊びの効いたビジュアル"。紙袋などショップの定番ツールでは、基本カラーに"ベーシックなイメージ"のある茶系色を使い、男女問わず受け入れられるテイストにしている。

3 key words

Create a brand consumers identify with "now"

This brand is a boutique retail chain. Brand's concept is "no age limit" and "unisex". The latest items from hot new creators in Japan and abroad make up three product lines, Basic, Work and Military Style. The store seeks a brand image that says "now".

Improve brand value with unique promotional tools

Create sales promotion tools, beginning with catalogs and novelties, that increase the value of the brand's "face" -- its product line. Develop the catalog around seasonal themes, and make it high enough quality to be looked at just for pleasure.

"Simple design tempered with playfulness"

The overall theme of the graphics is "material quality and feel" and "visuals that take the basic and add something new, something playful". Store bags, and other standard items, are rendered in brown tones which convey a basic image and appeal to both men and women alike.

Naming

メディア関連の言葉であるJOURNALと、基準を意味するSTANDARDを組み合わせ、"時流に乗った新しいスタンダードスタイルを発信する"というコンセプトを表現した。

The media connotations of "Journal" combines with "Standard", here meaning basic or common, to express the concept "bringing you today's standard in style".

JOURNAL STANDARD

Shop

ショップカード Shop card

ショップバッグ Shop bag

■CL= ベイクルーズ BAYCREW'S Co., Ltd.
■CD= 鈴木ひとみ Hitomi Suzuki ■Graphic Design= 黒田裕紀 Yuki Kuroda ■Planning & Production= 福田十詩子 Toshiko Fukuda ■S= ベイクルーズ BAYCREW'S Co., Ltd.

ノベルティ（ワイン） Novelty (Wine)

インビテーション Invitation

ギフト用ラッピング
Gift wrappings

シール Sticker

ノベルティ
新宿店のオープンに合わせて制作。"ピクニック、キャンプ" をコンセプトにしたカフェを併設しているため、そのイメージを伝えるノベルティとして布製バッグとタオル、ミネラルウォーター入りペットボトルをセットにした。

Novelty
Produced for the opening of the Shinjuku store and cafe annex, a novelty cloth pouch containing a towel and bottle of mineral water convey the picnic/camping theme of the cafe.

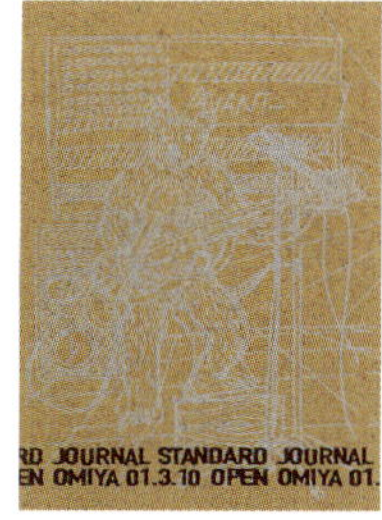

DM

ノベルティ Novelty

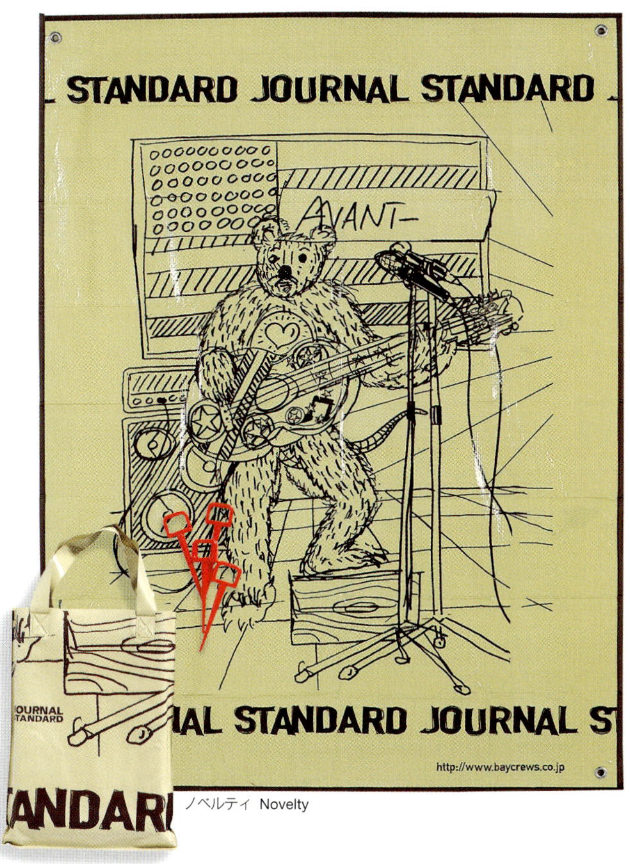

ノベルティ Novelty

2003 春／夏のレディースカタログ
シーズンテーマは「ONE TRIP WITH A BOSTONBAG」。小旅行に持っていくワードローブをイメージした商品構成であったため、カタログのビジュアルも“気軽に楽しむ小さな旅”をテーマとした。

2003 S/S Lady's Catalog
The season's theme: "trip with a Boston bag". As the product lineup proposes wardrobe to be taken on a short trip, the catalog visuals support the image of a fun and easy-spirited little journey.

ノベルティ Novelty

2002-2003 秋／冬のレディースカタログ
シーズンテーマは「CONTRAST」で、クール＆ガーリッシュなど対照的テイストのアイテムの組みあわせを楽しむスタイルを提案。カタログは小型のノートブックの体裁を選び“お気に入りのものをスクラップしているイメージ”を演出した。

2002-2003 A/W Lady's Catalog
The season's theme: "contrast", proposing a fun-filled style combining items, such cool and garish, of contrasting tastes. The catalog's small notebook format is imaged as a scrapbook documenting "the things I like".

ノベルティ Novelty

2003 春／夏のメンズカタログ
シーズンテーマは「WET BACK」で、メキシコからアメリカ・テキサスへ大河を泳いで越境する人々を指す俗語。現地の言語では「EL MOJADO」といい、それをカタログのタイトルに冠した。デザインモチーフはタブロイド版であり、写真は全てメキシコとテキサスで撮影したもの。

2003 S/S Men's Catalog
The season's theme was "wet back", slang for people that swim across the river between Mexico and Texas to enter the U.S. South of the border, the term is "el mojado" -- the catalog title. Formatted like a tabloid, the photographs were all shot in Mexico and Texas.

2002-2003 秋／冬のメンズカタログ
シーズンテーマは「新世代のトラディショナル」。ブランドが扱う世界中のクリエイターを紹介することを目的に、ペーパーバックをモチーフにして制作。わざと折り目をつけたりかすれさせたりといった加工を施し、古ぼけた印象を演出した。

2002-2003 A/W Men's Catalog
The season's theme: "new generation traditional". Designed with a paper bag motif to support the brand's objective -- introducing brand-related creators from around the world. The paper was purposely creased and smudged to give it a timeworn look.

edit.for Lulu エディット・フォー ルル

コラボレーション企画を核にした、ショップ主体のイメージ戦略
Planned collaboration grows into a shop-based image strategy

戦略を読み解く 3 key words

キュートな大人の女性に提案するミックススタイル

お洒落を楽しむ全ての女性に向けたショップで、商品は最新モードを採り入れたアイテム、ヴィンテージアイテム、ショップのオリジナルアイテムという3つのラインで構成。"キュート、ピュア、エレガント" をキーワードに自由なミックススタイルを提案する。

プロモーションの主体はあくまでショップ

ショップまわりの小型グラフィックをはじめ、2か月に1度の割合で行うショップお勧めのアーティストとのコラボレーション企画と、それに付随して制作するグッズによって、ブランドコンセプトの訴求とイメージの浸透を図っている。

目標は "思わず顔がほころぶキュートなデザイン"

コラボレーションの企画とツールの制作に共通するテーマは、"思わず笑みがこぼれるキュートなビジュアル"。遊び心をエッセンスとして加味した質の高いデザインによって、大人の女性のセンスに訴える "可愛らしさ" の表現に努めている。

3 key words

Mixed styles appeal to the girlish side of adult women

The shop targets every woman who likes dressing up with three lines of merchandise: items following the latest fashion trends, vintage fashion and store original items. "Cute, pure, elegant" are the watchwords for this mixture of styles.

The shop as the primary promotional medium

A plan for small-size graphics around the store calls for collaboration with a featured artist once every two months, and the production of accompanying promotional goods to define brand concept and increase image penetration.

Design that brings out an unwitting smile

The planned collaboration and the accompanying promotional goods are themed around cute visuals that bring an unwitting smile to viewers' faces. High-quality design that captures the essence of playfulness expresses the "cuteness" that adult women love.

Naming

「ルル」とは架空の女の子の名前。ショップは彼女の家であり、そこに置いている商品は彼女のクローゼットのために編集された物という設定。

"Lulu" is the name of the imaginary woman who owns the house in which this store is her closet and all the merchandise her things.

Shop

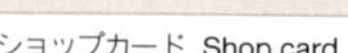

ショップカード Shop card

シール Sticker

■CL= ベイクルーズ BAYCREW'S Co., Ltd.
■CD= 鈴木ひとみ Hitomi Suzuki ■Graphic Design= 山川伊久 Iku Yamakawa ■Planning & Production= 河村純子 Junko Kawamura ■S= ベイクルーズ BAYCREW'S Co., Ltd.

ノベルティ
オープン1周年を記念して制作したもの。

Novelty
Produced for the shop's one-year anniversary.

Shop

VIPカード VIP card

アテンションカード Attention card

タグ Tag

ショップバッグ Shop bag

edit.for Lulu

Hunt out at Lulu!

Wo shi Ribenren exhibition
ryokuhanooto

DM

DM

Sale by edit.for Lulu
Special thanks sale
from 27. July .....
special summer of Lulu COAT,COSTUME&GOWN MANUFACTURES PHONE +81.57.72.32.66

COLLECTION DEU YUKATA
2003.5.29.thu.~6.15.sun.
EDIT.FOR LULU

edit.for Lulu

"MIHO" EXHIBITION
2002.9.7(sat)~9.28(sat)

mobile
"QUEUE DE SAYOKO KOBAYASHI" EXHIBITION
2003.4.26.SAT

IT'S YOUR TURN!

SPRING CAME ON ALSO TO LULU!
THE SEA, THE SEXINESS, AND THE SUN FROM ACAPULCO.
edit.for Lulu

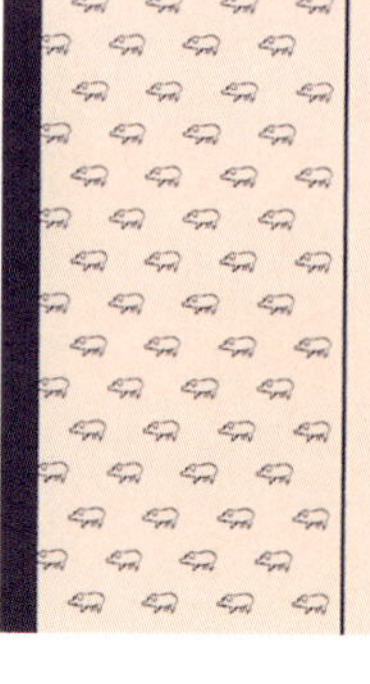

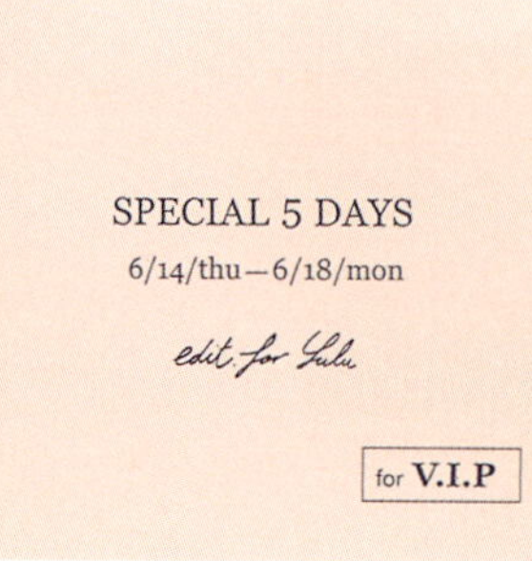
SPECIAL 5 DAYS
6/14/thu—6/18/mon
edit.for Lulu
for V.I.P

MEMBER'S SALE 6.8.sat.-6.11.tue.
"浴衣"
yukata collection 6.20.thu.-6.30.sun.
edit.for Lulu

オープンインビテーション Open invitation

招待状 Invitation

2003年春に行ったコラボレーション企画

イラストレーターの水森亜土氏とコラボーレート。企画展のオープニングイベントでは、"歌とお絵描き" のライブも行った。

Collaboration plan in 2003 spring

Collaboration with illustrator Ado Mizumori. The opening event included a live concert entitled "Song and Artist".

ノベルティ
小物作家とのコラボレーション企画を行ったときに制作した、オリジナルのぬいぐるみ。

Novelty
An original stuffed animal produced during the brand's collaboration with accessory artists.

限定商品 Limited product

DM

goldie H.P.FRANCE ゴールディ アッシュ・ペー・フランス

ショップのコンセプトを明確に表現する、テーマ性をもった空間
A themed space clearly expresses brand concept

戦略を読み解く 3 key words

作家の世界観と作品に込められた物語を伝えたい

主にヨーロッパのクリエイターの手によるアクセサリーと小物を扱うセレクトショップ。ただ単に商品として販売するのではなく、それぞれのクリエイターの世界観と作品に込められた物語を伝え、引いてはヨーロッパの文化を紹介していきたいと考える。

グラフィックも含めた空間作りで商品価値を高める

ブランドコンセプトを具現化する場所はショップであり、プロモーションの主役もショップであると考える。店舗のインテリアはもちろん、ギフトボックスなどのツール類も全て含め、商品のもつストーリー性に付加価値を与える空間作りを目指す。

デザインのテーマは “ヨーロッパ” と “アート性”

全体を通してのビジュアルコンセプトは、“ヨーロッパの香りやアート性を感じさせるテイスト”。店舗のインテリアは “ヨーロッパのプライベート美術館” をテーマにしたデザインで、美術品を展示するイメージで商品をディスプレイしている。

3 key words

Conveying creators' worldviews and creations' stories

A select shop that carries accessories and other small articles, mainly from the hands of European designers. More than a shop, however, it conveys the stories contained in the products and the worldviews of their creators, and in the process provides a taste of Europe to its customers.

Increasing product value with graphics and interior design

As the shop is the realization of the brand concept, it should be the star of the promotion as well. Design the shop interior, gift boxes and every sort of promotional tool to communicate the added value of the stories the products tell.

"Europe" and "Artistic" form twin design themes

The visual concept running throughout the promotion is "giving viewers a sense of the aura and artistic quality of Europe". Design the store interior as if it were a "European private museum", with product displays that treat the items as works of art.

Naming

いつの時代でも変わらずに愛すべきものをゴールドになぞらえ、自分だけの “ゴールド=特別なもの” を見つけてほしい” という思いを込めたネーミング。

Just as precious items throughout history have been traced in gold, the store's name reflects its desire for customers to find their own "gold" -- their own "precious thing".

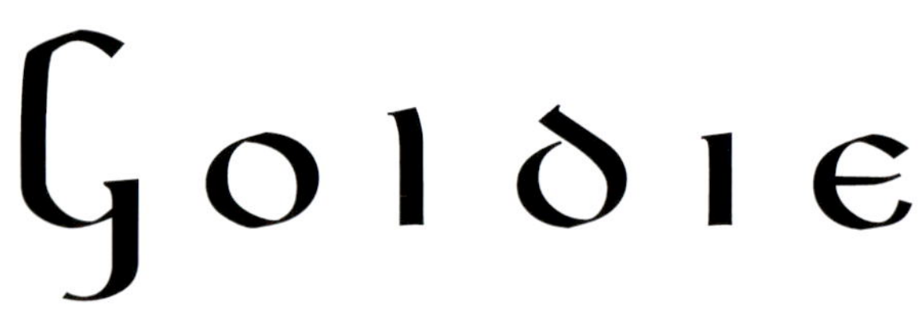

ギフトボックス Gift box

ギフト袋 Gift bag

ショップバッグ Shop bag

Shop

■CL= アッシュ・ペー・フランス H.P.FRANCE Inc.
■CD + Buyer= 町田小都美 Satomi Machida ■AD= 上尾智昭 Tomoaki Ueo ■D= DM 4 / 日野準子 Junko Hino ■D= DM 2.3.5 / 佐野智子 Satoko Sano ■D= DM 1 / 野中孝義 Takayoshi Nonaka ■P= DM 3 / 森田晃代 Akiyo Morita
■DF= ハレオ HArEO ■S= アッシュ・ペー・フランス H.P.FRANCE Inc.

DM 1

DM 2

DM 3

DM 4

DM 5

HaaT ハート

ブランドカラーをメインビジュアルに据えて認知度アップを狙う

Develop brand recognition with color and strategic visuals

戦略を読み解く 3 key words

"西洋と東洋の交差点" をテーマにした新ブランド

イッセイ・ミヤケのコレクションライン「PERMANENTE」と、インドの手織り布を使ったライン「ASHA」がひとつになって登場した新ブランド。ブランド名には英語のハート（心）と、インド語のハート（手仕事）の意味も込められている。

小型グラフィックを中心にブランドの世界観を主張

ADはロゴデザインなどブランドのアイデンティティ構築の段階から参画。プロモーションでは、ブランドの認知度を高める大切な手段として小型グラフィックを重視。特に毎シーズン制作するカタログによって、更なるブランド力のアップを図っている。

ブランドカラーの強調で存在感を高める

気品を感じさせつつも強いインパクトを与えるブランドカラーを選び、そのカラーを全てのグラフィックツールにおいて前面に出した。結果として2ブランドで展開していた当時の顧客だけでなく、幅広い新規顧客層へのアピールに成功した。

3 key words

A new brand at the crossroads of West and East

The Issey Miyake line "PERMANENTE" merges with the Indian hand-woven textile line "ASHA" to form a new brand. The brand name "HaaT" combines the meanings of "heart" from the English homonym and "handicraft" from Hindi.

Emphasize brand worldview through small-scale graphics

The artistic director participated in constructing brand identity from the logo design stage. In promotion, emphasis is placed on the small-scale graphics as devices for increasing brand awareness. Plans include strengthening the brand by producing seasonal catalogs.

Promote presence through brand color

Select a brand color that will give an elegant feel yet have strong impact, and use that color consistently throughout the graphics. The result successfully appeals to not only the customers of the previous two brands, but also a wide range of new customers.

Logo

ブランド名はサンスクリット語で「マーケット」の意味。たて組みにすることで、屋台（マーケット）の形を表現した。

"HaaT" also means "market" in Sanskrit. And, if you write the Japanese characters vertically, the result looks like a stand in an outdoor market.

Shop Design= 吉岡徳仁 Tokujin Yoshioka

Shop

タグ Tag

タグ Tag

ショップバッグ Shop bag

■CL= イッセイミヤケ Issey Miyake, Inc.
■AD= 東海林小百合 Sayuri Shoji ■P= DM 1, Catalog 1 / 紀里谷和明 Kazuaki Kiriya ■P= Catalog 2-5 / 富永よしえ Yoshie Tominaga ■P= Catalog 6 / 土井浩一郎 Koichiro Doi ■S= サユリ・スタジオ Sayuri Studio, Inc.

DM

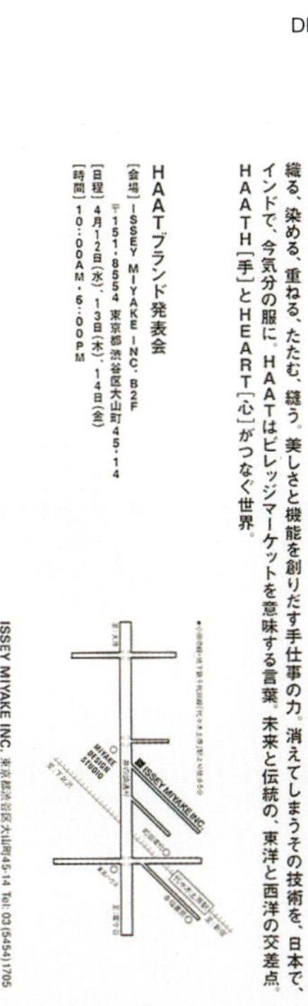

DM 1

ファイルケース File case

カタログ
たて組みのロゴを印象づけるために、
毎回たて長の体裁を選択。

Catalog
Vertically formatted items emphasize the vertically oriented logo.

1

2

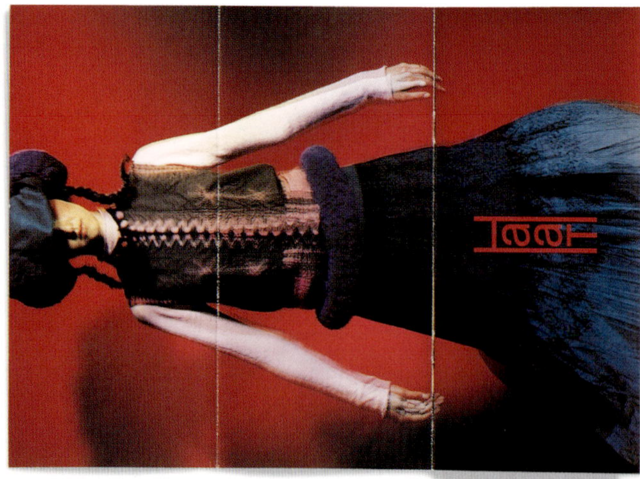

3

4

5

6

white trash charms　ホワイト トラッシュ チャームズ

あえて商品を露出しないSPツールでブランドのセンスを演出
Promoting sales without revealing the product

戦略を読み解く 3 key words

“日本人の胸元を元気にする” アクセサリー

ハリウッド生まれのアクセサリーブランド。もとはファッションスタイリストをしていたデザイナーが、「ロックなアクセサリーが欲しい」というミュージシャンの要望に応えて立ち上げたブランドで、遊び心のあるデザインが特徴。

自分流のオシャレを楽しむ女性に向けて発信

ブランドのもつ空気感や匂いを表現する要素としてショップまわりのツールに力を入れるほか、ノベルティで付加価値をつけている。また、新規ユーザーへのアプローチ手段としてポスターを重視している。

商品写真なしのSPツールでイメージを膨らませる

あえて商品の写真を使わないことで、ブランドのイメージを膨らませるビジュアルを実現。ベースカラーのピンクを使ってポップに仕上げながらも、大人っぽい雰囲気を演出する。また、ブランド発祥地の “アメリカっぽさ” を大切にしている。

3 key words

Accessories that "fill Japanese hearts with cheer"

A line of accessories born in Hollywood. Created by a designer working as a fashion stylist in response to the demand from musicians for "rock accessories", the brand's characteristic is its playfulness.

Targeting women who enjoy dressing as a personal statement

Develop promotional tools for use in and around the shop that communicate the atmosphere and aura of the brand and novelty gifts that add value. Posters as a way to draw new customers into the stores are also important.

Expand brand image by omitting product photographs

Consciously avoiding product photographs, create visuals that expand the image of the brand. Use pink as the base color to add some pop flavor, but make the overall atmosphere an adult one. As well, the ads must communicate some of the "American flavor" of the brand's birthplace.

Logo

本国のテイストを基本にしつつ、日本国内向けにオリジナルのロゴをデザイン。ベースカラーにピンクを選んだ。

Design an original logo for use in Japan, based on America sensibility. Choose pink as the base color.

ポスター　Poster

■CL= ホワイト トラッシュ チャームズ ジャパン White Trash Charms JAPAN Co., Ltd.
■CD + AD + D= 青木克憲 Katsunori Aoki　■D= 高桑佳奈 Kana Takakuwa　■I= 村田篤司 Atsushi Murata　■Agency & Production= バタフライ・ストローク butterfly·stroke inc.　■S= バタフライ・ストローク butterfly·stroke inc.

ノベルティ（鏡） Novelty (Mirror)

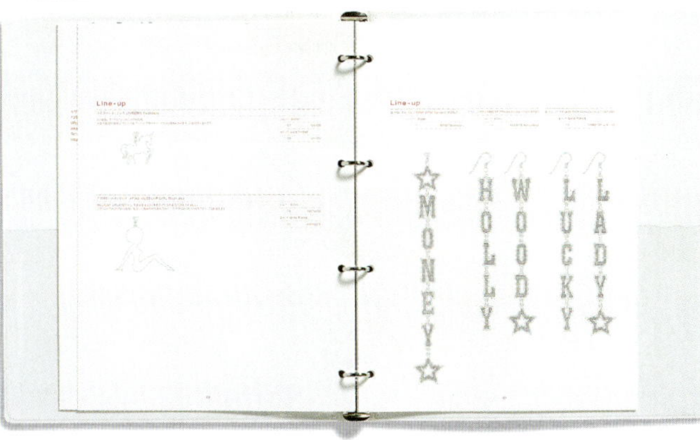

カタログ Catalog

ショップバッグ Shop bag

店頭用シート Sheet for shop-front

HPH エイチ・ピー・エイチ

バイヤー自身がディレクターも務めてショップの個性を演出

A unique store whose buyer also works as a creative director

戦略を読み解く 3 key words

洗練された大人の男の美意識とスタイルを追求

大人の美意識をもつ男性に向けた、洋服とアクセサリーのセレクトショップ。"グラマラスの時代を過ごした、次のセンス"をキーワードに、CDも兼ねるバイヤーが国内外からクリエイティブなアイテムを集め、洗練された大人の着こなしを提案する。

ショップツールで美意識の高さを演出する

バイヤーの審美眼＝ショップで扱う商品のラインナップ自体がブランディングの核。その価値を更に高めるものとして、ショップまわりのグラッフィクツールを重視しており、ショップ全体を俯瞰したときに"クリエイティブな印象"を感じさせることを目指す。

デザインのテーマをブランドカラーで象徴

デザインのキーワードは"シック、シンプル"で、プラスαとして"とんがった雰囲気"の演出を心がける。その象徴としてブランドカラーに黒、白、こけ色の緑の組み合わせを選んだ。またアイキャッチに"BEAUTYとLUCKYのシンボル"としてフクロウを使う。

3 key words

Seeking an aesthetic for the sophisticated gentleman

A select shop carrying clothing an accessories for the gentlemen with refined taste. "Fashion sense for the post-glamour era" is the watchword for the store's buyer, who seeks out creative items both inside and outside Japan to assemble a lineup of stylish fashions for the sophisticated gentleman.

Promoting the store's high aesthetic sense

The buyer's keen eye translates into the store's product offerings -- and forms the core of the brand. In order to increase the value of that branding even further, emphasize the use of graphic tools in the area around the store, giving consumers a "creative impression" of the store as a whole.

Symbolizing design themes with brand color

Keywords for the promotion's visual design are "chic" and "simple", with an added overtone of "discriminating atmosphere". Use a combination of black, white and subdued green to symbolize these themes, and the image of an owl as a symbol of "beauty" and "luck".

Logo

シンプルなロゴに"フクロウ"と"黒い月"を組み合わせてロゴマークとした。フクロウはバラの茨を感じさせるタッチを得意とするイラストレーターによるもの。

The symbolic logo mark combines an owl with a black moon. The image of the owl was drawn by an illustrator with a style reminiscent of a rosebush's thorns.

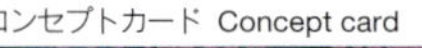

コンセプトカード Concept card

Shop

ショップバッグ
Shop bag

■CL= ジェネレーション Generation Inc.
■CD + Buyer= 上尾智昭 Tomoaki Ueo ■D= 佐野智子 Satoko Sano ■D= 高橋史明 Fumiaki Takahashi ■D= 鈴木祐子 Yuko Suzuki ■I= GEM ■DF= ハレオ HARÉO ■S= ジェネレーション Generation Inc.

DM

HPH

オープニングカタログ
Opening catalog

Chez Toi シェトワ

ブランドのメッセージをイラスト中心のグラフィックに込めて発信
Disseminating brand message through illustration-based graphics

戦略を読み解く 3 key words

"普通の服" と生活を楽しむ心で毎日をお洒落に

20代を中心とする女性向けのファッションブランド。"お洒落というのは決して着飾ることだけではない。毎日着たい -普通の服- に身を包み、生活のなかからお洒落なものを見つけることで、日々の暮らしを素敵なものにしてほしい" というメッセージを送る。

小型ツールを通した顧客とのコミュニケーション

ユーザーの手に届く小型グラフィックの制作を大切にし、ひとつひとつのツールにメッセージを込める。特に力を入れているカタログには「Chez Moi（わたしの家）」と名付け、ブランドのコンセプトを伝えるメッセージブックとしての役割も与えている。

イラストのみのビジュアルでイメージを膨らませる

"毎日の一部として楽しむお洒落" をイラストによって表現。イラストに登場する洋服はもちろん商品をモチーフにしたものではあるが、写真は使わずにイラストのみのビジュアルによって、見る人が感じるイメージを更に膨らませたいと願う。

3 key words

Dress up every day with fun-loving everyday clothes

The fashion brand targets women in their twenties with the message, "Chicness is not merely dressing up". Discover elegance in your daily lifestyle with these everyday clothes, and make each moment marvelous."

Communicating with customers through small-scale promotional tools

Focus on small-scale graphics that each bring a message directly into the customer's hands. Make the catalog the centerpiece, creating a message book that conveys the brand concept and naming it "Chez Moi (my house)".

Illustrated visuals expand brand image

Illustrations represent the concept, "enjoy a little bit of elegance each day". Using illustrations of product items that follow the brand motif rather than photographs lets the brand image expand in the mind of the viewer.

Naming

ショップ名はフランス語で「きみの家」という意味。友達の家に遊びに行くような感覚で、ショッピングを楽しんでもらいたいという気持ちを込めた。ロゴはイラストレーターによる手書き文字。

The store name means "your house" in French, conveying the sense that the company wants customers to come in and enjoy themselves as if they were visiting a friend's house. The logo consists of letters hand-drawn by an illustrator.

ショップカード Shop card

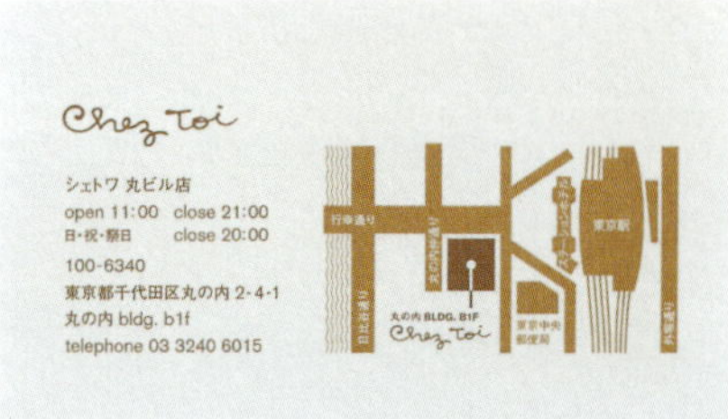

ショップバッグ Shop bag

■CL= シェトワ Chez Toi co., ltd.
■D= 三木俊一 Shun-ichi Miki ■I= 川口澄子 Sumico Kawaguchi ■DF= 文京図案室 Bunkyo-Zuan-Shitsu ■S= 文京図案室 Bunkyo-Zuan-Shitsu

タグ Tag

Shop

ノベルティ Novelty

カタログ Catalog

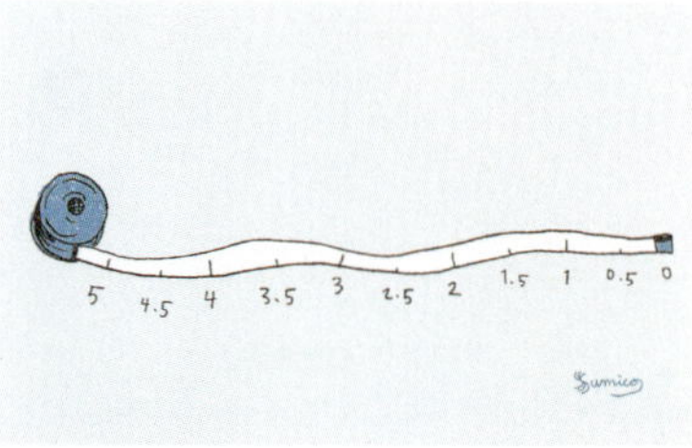

ポストカード Postcard

カタログ Catalog

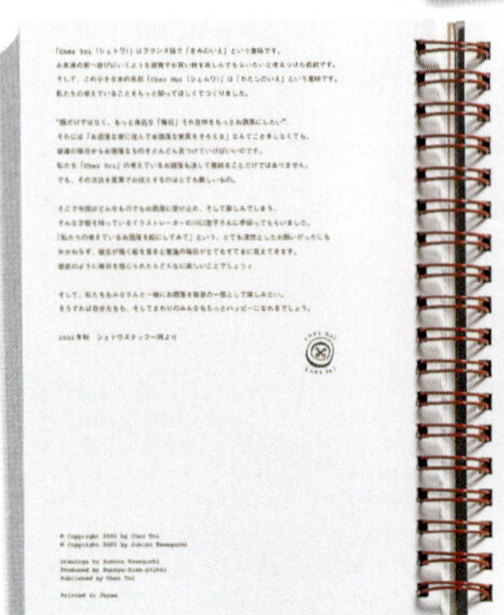

カタログ Catalog

LOCOMOTION

Chez moi series #3

DM

CANNABIS カンナビス

ユニークなショップコンセプトそのもので同業他店と一線を画す
Distinguishing a unique shop from its competitors

戦略を読み解く 3 key words

テーマは "アウトサイダーが引き寄せられる場所"

メンズファッションのセレクトショップで、"カルチャーやアート" を切り口にした商品構成にこだわる。"タバコも酒も女も全部好き" というのがショップの個性を語るフレーズであり、"アウトサイダーの集う場所" としての店作りが目標。

PRの一環でクリエイターに作品発表の場を提供

クリエイター達の合同展示会をプロデュースし、ショップの一角をギャラリースペースとして開放。そうした意欲的な取り組みやスタンスをブランディングの柱に据えながら、グラフィックも含めた店自体が醸し出す空気感でショップの個性を主張する。

"知的でセンスのいい不良" をイメージして制作

グラフィックのキーワードは "不良性と洗練性"。アウトサイダー的な不良っぽさをメインテーマとしながらも、下品な方向に走っていない知的なビジュアルを目指す。商品そのものを前面に出すことはせず、あくまでイメージを重視したデザインにこだわっている。

3 key words

A place where outsiders are insiders

The shop carries a selective lineup of men's goods chosen for their artistic or cultural value. The catchphrase "there's no tobacco, alcohol or woman we don't like" expresses the individuality of the store, founded as a "place where outsiders can gather".

Creating exhibition opportunities for creators as part of PR

As part of the promotional campaign, turn a corner of the shop into a gallery space for exhibitions of creator groups. Make that enthusiastic support for creators a cornerstone of the branding effort, and use the atmosphere of the store to emphasize its individuality in graphic promotional tools and other means.

"Intelligent, fashionable delinquency" as an image

The keywords for the graphic design are "delinquency" and "intelligence". Use smart, savvy visuals to avoid making the products look low-quality, but make "rebellious hooligan" the main theme. Design should give precedence to image, rather than product.

Naming

CANNABISは英語で「マリファナ」の意味で、ショップコンセプトを象徴させる言葉として選んだ。

Cannabis is another word for "marijuana", and was selected to symbolize the shop concept.

CANNABIS

Shop

ショップバッグ Shop bag

■CL= ジェネレーション Generation Inc.
■CD + Buyer= 南 貴之 Takayuki Minami ■AD= Catalog / HIRO (FEMME) ■AD= DM 5 / Virgin Tryhard ■AD + D= DM 1 - 4 / 野中孝義 Takayoshi Nonaka ■P= Catalog / KEITARROW (F.I.O)
■P= DM 1 / 東 花行 Hanayuki Higashi ■S= ジェネレーション Generation Inc.

2003春／夏カタログ 2003 S/S Catalog

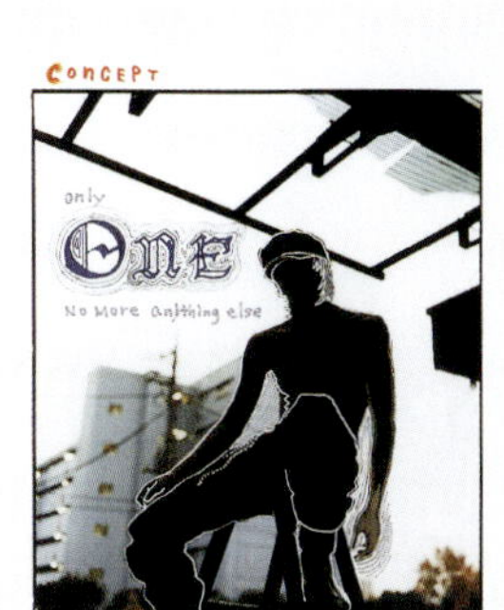

DM 1

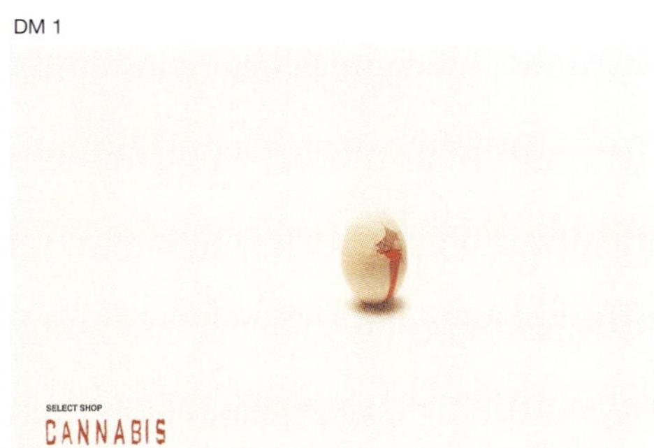

展示会DM 2 Exhibition DM 2

展示会DM 3 Exhibition DM 3

DM 4

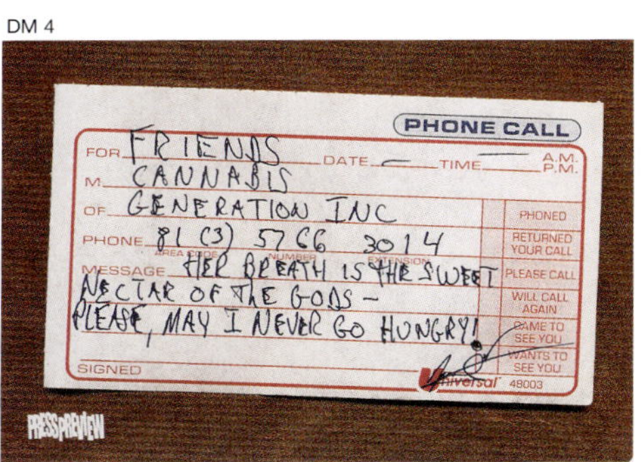

展示会DM 5 Exhibition DM 5

Rouge vif ルージュ・ヴィフ

何気ない日常を大切に。女性を輝かせるスタイリングを提案

Radiant style for women's casual, everyday lives

戦略を読み解く 3 key words

大人の女性のカジュアルな日常着を提案

自然な大人っぽさとプライベートで見せる無邪気さを織り交ぜたスタイリングを基本にカジュアルな日常着を提案している。この基本ラインのほかに、おでかけ着を提案する「Rouge Foncé（ルージュ・フォンセ）」がある。

年5回の展示会でブランドイメージを確立

春夏と秋冬のシーズンに合わせ5回の展示会を開催。シーズンテーマに添ったツールを制作している。カタログ、DMは顧客を中心に配付。雑誌広告の際は20代半ばの女性が購読層である雑誌へ出稿し、ターゲットに照準を合わせたプロモーションを展開している。

シーズンテーマに添ったビジュアルを展開

ショップバッグや下げ札など通年使用するツールは色を抑え、デザインもシンプルに統一。シーズン立ち上げごとに用意するビジュアルでテーマおよびブランドコンセプトを発信し、ブランドイメージの確立を訴求している。

3 key words

Casual, everyday clothing for women

The company offers a line of casual clothing for women styled on a natural sense of maturity mixed with the childlike innocence in every woman's heart. Additionally, they offer a line of dress wear under the label "Rouge Forcé".

Five shows a year establish brand image

Hold five fashion shows per year planned around the spring-summer and fall-winter fashion seasons. Create promotional tools around each season's theme. Distribute catalogs and direct mail advertisements, focusing on pre-existing customers. Use advertisements in magazines with strong readership among women in their mid-to-late twenties, and target them with focused promotions.

Visuals match each season's theme

Control the colors of year-round items, such as shopping bags and hang tags, and keep the design simple and consistent. Use the seasonal visual advertisements to communicate the seasonal theme and the overall brand concept, continually seeking to reinforce brand image.

Naming

フランスの伝統色のひとつで、生き生きとした輝く赤を意味する。

One of the traditional French colors, "rouge vif" is a bright, vivid shade of red.

Rouge vif

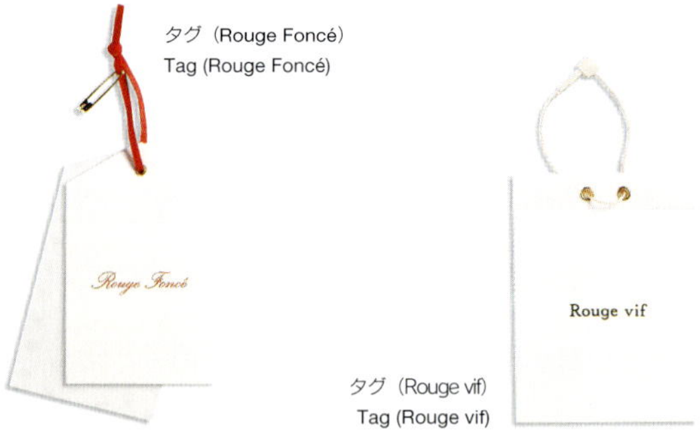

タグ（Rouge Foncé）
Tag (Rouge Foncé)

タグ（Rouge vif）
Tag (Rouge vif)

ショップバッグ Shop bag

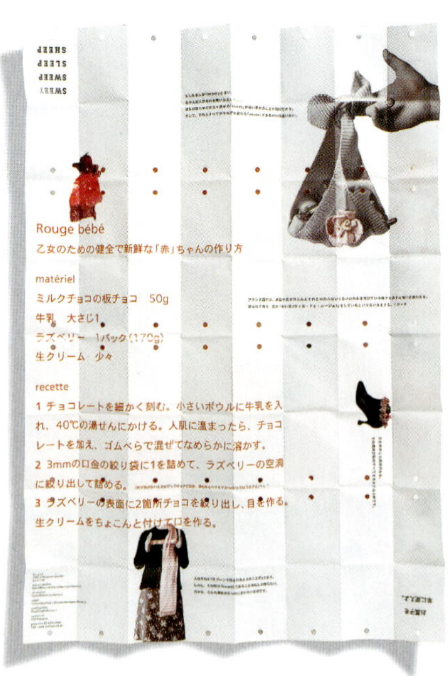

イメージビジュアル兼ノベルティ Image visual & Novelty

2002 - 2003 秋／冬「Sweet trad」

女性が甘さの裏に秘めている毒をさらりと表現。イメージビジュアルを小さく折りたたみ、穴を開けてリングで止めた。表面にはSweetsの写真、裏面には『Rouge bebe 乙女のための健全で新鮮な「赤」ちゃんの作り方』というレシピが載っている。

2002 - 2003 Autumn/winter 「Sweet trad」

Expresses the bite lurking behind a woman's sweetness. Image visuals are folded up and ring bound. The front cover features a photograph of sweets, the back a recipe for how to create a fresh and wholesome "Rouge bebe".

■ CL= アバハウスインターナショナル Abahouse International
■ S= アバハウスインターナショナル Abahouse International

カタログ Catalog

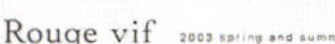

Shop

DM

ポスター Poster

2003 春／夏「Working girl」

June & Luluという姉妹をメインビジュアルに設定。アクティブで格好いいイメージのJuneと、キュートで清楚なイメージのLulu。タイプの異なる2人のワードローブをハイセンスな日常着として提案している。

2003 Spring/summer 「Working girl」

Two sisters -- active, good-looking June and cute and tidy Lulu -- as the main visuals proposing high-sensibility, everyday wardrobes for two different personalities.

no quiet ノークワイエット

トータルプロデュースで“ブランドイメージのデザイン”を実践
Total brand image design in practice

戦略を読み解く 3 key words

オリジナルスタイルにこだわった物作りを目指す
プロダクトからグラフィックまで幅広く手がけるデザイナーが主宰するワークショップ的スペース。“万人に受けることを目的としない、独自のスタイルをもった物作り”をコンセプトに、身近なアイテムを新しい視点で捉えた、企画性のある商品を提案する。

万人ではなくブランド賛同者に向けたイメージ作り
“万人受けを目的としない”ショップであるため、あえてマス媒体でのプロモーションは重視しない。商品企画・デザインはもちろん、店舗設計からあらゆるショップツールのデザインまでを主宰者本人が行い、“ブランドイメージをデザイン”している。

商品の個性や空気感を伝えるショップツール
店舗やロゴも含めたショップツールの制作では、どこをクローズアップしても一貫して「no quiet」のイメージが感じられるようにデザイン。“浮遊感、透明感、反復、微妙なバランス感覚”といった、商品特性のキーワードをビジュアル化している。

3 key words

Creating products with entirely original style
A workshop-like space overseen by a designer involved in everything from product to graphic design. It offers a lineup of familiar items inventively redesigned from a new viewpoint, under the concept "creating not to appeal to the masses, but to make things with a unique style".

A brand image aimed at like-minded people, not the masses
Since the shop "does not appeal to the masses", spend little effort on promoting it through the mass media. Communicate the brand image through the product planning and design, store interior and promotional tools designed by the principal director.

Promotional tools stress the shop's uniqueness and atmosphere
Design the brand logo and store promotional tools to consistently project the "no quiet" image even in their smallest details. Create a visual representation of the product characteristic keywords, "floating -- transparent -- recursive -- delicate sense of balance".

Naming

“no quiet=黙ってはいられない”という意味のブランド名に、物作りに対するこだわりの気持ちを込めた。

The brand name "no quiet" implies "one cannot be silent", referring to the store's attitude towards creativity.

kunikazu hoshiba

ショップカード＆DM Shop card & DM

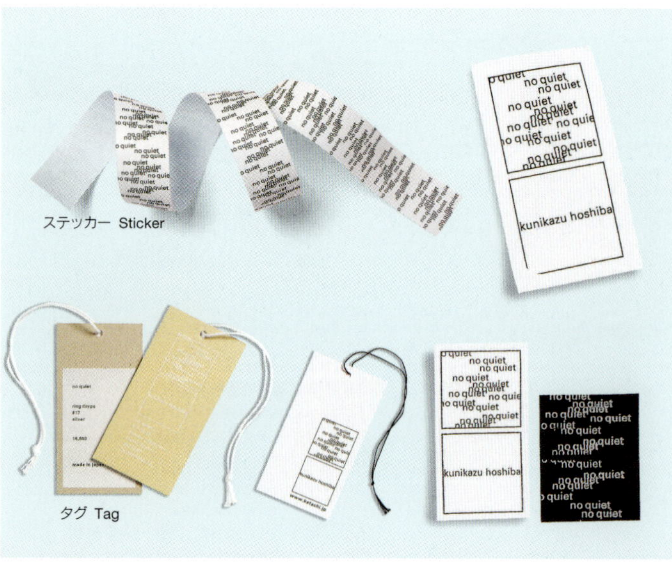

ステッカー Sticker

タグ Tag

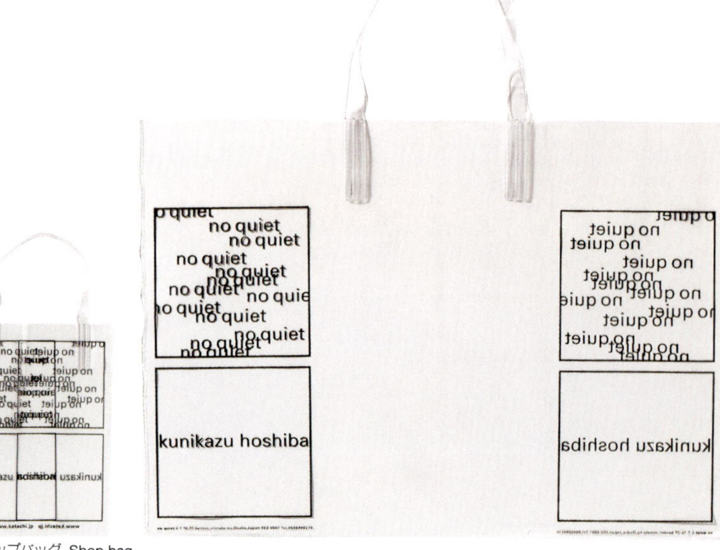

ショップバッグ Shop bag

■CL= カタチ katachi
■D= 干場 邦一 Kunikazu Hoshiba ■S= カタチ katachi

ポスター Poster

ポスター Poster

Shop

DM

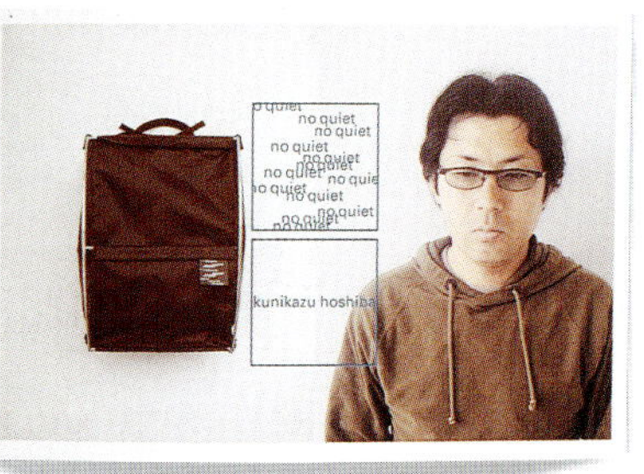

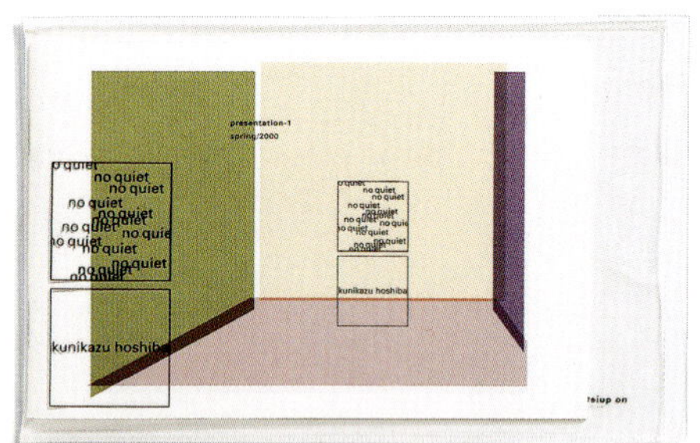

カタログ Catalog

カタログ Catalog

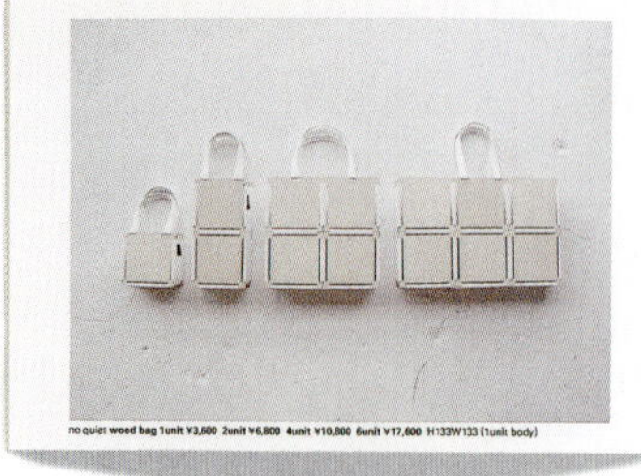

DM

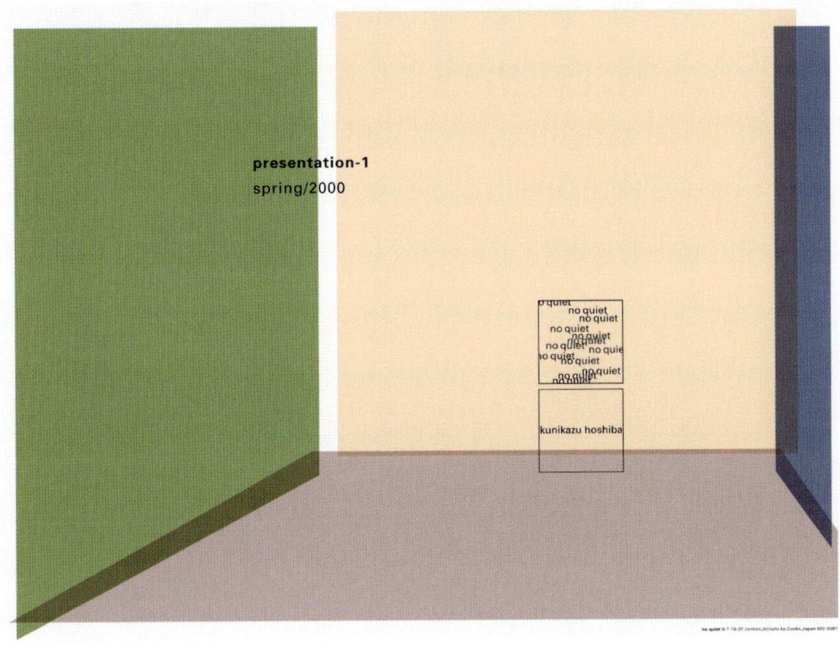

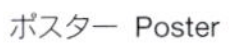

ポスター　Poster

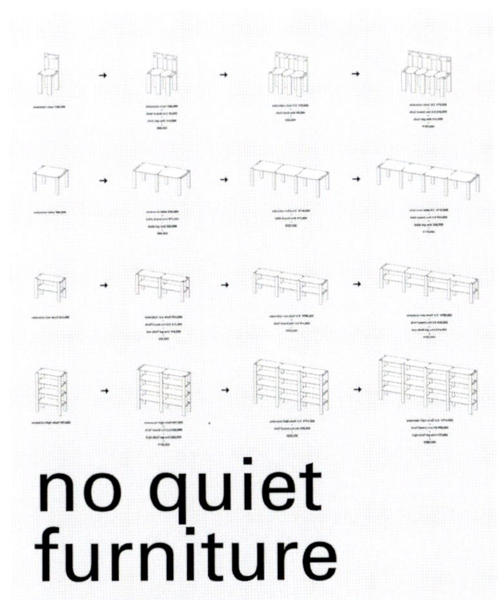

ポスター　Poster

現状のマーケットに合わせて再構築したVIの浸透を図る

Resigning visual imagery in response to today's market

戦略を読み解く 3 key words

キーワードは“クリエイティブでフレンドリー”

ウイメンズにメンズ、キッズ、マタニティ、雑貨など幅広いラインを揃えた、洋服と雑貨を扱うショップ。“クリエイティブでフレンドリー”をキーワードにした商品の提供で、“洋服というものの楽しさ、生活の楽しさ”を提案していきたいと考える。

長期的ビジョンに立ってショップのVIを再構築

既存のロゴマークと現在のショップコンセプトの間にズレが生じていた2002年春、新規3店舗のオープンを機にVIを一新。“時代に左右されない不変的価値”がテーマの新たなロゴマークは“葉”をモチーフとしながらも展開によって様々にイメージが膨らむ。

ショップの新たな“顔”と、“空気感”をアピール

マス広告から小型のSPツールまで、あらゆるグラフィックにロゴマークを展開させることで新たなVIの浸透を図る。それにプラスして新聞の折り込み広告などではショップのもつ“空気感”を伝えたいと考え、イメージ写真や印象的なコピーで構成した。

3 key words

Keywords: "Creative" and "Friendly"

The shop carries a wide variety of clothing and miscellaneous goods, including men's, women's, kids' and maternity clothing and sundry other products. Offering products that are "creative" and "friendly", the store provides customers "the fun of clothing, and the fun of life".

Redesigning visual imagery along a long-term vision

Resolve the gap between the store concept and the existing logo by using the opening of three new shops as an opportunity to renew the brand's visual imagery. Develop a new brand logo that will have "lasting value, unaffected by time", designing it with a "leaf" motif and developing it into a wide variety of promotional imagery.

Appealing to customers with a new retail face and atmosphere

From mass media advertisements to small-scale promotional tools, increase brand penetration by using the new visual imagery, developed using the new brand logo, far and wide. Use newspaper inserts with photos and impactful copy to communicate to consumers the store's new retail atmosphere.

Naming

ネーミングは、不変的な価値観を大切にするというショップのスタンスを、いつの時代でも人間が常に必要とする“自然”を強くイメージさせる“緑”に投影したもの。

The brand name reflects the importance the store places on lasting value through the word "green", which strongly suggests images of "nature" -- a lasting necessity for humanity.

united arrows
green label relaxing

ショップカード Shop card

タグ Tag

ショップバッグ Shop bag

■CL= ユナイテッドアローズ UNITED ARROWS LTD. ■S= ユナイテッドアローズ UNITED ARROWS LTD.
<Shop card, Tag> ■Production= ユナイテッドアローズ UNITED ARROWS LTD. ■D= 伊東淳一 Junichi Ito <Shop bag> ■Agency & Production= サン・アド SUN-AD COMPANY LIMITED ■AD= 葛西 薫 Kaoru Kasai
■D= 池田泰幸 Yasuyuki Ikeda ■D= 戸田かおり Kaori Toda ■Producer= 守屋その子 Sonoko Moriya ■Producer= 徳永あかね Akane Tokunaga ■DF= サン・アド SUN-AD COMPANY LIMITED

新聞折り込み広告
2003年春の小倉店のオープンに合わせたもので、観音開き4面の構成。1～3面では恋人同士が出会った頃を懐かしく振り返るストーリーが展開し、最終面では "Boy meets girl" のコピーが大きく躍るという、"出会いの春" を予感させる作り。"私たちブランドもあなたと出会いたい" という気持ちを込めた。

Inserted bill of newspaper
Four-page ad produced in conjunction with the Kokura store opening in spring 2003. Pages one through three, entitled "Boy meets girl" depict fond reminiscences of two lovers' first encounter, alluding to the coming of "a spring encounter" with the brand.

中吊り広告 Traffic AD

<Inserted bill of newspaper> ■ Agency & Production= サン・アド SUN-AD COMPANY LIMITED ■ CD= 葛西 薫 Kaoru Kasai ■ AD= 福地 掌 Sho Fukuchi ■ D= 安藤基広 Motohiro Ando ■ P= 上原 勇 Isamu Uehara ■ CW= 一倉 宏 Hiroshi Ichikura ■ I= 北山雅和 Masakazu Kitayama ■ Producer= 守屋その子 Sonoko Moriya ■ Producer= 徳永あかね Akane Tokunaga ■ DF=サン・アド SUN-AD COMPANY LIMITED
<Traffic AD> ■ Agency & Production= サン・アド SUN-AD COMPANY LIMITED ■ AD= 葛西 薫 Kaoru Kasai ■ D= 池田泰幸 Yasuyuki Ikeda ■ CW= 一倉 宏 Hiroshi Ichikura ■ Producer= 守屋その子 Sonoko Moriya ■ Producer= 徳永あかね Akane Tokunaga ■ DF= サン・アド SUN-AD COMPANY LIMITED

新聞折り込み広告
VIを一新した2002年春に出稿したもので、観音開きの8面という大きなスペースを使った。コンセプトは"買物に行こう"という気分に誘うこと。外側の4面は新たなVIを伝える情報面、内側の4面は春の開放感を感じさせるイメージ写真という構成になっている。

Inserted bill of newspaper
A generous eight pages devoted to promoting the brand's changed visual identity in spring 2002. Inspires the feeling "let's go shopping". The four outer pages convey the new visual identity, the inner pages feature photographic images that communicate the free and open spirit of spring.

<Inserted bill of newspaper> ■Agency & Production= サン・アド SUN-AD COMPANY LIMITED ■AD= 葛西　薫 Kaoru Kasai ■D= 長谷川美幸 Miyuki Hasegawa ■P= 辻　佐織（イメージ） Saori Tsuji (Image photo) ■P= 上原　勇（商品） Isamu Uehara (Product photo) ■CW= 一倉　宏 Hiroshi Ichikura ■Producer= 守屋その子 Sonoko Moriya ■Producer= 徳永あかね Akane Tokunaga ■DF= サン・アド SUN-AD COMPANY LIMITED

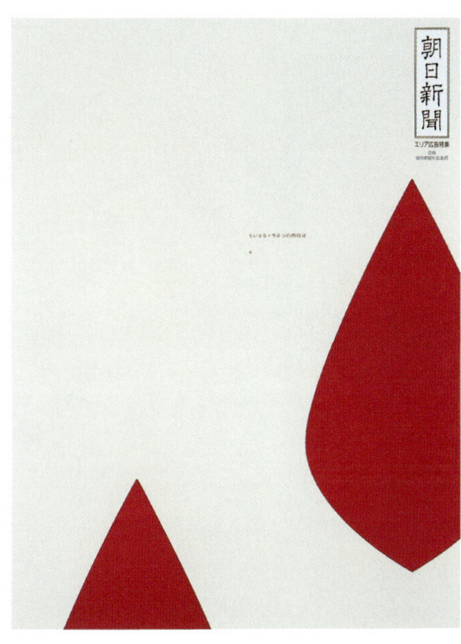

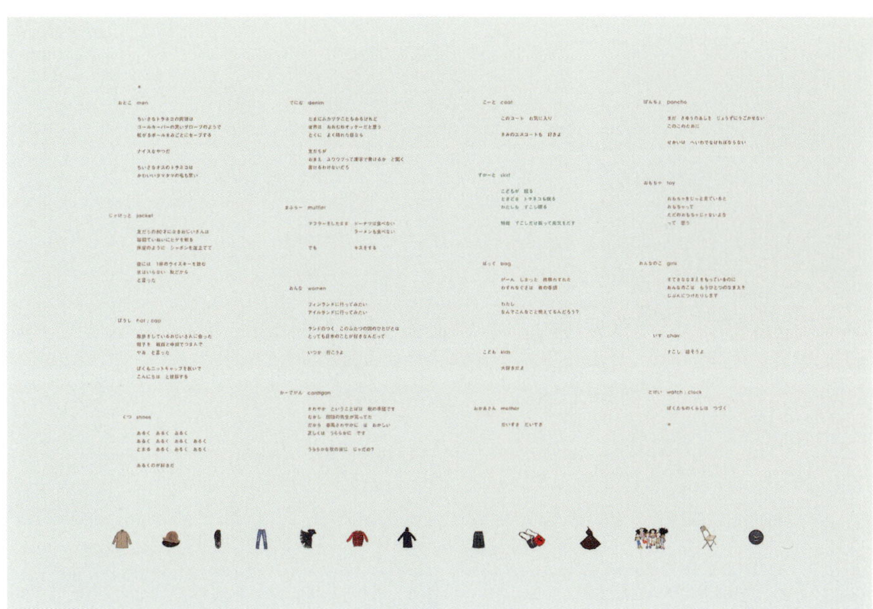

新聞折り込み広告
福岡店と名古屋店のオープンに合わせて2002年秋に出稿。春と同様の紙面構成になっている。

Inserted bill of newspaper
Printed in conjunction with the Fukuoka and Nagoya store openings in autumn 2002. Same page composition as the spring campaign.

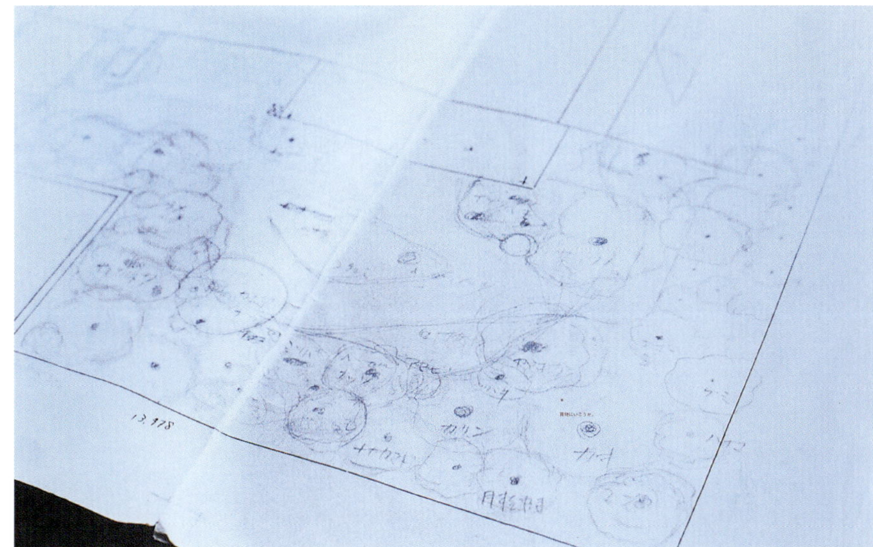

<Inserted bill of newspaper> ■Agency & Production= サン・アド SUN-AD COMPANY LIMITED ■CD= 葛西 薫 Kaoru Kasai ■AD= 福地 掌 Sho Fukuchi ■D= 安藤基広 Motohiro Ando ■P= 白井 綾（イメージ） Aya Shirai (Image photo) ■P= 上原 勇（商品） Isamu Uehara (Product photo) ■CW= 一倉 宏 Hiroshi Ichikura ■Producer= 守屋その子 Sonoko Moriya ■Producer= 徳永あかね Akane Tokunaga ■DF= サン・アド SUN-AD COMPANY LIMITED

2002-2003 秋／冬カタログ
2002-2003 A/W catalog

2003 春のカタログ 2003 Spring catalog

2003 夏のカタログ 2003 Summer catalog

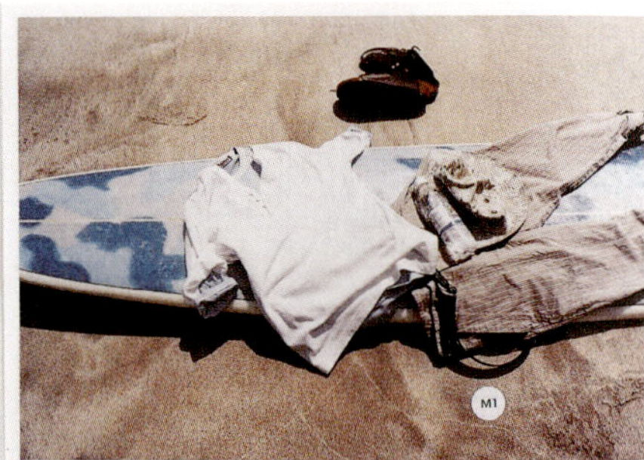

<2002-2003 A/W catalog> ■Agency & Production= サン・アド SUN-AD COMPANY LIMITED ■AD= 福地 掌 Sho Fukuchi ■D= 安藤基広 Motohiro Ando ■P= 白井 綾（イメージ） Aya Shirai (Image photo) ■P= 上原 勇（商品） Isamu Uehara (Product photo) ■Stylist= マツイ カヲリ Kaori Matsui ■Producer= 守屋その子 Sonoko Moriya ■Producer= 徳永あかね Akane Tokunaga ■DF= サン・アド SUN-AD COMPANY LIMITED

<2003 Spring catalog> ■Agency & Production= サン・アド SUN-AD COMPANY LIMITED ■AD= 福地 掌 Sho Fukuchi ■D= 安藤基広 Motohiro Ando ■P= 野口貴司 Takashi Noguchi ■I= 北山雅和 Masakazu Kitayama ■Stylist= マツイ カヲリ Kaori Matsui ■Producer= 守屋その子 Sonoko Moriya ■Producer= 徳永あかね Akane Tokunaga ■DF= サン・アド SUN-AD COMPANY LIMITED

<2003 Summer catalog> ■Agency & Production= サン・アド SUN-AD COMPANY LIMITED ■AD= 福地 掌 Sho Fukuchi ■D= 安藤基広 Motohiro Ando ■P= 永禮 賢 Satoshi Nagare ■Stylist= マツイ カヲリ Kaori Matsui ■Producer= 守屋その子 Sonoko Moriya ■Producer= 徳永あかね Akane Tokunaga ■DF= サン・アド SUN-AD COMPANY LIMITED

メンズスーツのカタログ
メンズスーツ「green label relaxing SUIT」のカタログ。"男を感じさせる"イメージとして、外国製のシガレットボックスをモチーフにしてパッケージをデザイン。中身はカード型のカタログになっており、プラスαとして「緑の男」というショートストーリーを挿入。物語に登場する5人の男のイニシャルをつなげると"GREEN"になるという仕掛け。

Men's suit catalog
The men's suit line catalog. Packaging design with foreign cigarette packages as a motif for a masculine-feeling image. The inside pages are structured like a card catalog, featuring the "Green men" story. The first initial of the five characters spell "GREEN".

マタニティウエアのカタログ Maternity catalog

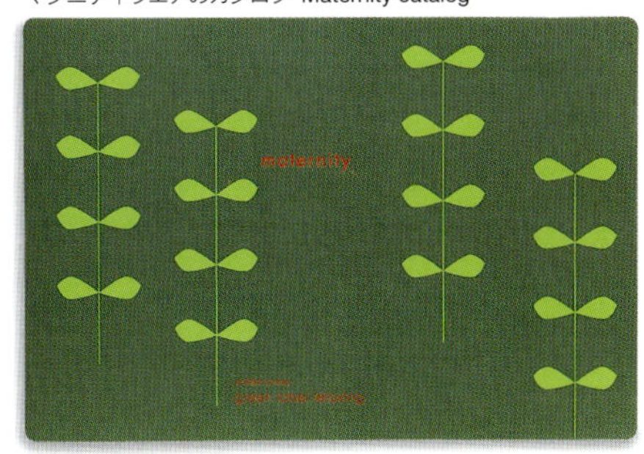

<Men's suit catalog> ■Agency & Production= サン・アド SUN-AD COMPANY LIMITED ■AD= 小島潤一 Junichi Kojima ■P= 上原 勇 Isamu Uehara ■D= 白井陽平 Yohei Shirai ■CW= 蛭田瑞穂 Mizuho Hiruta ■Stylist= マツイ カヲリ Kaori Matsui ■Producer= 守屋その子 Sonoko Moriya ■Producer = 徳永あかね Akane Tokunaga ■DF= サン・アド SUN-AD COMPANY LIMITED
<Maternity catalog> ■Agency & Production= サン・アド SUN-AD COMPANY LIMITED ■AD + D= 青葉淑美 Yoshimi Aoba ■P= 上原 勇 Isamu Uehara ■Stylist= マツイ カヲリ Kaori Matsui ■Producer= 守屋その子 Sonoko Moriya ■Producer= 徳永あかね Akane Tokunaga ■DF= サン・アド SUN-AD COMPANY LIMITED

CLASSICS the Small Luxury クラシクス ザ スモール ラグジュアリ

ハンカチーフに付加価値を付け、特別な一枚へ
Adding value to the handkerchief

戦略を読み解く 3 key words

世界初のハンカチーフ専門店

六本木ヒルズのウエストウォークにオープンした世界で初めてのハンカチーフ専門店。100年以上にわたってハンカチーフづくりに携わってきた老舗・ブルーミング中西が、長年の知識・経験を生かして、新しいハンカチーフの在り方を提案している。

商品&ディスプレイの独自性で広がる世界

大規模な広告展開はしていないが、唯一、ここだけで購入できる商品というオリジナリティが注目を集め、集客に結び付いている。店内は、ハンカチーフをオブジェ風に展示する、額縁に入れるなど、各コーナーごとに変化を持たせたディスプレイとなっている。

世界で一枚の特別なハンカチーフを提供

オリジナルのハンカチーフにさらに付加価値をプラスするよう、動植物や天使など101種類にもおよぶモチーフをアイコン化し、ハンカチーフに刺繍するオーダーメイドコレクション（ボディーガード）を展開。イニシャル（アルファベット1文字）の刺繍もあり。

3 key words

The world's first handkerchief specialty shop

The world's first handkerchief specialty shop, opened on the West Walk of Roppongi Hills. With over one hundred years of experience in making handkerchiefs, the long-established Blooming Nakanishi decided to put its knowledge and experience to work in a search for a new paradigm for the handkerchief.

Unique products and display draw customers

Without performing a large-scale promotional campaign, the singular nature of the store and its products capture public attention and draw customers. Within the store, the handkerchiefs are treated like objets d'art, framed and displayed slightly differently in each corner of the store.

Offering unique, only-one-in-existence handkerchiefs

The company's bespoke collection, "Bodyguard", adds value over and above the company's high-quality original products with design motifs -- 101 varieties of fauna and flora, earthly and heavenly -- embroidered on demand. They also offer monogram embroidery.

Naming

「第一級の、上品な密やかな贅沢」という意味を持つ。

The brand name communicates the idea of "top-class, high quality secret luxury".

CLASSICS THE SMALL LUXURY

Shop

リボン Ribbon

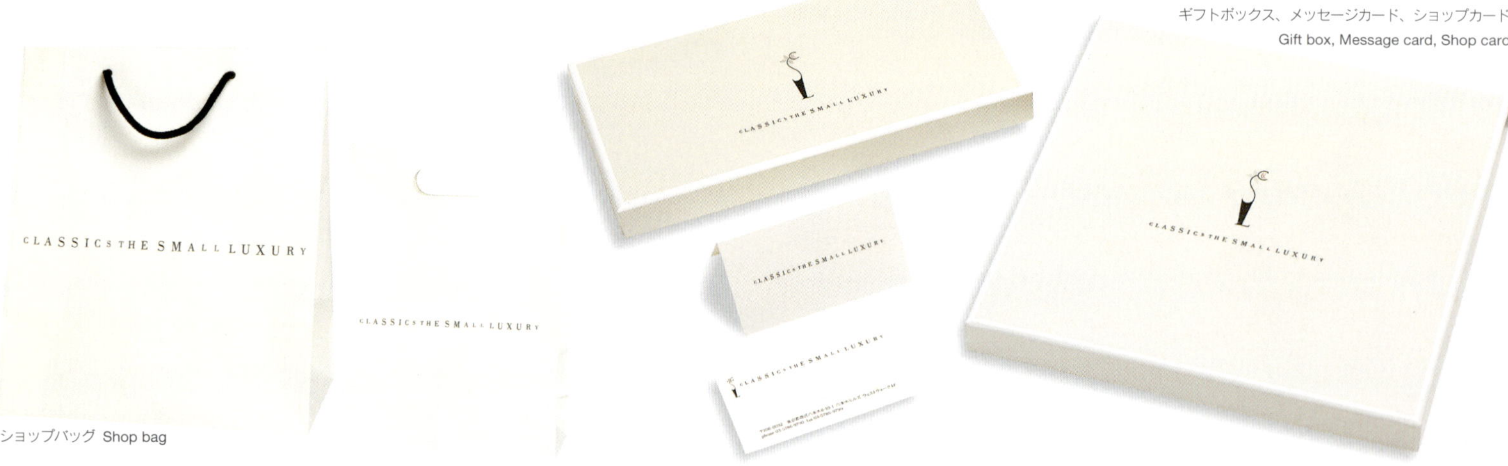

ショップバッグ Shop bag

ギフトボックス、メッセージカード、ショップカード
Gift box, Message card, Shop card

■CL= ブルーミング中西 BLOOMING NAKANISHI
■Producer= 秋山道男 Michio Akiyama ■AD + D= 奥村靫正 Yukimasa Okumura ■D= 井上嗣也 Tsuguya Inoue ■D= 三浦太郎 Taro Miura ■D= 高橋 歩 Ayumi Takahashi
■DF= ザ・ステューディオ・トウキョウ・ジャパン The Studio Tokyo Japan ■S= ブルーミング中西 BLOOMING NAKANISHI

Shop

カタログ（オーダーメイドコレクション）
「ボディーガード」とアルファベットの2種。アルファベットは各字とも28種のデザイン、12色から好きなものを選べる。

Catalog (A custom made collection)
"Bodyguard" and two alphabets. Customers can choose from these typestyles for individual letters, as well as 28 designs and 12 colors.

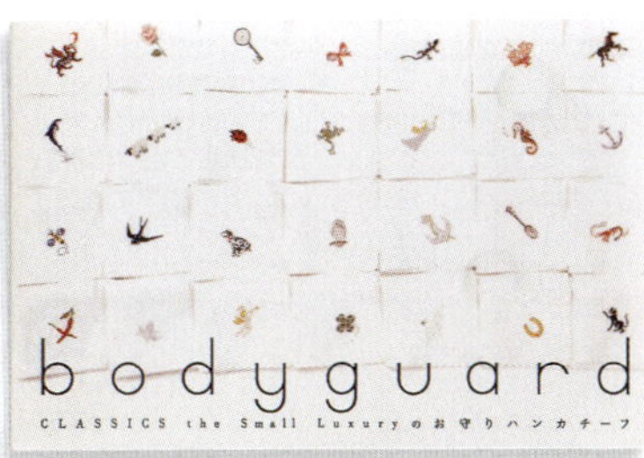

リーフレット Leaflet

TOUCH タッチ

流通販路を絞った“特別な商品”の価値を高めるグラフィックと空間

Graphics and spatial design add value to a unique product line

戦略を読み解く 3 key words

肌の感覚を大事にすることは生活を豊かにすること

“肌がうれしいと、生きていることがうれしくなる”をキャッチフレーズに、天然素材のタオルや無添加の石鹸など、素材にこだわった生活用品を販売する。“身体に触れる様々な物について考えることを通して、生活文化を豊かにしていく”ことを提案。

“特別な”商品価値を更に高めるブランディング

メーカーブランドの直営ショップであるため、取り扱う製品は「TOUCH」でしか買えない“特別なもの”ばかり。その商品価値を高めるプロモーションとして、ショップの空間設計をはじめ、ロゴマークのデザインやギフトボックスの制作にこだわった。

“簡素な贅沢”にブランドの誇りを添えたデザイン

商品と空間（店舗）、グラッフィックの全てに通じるキーワードは“簡素な贅沢”。グラフィックではベーシックな基本ロゴをもとに、素材をイメージさせる“綿の花”や“綿畑”を添えて、メーカーブランドならではの強みやこだわりを表現している。

3 key words

Take care of your skin for full and happy life

"Happy skin makes living happier" is the catchphrase for this line of products made from select ingredients, such as natural-fiber towels and soaps with no artificial ingredients. The company "makes your life richer by improving the many things that touch your body".

Branding that emphasizes the value of "special" products

Retail outlets directly managed by the manufacturer sell products consumers have to TOUCH to buy. The promotion increases the value of this special product line by designing store interiors and a brand logo, and creating gift bags.

Design that promotes a "simple elegance"

The products, store interiors (i.e., the retail outlet) and promotional graphics all communicate the keyword "simple elegance". The graphics are based on a simple logo accompanied by images of cotton flowers or fields of cotton, expressing the singular nature of the brand's products and the select ingredients used in making them.

Logo

基本ロゴはベーシックでありながらテイストを感じさせるデザインにし、“浄化することによって生まれる豊かさ”を表現。このロゴをスタンダードにして様々なビジュアルに展開させている。

The brand logo has a basic yet tasteful design that expresses "richness born from purification". The brand logo becomes a uniform element in a variety of visual images.

TOUCH

Shop

ギフトボックス Gift box

メッセージカード Message card

■CL= 内野 UCHINO CO., LTD.
■CD= 秋山道男 Michio Akiyama ■AD + D= 仲條正義 Masayoshi Nakajo ■Space Planner= 植木莞爾 Kanji Ueki ■DF= 仲條デザイン事務所 Nakajo Design Office ■S= 内野 UCHINO CO., LTD.

Shop
"知性、秩序、素朴"をテーマに設計された店舗。木材や溶岩といった自然素材の質感を生かした空間になっている。

Shop
Store designed based in the theme "intelligence, systematic, simple" exploiting the qualities of wood and lava stone as materials.

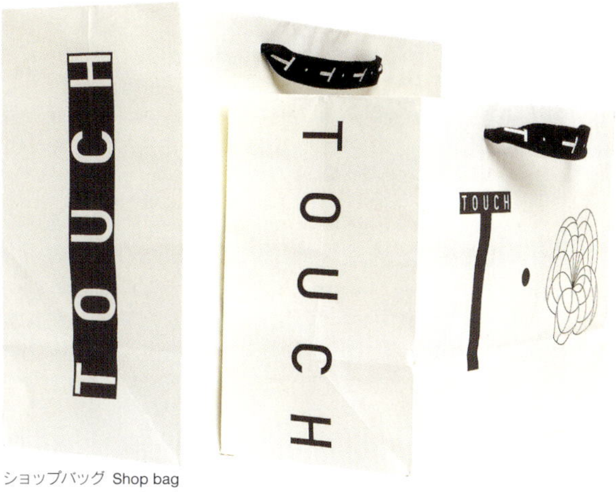

ショップバッグ Shop bag

商品 Product

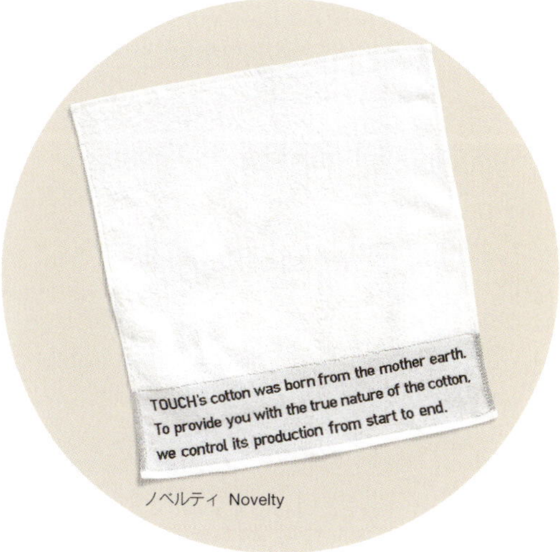

TOUCH's cotton was born from the mother earth.
To provide you with the true nature of the cotton,
we control its production from start to end.

ノベルティ Novelty

ポストカード Postcard

私たちの、身体という小自然に呼応する、自然からの希少な贈り物。
"マザーコットン"コレクション：スビンゴールド
Suvin Gold

スビンはインドの在来種スジャータを父に、海島綿を母に生まれた、栽培種としては世界一細くしなやかな繊維を持つ超長綿です。スジャータという品種名と海島綿の栽培されるセントビンセント島からスビンと銘名されました。現在では世界でただ一ヶ所、インド南部、タミールナドゥ州のアップスァミ氏の農場だけで栽培され、手作業を中心とした農法によって宝石のように大切に育てられています。ＴＯＵＣＨはこの希少な綿花をさらに厳選し、44ミリ以上の超長繊維だけを使用し、この超長繊維の特性をフルに活かすために、コーミング加工によって短繊維を取り除き、均一な長い繊維だけの美しい糸に仕上ました。利点は、強く清浄な糸をうむこと、均一に引き揃えられた超長繊維が素早く水分を吸収すること、に加え、スビンの特徴である繊細でしなやかな風合を際立たせています。使用を重ねるごとに吸水性が増し、弾力性としなやかさが長期に持続します。

With the Indian native variety of Sujata as its father and Sea Island cotton as its mother, Suvin was born as an extra-long staple cotton with the world's most superfine and supple fibers of all cultivated varieties. The name Suvin was taken from Sujata and the island of Saint Vincent, where Sea Island cotton is grown. Currently, this is cultivated in only one place in the world, on the farms of Mr. Apswami in Tamilnadu of south India. With agricultural methods mainly done by hand, it is raised with the care worthy of a jewel. TOUCH has gone a step further, carefully selecting among this rare cotton, using only extra-long fibers over 44mm. To fully maximize the qualities of these extra-long fibers, short fibers are removed with a combing process, leaving only beautiful yarns of evenly long fibers. An advantage of this is the creation of a strong and pure thread. Also, the evenly pulled extra-long fibers absorb moisture quickly, while the delicate and supple texture characteristic of Suvin is enhanced. As you use it over and over, absorption improves, and elasticity and suppleness is sustained for a long time.

WHITE HOUSE ホワイトハウス

"LOOK INSIDE" 中身を見たい! と思わせる仕掛けを展開

Inspiring people want to "look inside"

戦略を読み解く 3 key words

最先端技術とアイデンティティで新スタイルを提案

設立30年の老舗サロン。最先端の技術とアイデンティティを持ってヘアスタイルを提案しつづけることで、美容業界をリードし、躍進することを目指す。今回はリニューアルオープンにあたり、"LOOK INSIDE" をテーマに掲げた。

「見たい！ 開けたい！ 行きたい！」を狙って

テーマ "LOOK INSIDE" に基づき、「中身が見たくなる＝開けたくなる＝行きたくなる」を意識したプロモーションを展開。街で配布したノベルティにはプライスリストのほかにカード型の鏡をパッケージ。ポスターもノベルティと連動させて制作した。

イメージは鏡。光を反射する素材をセレクト

「自分を映す」のコンセプトから鏡をイメージ。ノベルティ・パッケージ、ポスターともに、光を反射する素材を使用した。ポスターにはタバコのパッケージに使用されている銀紙を使い、端のリブ部分はシルク印刷で表現している。

3 key words

Proposing new styles with cutting-edge technology and identity

A salon with a 30 year history. Lead and advance the beauty industry by continually proposing hair styles with identity that employ cutting-edge technology. Salon renovation based on the theme "look inside".

Making people want to look! open! go!

Develop promotion based on the premise that wanting to "look inside", inspires the desire to open (the door) and go (in). Distribute novelties around town that include a price list of services and a small card-sized mirror in the package. Design the poster to work in tandem with the novelties.

Mirror as image -- reflective materials

The mirror as an image stems from the concept of "reflection yourself". Use reflective materials for the novelty package and poster as well. The poster is printed on foil used in cigarette packaging; the ribbed section is silkscreen printed.

Naming

米国のホワイトハウスと同様に、「ホワイトカラー＝知的集団＝ハイクオリティ＝クリエイティブ」といった意味を持つ。カラーは大阪のメインストリート・御堂筋に面することから、ポプラ並木にちなんでグリーンをメインに据えた。

Like the American White House, white stands for an intellectual collective, high-quality, and creativity. The main color green is taken from the poplar-lined street in Osaka, Midosuji, the store looks out on.

THE HAIR
WHITEHOUSE
www.wh-style.com

ノベルティ Novelty

■ CL= ホワイトハウス WHITE HOUSE
■ CD + AD + D= 舛田 忍 Shinobu Masuda ■ P= 小野晃蔵 Kozo Ono ■ CW= 工 岳 Takeshi Takumi ■ Image Perth Design= 岡山伸也 Shinya Okayama ■ Producer= 寺谷真由美 Mayumi Teratani
■ Coordinator= 上田廉次郎 Renjiro Ueda ■ Planner= 遠藤美和子 Miwako Endo ■ Planner= 小塚奈歩 Naho Kozuka ■ DF= バーナーグラフィックス BURNER GRAPHICS ■ S= バーナーグラフィックス BURNER GRAPHICS

ポスター
「思わず開けたくなる（行きたくなる）」を狙って、ふわふわとした厚みを持たせている。

Poster
Thick and fluffy, designed to inspire viewers "open and enter"

ポスター Poster

Dear Men & Women

THE HAIR
WHITEHOUSE
www.wh-style.com

RENEWAL OPEN CAMPAIGN 〈キャンペーン期間▶11月末日まで〉

Part1 \ 下記コース&プログラムをキャンペーン特別価格《¥3,000》にてご体験!
（お一人様A.B.C.の中から、いずれか1つ1回のみ特別価格でご利用いただけます／要予約）

A.ネイルケア&カラーコース（アート2本付）	B.ウォーターサプライプログラム（シャンプー・ブロー付）	C.ヘッドスパプログラム（シャンプー・ブロー付）
通常価格〈ケア&カラー3,500円＋アート1,000円相当×2本＝¥5,500〉	通常価格〈¥7,000〉	通常価格〈¥8,000〉

Part2 \ ご来店のお客様に抽選でペア25組50名様、
「タラサ志摩全日空リゾート1泊（朝食付）タラソテラピー付プラン」ご招待!

ホワイトハウス心斎橋店はリニューアルに伴い、より一層お客さまに満足していただける新メニューを用意しました。ぜひご利用ください。

NEW MENU

Head Spa Program（ヘッドスパ プログラム）	Water Supply Program（ウォーターサプライ プログラム）	Hair Restoration Program（ヘアレストレーション プログラム）	Color Bath（カラーバス）	Nail（ネイル）
バックシャンプーをしながらの頭の温浴、マッサージ。頭から肩にかけてまるでスパに入ったような贅沢なリラクゼーションの世界に誘います。	毛根と毛髪から汚れを根こそぎ取り除き、髪に不足した水分とミネラルを特殊技術で効果的に補給することで、髪と地肌の美しさと健康を呼び覚まします。	クレンジング効果、育毛促進効果、ヘアトリートメント効果が3つ同時に得られるプログラム。抜け毛や髪の痩せ衰え、髪の傷みが気になる方はお試しください。	カラーリング後、色落ちした方のためにシャンプーをしながら短時間に手軽にカラーを入れ直します。	ヘアカラーやパーマの施術中に、ネイリストによるネイルを楽しんでいただきます。ブースでのスカルプチュアやアートもご用意してます。

OPEN
2002.10/11FRI.
WHITEHOUSE SHINSAIBASHI RENEWAL OPEN

ホワイトハウス心斎橋店
大阪市中央区西心斎橋1-4-5
御堂筋ビル3F
受付/AM11:00～PM8:00
1/1,2,3を除き年中無休
0120-66-7121

DM・年賀状 DM & New Year's card

Shop

HEAVENS ヘブンス

プレスの審美眼を意識した、明確なブランディングで集客に成功

Distinct branding, sensitive to the media aesthetic

戦略を読み解く 3 key words

質の高い“スタンダード・スタイル”を創り出す

“Tokyo Provides The New Standard” をコンセプトに掲げ、10代~20代のファッション感度の高い女性をメインターゲットとする美容室。奇をてらった極端なスタイルではなく、“ニュートラルななかに上品さを感じる” スタイルを提案する。

編集者へのアピールを通じて集客力をアップ

雑誌の記事ページにどれだけ紹介されるかが集客の鍵を握るという事実を踏まえ、編集者の目を意識したプロモーションを行う。美容室としては珍しい駅貼りポスターをはじめ、センスの良さを感じさせるツールの数々で、他店との差別化を図っている。

ひねりの効いた知的なデザインが見る人の心を掴む

ブランディングを盤石にするため、ひとりのADが一貫してディレクションを担当。目の肥えた編集者をも引きつけるデザインを目指し、品のよさを感じさせつつ、ひねりの効いたビジュアルを心がける。また、外人モデルは使わないというポリシーを貫く。

3 key words

Creating a high-quality standard in style

A chain of hair salons that targets highly fashion-conscious young women in their teens and twenties under the concept "Tokyo Provides The New Standard". Rather than ostentatious, extreme style, the company offers style that is "neutral, but elegant".

Increasing editorial appeal to increase customer appeal

Run a promotion designed to appeal to the eyes of magazine editors, relying on the fact that being introduced in the pages of a magazine is the key to attracting customers. Starting with railway station posters -- rare for a salon -- distinguish the chain from its competitors through a variety of promotional tools that communicate fashion sense.

Intelligent, witty design grabs the viewer's attention

To solidify branding efforts, one art director coordinates and directs the projects. Create design that will catch even the jaded eyes of magazine editors and communicate the high quality of the product, while incorporating witty and intelligent visuals. As well, stick to a policy of only using Japanese models.

Logo

店のコンセプトでもある “一見ベーシックだが、ちょっとひっかかりのあるデザイン” を心がけ、オリジナルのタイポグラフィをデザインした。

In keeping with the store's concept of "simple at first glance, but somehow entrancing", an original font is designed for use in the promotion.

ショップカード
Shop card

ステッカー
Sticker

チケット
Ticket

■CL= ヘブンス HEAVENS CO., LTD.
■AD= 野尻大作 Daisaku Nojiri ■P= 皆川 聡（'02ポスター、カタログ） Satoshi Minakawa ('02Poster, Catalog) ■P= 石坂直樹（'01ポスター、リーフレット） Naoki Ishizaka ('01Poster, Leaflet) ■Agency= レマン プラス Lesmains Plus Inc.
■S= レマン プラス Lesmains Plus Inc.

'02ポスター '02 Poster

'01ポスター '01 Poster

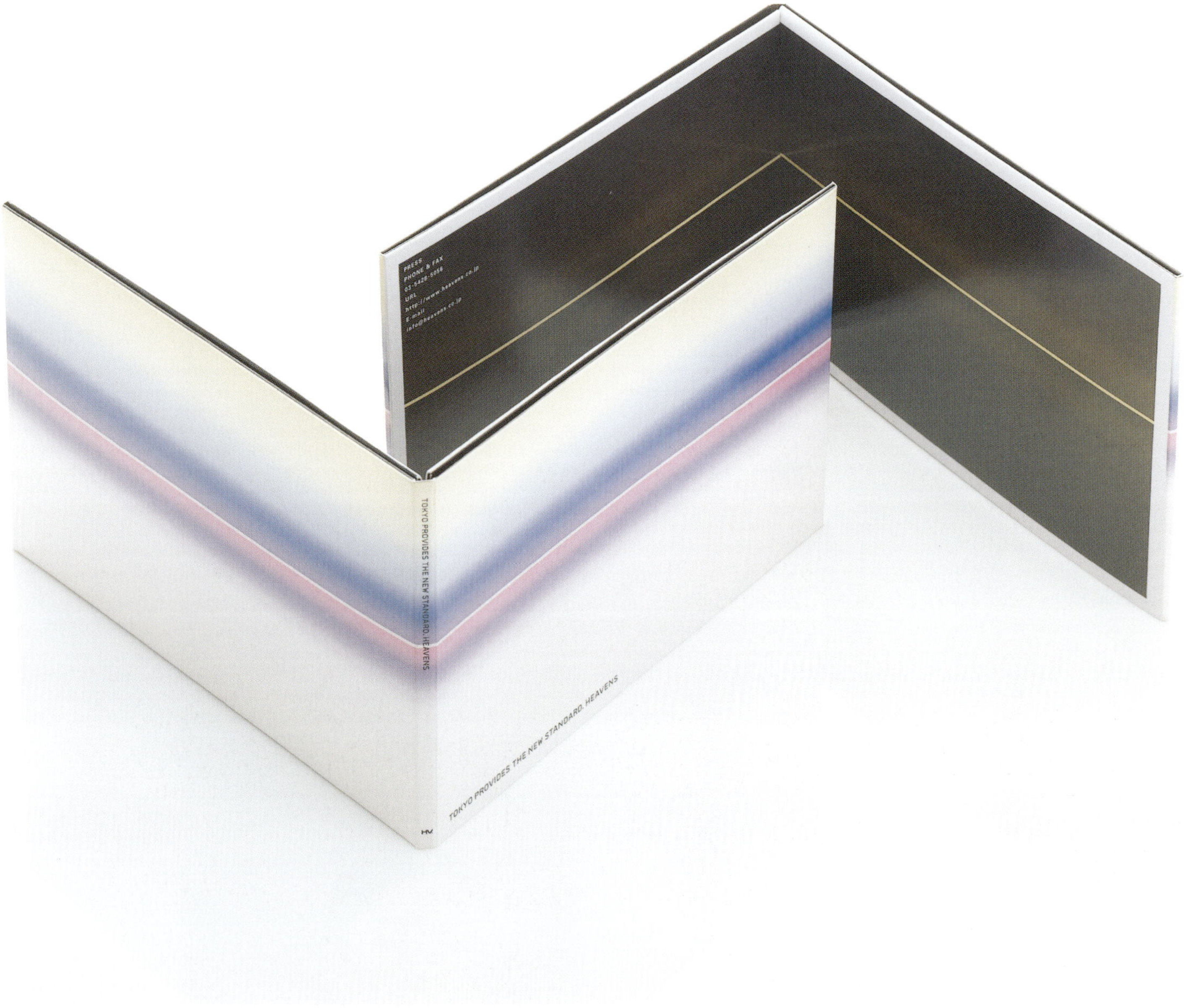

リーフレット Leaflet

カタログ Catalog

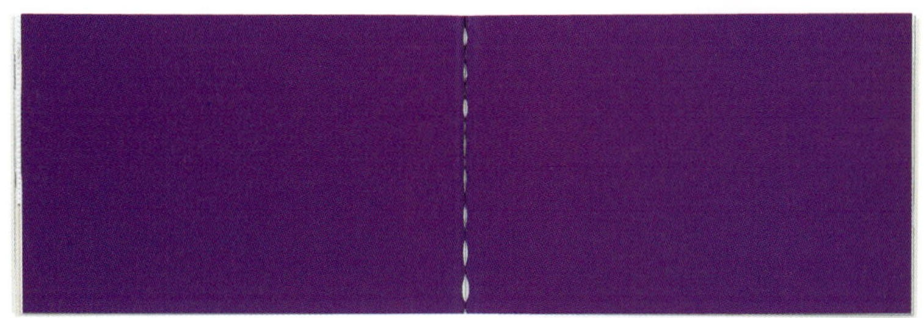

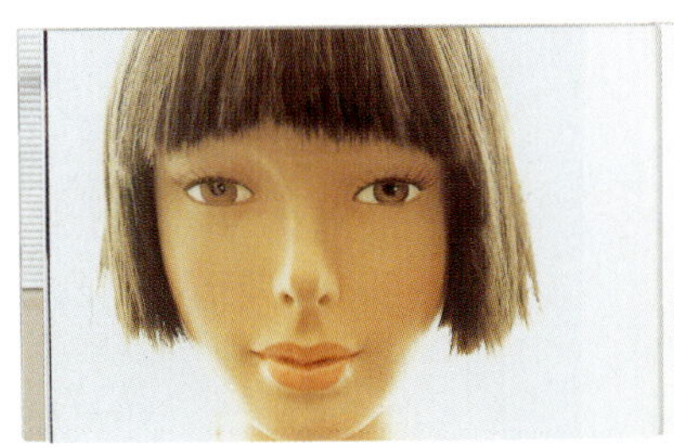

FRESH FLOWER SERVICE フレッシュ・フラワー・サービス

“さりげない主張”をグラフィックで実現するバランス感覚とデザイン

Balanced graphics create an "indifferent assertion"

戦略を読み解く 3 key words

有機栽培の花の提供で“健康的な暮らし”を彩る

“健康的な生活を楽しく送るお手伝いをしたい”との考え方から、有機栽培の花をできるだけ多く取り扱うフラワーショップ。花卉の流通会社が経営する店であるため、花の鮮度を保つ技術には自信をもっており、顧客からも定評がある。

“コンセプトの感じられる花屋”を目指して

チェーン店ではない小さなショップであるため、大々的な広告は打っていない。しかし、それだけにショップツールの制作にはこだわり、ひとつひとつのツールに店のコンセプトを込め、“あそこは他の花屋とはちょっと違う”と感じてもらえることを目指す。

声高にではなく、さりげなく主張するデザイン

“有機栽培＝虫がついているのが当たり前”なことを、ネガティブではない方向で表現したいと考え“てんとう虫とちょっぴり虫に食われた葉”をデザイン。てんとう虫にはアイコン的役割もあるが、さりげなさを大切にするため、あえてロゴマーク化はしない。

3 key words

Add color to a healthy lifestyle with organically grown flowers

A flower shop that "helps you add some fun to a healthy lifestyle" by offering all possible varieties of organic flowers. As the retail outlet of a flower delivery company, it has the technology and knowhow to assure freshness and an established reputation among customers.

A flower shop with a recognizable concept

A wide-scale advertising campaign is inappropriate for a small, non-franchise shop -- so scrupulously create promotional tools imbued with the store concept which inspire customers to feel that "this flower shop is a little bit different".

Soft-spoken, nonchalantly assertive design

Turn the popular notion, "organic means bug-ridden, of course", into a positive with imagery of a slightly bug-eaten leaf and a ladybug. Use the ladybug as an icon, but in keeping with the nonchalance of the campaign, avoid use of logos.

Logo

“主役はあくまで花”なので、ロゴで印象づけたくはないと考え、花を引き立てるシンプルでスタンダードなロゴをデザインした。

"To the utmost, flowers take the leading roll", so create a simple, "standard" logo that gives prominence to the flowers.

FRESH FLOWER SERVICE

Shop

ショップカード Shop card

ポストカード Postcard

ショップバッグ Shop bag

シール Sticker

リボン Ribbon

■CL= ヨシカワスタンダード Yoshikawa Standard
■AD + D= 菊地敦己 Atsuki Kikuchi ■Shop Planner= 松島弘幸（ダブルエムアーキテクツ） Hiroyuki Matsushima (Double M Architects) ■S= ブルーマーク Bluemark Inc.

INDEX

CLIENTS

SUBMITTORS

ブランド戦略とデザイン
Brand Strategy and Design

JACKET DESIGN
ウルトラグラフィックス
UltRA Graphics
山田英二（AD）
Eiji Yamada
野寺尚子（D）
Naoko Nodera

ART DIRECTOR
三芳伸吾
Shingo Miyoshi

EDITOR
山本章子
Akiko Yamamoto

WRITER
塚本朋子
Tomoko Tsukamoto
織原靖子
Yasuko Orihara

DESIGNER
高松セリアサユリ
Célia Sayuri Takamatsu

PHOTOGRAPHER
藤本邦治
Kuniharu Fujimoto

TRANSLATOR
パメラ・ミキ
Pamela Miki

PUBLISHER
三芳伸吾
Shingo Miyoshi

2003年10月10日　初版第1刷発行

発行所　ピエ・ブックス
〒170-0005　東京都豊島区南大塚2-32-4
編集　Tel:03-5395-4820　Fax:03-5395-4821
e-mail:editor@piebooks.com
営業　Tel:03-5395-4811　Fax:03-5395-4812
e-mail:sales@piebooks.com

印刷・製本
大日本印刷(株)

ISBN4-89444-295-7 C3070

Printed in Japan